When
Millennials
Rule

THE RESHAPING OF AMERICA

DAVID & JACK
CAHN

A POST HILL PRESS BOOK

WHEN MILLENNIALS RULE
The Reshaping of America
© 2016 by David Cahn & Jack Cahn
All Rights Reserved

ISBN: 978-1-68261-075-6
ISBN (eBook): 978-1-68261-076-3

Cover Design by Quincy Alivio
Interior Design and Composition by Greg Johnson, Textbook Perfect

Post Hill Press
275 Madison Avenue, 14th Floor
New York, NY 10016
posthillpress.com

Printed in the United States of America

1 2 3 4 5 6 7 8 9 10

Contents

To America's young leaders,
the buck stops with you.

To the Junior State of America,
for investing in a civically engaged electorate.

Introduction

On a recent afternoon, Jack was riding the New York City subway when an older woman walked on, and he stood up to offer her his seat.

"How old are you?" she asked, surprised by the gesture. "You're so unlike those obnoxious millennials with poor manners who can't keep their legs crossed and don't clean up their own messes," she said bitterly.

Of course, as 20-year-old identical twins, we most certainly are members of the millennial generation, born between 1980 and 2000. Even if the term were based on time spent on Facebook, we'd still make the cut. How could we miss pressing updates on the most recent Kardashian exploits?

But for many adults, the millennial generation is irritating and confusing. "What with their stupid iPhones, and their apps, and their selfies, and their social networks, and their narcissism, and their job-hopping, and their potatoes, and—well, you get the picture," wrote *The Washington Post*'s Christopher Ingraham."[1] *The New York Times* once noted that "among Americans age 40 and older, there's a pastime more popular than football, Candy Crush or HBO. It's bashing millennials."

Perhaps nowhere are millennials as mystifying as in Washington, D.C. In 2012, we delivered President Obama his margin of victory.[2] But then in 2014, we flipped and delivered Republicans a majority in the Senate.[3] Millennials support background checks, but oppose gun control,[4] believe in small government but want to help the poor, and promote social justice but push for cuts to Social Security. Vox concluded that our opinions are "incoherent." What's going on?

Whether older generations understand us or not, millennials—along with our perplexing views—will play a critical role in responding to a unique set of challenges that threaten our way of life.

ISIS is on the rise in the Middle East and terrorists threaten our homeland. President Assad is winning a brutal civil war in Syria, and millions of refugees are fleeing the region for a better life. A tenuous agreement in Iran has slowed a Middle Eastern nuclear arms race ... for now. Putin's Russia is flexing its muscles, with aggression in Eastern Europe threatening a decades long détente. China is asserting its influence in East Asia.

At home, Social Security is on the verge of going bankrupt, as is Medicaid. Universal health care is now the law of the land, much to the chagrin of millions of voters. The struggle to balance gun rights with safety continues to rage in our streets. A new civil rights movement is forming as evidence of systemic racism becomes all too apparent. Climate change threatens to create the biggest migrant crisis in history, upending millions of people across the world. Meanwhile, the War on Drugs is costing taxpayers billions of dollars and creating a crisis of mass incarceration.

If America today is at a crossroads, it is millennials who will need to make the tough choices to shape the future of our country. Today, we are America's largest voting bloc, with 78 million eligible voters. "Ignore millennial voters at your peril," wrote Harvard's Maggie Williams.[5]

This seismic shift—from millennials being the laughingstock of every boardroom and newspaper, to being a politically powerful force to be reckoned with—has been a long time in the making.

Over the past five years, we've had front row seats to this transition. When we first embarked on our careers as competitive debaters during our freshmen year of high school, we didn't fully understand what we were witnessing. But over time, as we talked with more than 10,000 young people and traveled all across the country, from Minneapolis to Chicago and Boston, we began to form a clearer picture of what was happening: millennials were forming their political beliefs—and the dialogue they were having was radically different from the one happening at the national level.

Soon, we set out with a much more conscious goal: to figure out how millennials are going to reshape our country's future. We slept in a train station in Boston, a Starbucks in Cleveland, and flew to the beautiful city of San Jose. Everywhere we went, we challenged a diverse group of young people of different backgrounds—racial, socioeconomic, and political—to explain how they think about the most important issues confronting America today. We organized focus groups and listened to young people argue among themselves.

Along the way, we met a diverse group of young people who helped bring our generation's views to life. A young woman described being shocked and deeply saddened when her father was deported. A teen-ager described the struggles of working through school, and coming home to an empty refrigerator. A young man vocally challenged the pro-minimum wage millennial consensus, saying he opposes it even though his mother earns it. A student described fearing gun violence, after experiencing six gun-scares on her campus. These conversations drove home just how uniquely millennials are engaging with some of America's most complex issues.

With Jack serving as the National Director of Public Relations for the Junior State of America and coordinating speaking engagements in the Northeast, we had the privilege to meet with important national figures, from former Federal Reserve Chairman Ben Bernanke to former Rep. Barney Frank (D-MA), whose Dodd-Frank law is reshaping Wall Street, and 2016 presidential candidate Bernie Sanders. After their speeches, we asked these leaders questions about what Washington is doing for our generation. The answer was usually: not enough.

At the same time, we dug into available data and polls. After all, that's what we spent years training to do as debaters. When we finally synthesized our findings, we discovered much more than just a portrait of the millennial generation. We uncovered an insurgency of young voters who are silently breaking the rules of Washington politics. Instead of buying into the yes-no ideological dichotomies pedaled by talking heads in Washington, our generation unifies around pragmatic, commonsense solutions. In the age of the Internet, millennials have adopted extremely nuanced and informed stances on some of America's most pressing issues.

Our thesis is that these pragmatic, resilient, and optimistic young people will use their votes to wage a silent war against the Washington elite. By ousting ideologues and voting for politicians who share our values—namely, authenticity, optimism, and tolerance—millennials will usher in an era of reform. Using compromise to implement change, millennials will translate their political consensus into actual public policy and break the gridlock in Washington.

Our friends will disrupt Washington in the same way they have disrupted everything from driving to shopping to television. Just like we replaced cabs with Uber, hotels with Airbnb, and movies with Netflix, millennials are fundamentally reimaging what politics will look like. Instead of accepting Washington as being corrupt and broken, millennials seek new reforms.

Our enemy is not a specific political ideology, but cronyism and "dependency corruption" in Washington that allows special interest groups to step ahead of the American public in setting the public policy agenda. On everything from jobs, to gun rights, the environment, entitlements, and education, our priorities are ignored, as unions and corporations wield their influence to stifle progress. We oppose the divisive rhetoric used to divide the American public and rally votes, because it prevents progress. The Harvard Institute of Politics reports that "cynicism toward the political process has never been higher."[6]

"They've been told all their lives to wait in line," explained former Republican National Committee Chairman Michael Steele. "But they're of a mind to say, 'OK, while I'm waiting in line, I'll blow your stuff up,'" he said. "That scene tells you all you need to know about what millennials are poised to do to Washington. ... They are going to destroy the old silos, scatter their elements to the wind, and reassemble them in ways that make sense for them and the new century."[7]

By fighting against machine politicians in Washington, millennials strive to restore reason and hope to American public policy and take back our country's future.

In *When Millennials Rule*, we travel from Paris, where a 15-year-old American speaks at an international climate summit, to the halls of the West Virginia legislature, where the youngest elected legislator in the U.S. is fighting to protect gun rights.

In each chapter, another angle of the millennial platform is revealed. What emerges is a full-scale manifesto of millennial political beliefs that is radically different from the platforms of Democrats and Republicans. We find a generation that rejects the partisan dichotomy that offers us bad jobs or fewer jobs as our economic choices, and dead soldiers or appeasement as our foreign policy options.

Do millennials have the resilience and tenacity to win the war for America's future, or will young people find themselves stifled by the political machine, as so many others have before us?

You be the judge.

PART 1

Welcome to Millennial America

Social Security is going bankrupt. Radical Islamic terrorists threaten our safety. Our planet is on the brink of disaster. Meanwhile, our leaders line their pockets with dirty money while pounding their chests in ideological wars that enrich lobbyists at the expense of voters. "Welcome to Millennial America" follows our journey from Chicago to Mineola, N.Y., and San Jose, and tells the story of how young Americans are tackling these problems and re-shaping America's future.

Safer Streets: A Call for Reasonable Restrictions on Guns

NEW HAVEN, CONNECTICUT

We arrived in New Haven, just a few months after the Newtown school shooting, a tragedy during which a lunatic gunned down 20 innocent children. As we walked up the stairs into a Yale University library, we saw dozens of young millennials like us sitting on benches and running around, preparing to spend the next weekend discussing and debating solutions to America's gun violence epidemic.

But throughout the building there was an eerie undercurrent: this wasn't a debate topic, not really—it was a matter of life and death. On the streets, one in five teenagers has witnessed a shooting, according to the Justice Department,[1] and more than half of all people murdered with guns since 2010 were under the age of 30, making homicide the second leading cause of death for our generation.[2]

As a result, for young Americans on both sides of the aisle, there is perhaps no issue closer to our hearts than the issue of gun violence, which has killed so many of our friends and family members. And yet, our generation has not seen any significant gun reform since before many of us were even born.

When asked how they'd solve today's gun violence problem, millennials say they don't want to ban guns—semiautomatic or otherwise. In fact, we've been labeled as America's most pro-gun generation. But in the face of so many of our friends dying at the point of a gun barrel, young people want Congress to pass reasonable restrictions on gun ownership to protect our and future generations from the havoc that we've witnessed since our childhoods.

We are Dying: Millennials Caught in the Crossfire

David remembers his first experience with gun violence. He was sitting in an office two blocks from New York's Empire State Building when the shots were fired, but he heard nothing but the buzz of his phone. "u OK?" he read, checking his messages. "Yeah man, what's up?" Another buzz. "Shooter at Emp. State. Dude be careful." He quickly scrolled to update Facebook. People thought there was a terrorist attack. Soon his newsfeed was updated with new posts. Apparently a man attacked his former employer over a financial dispute. Nine bystanders were injured in the ensuing shootout.

The most frightening part of the attack was its senselessness, the seeming randomness of it all. In the first of many *Huffington Post* editorials, David explained: "On a more fundamental level, we are shocked by the arbitrariness of the murder. Murder for the sake of murder, murder of unsuspecting civilians, hits us harder than any other crime—it is raw evil. In these unique and public cases, we realize that we, or those we love, could be the victims of these crimes."

Even though David was just 16 at the time, this was not his first exposure to gun violence. David recalls that when he was just beginning public high school in New York, the threat of gun violence was all too real. During routine lockdown drills, students were required to practice their response to an armed invader—the modern day equivalent of hiding under desks from nuclear attacks. "Code Blue, Code Blue," a voice would boom over the school's intercom and like clockwork, students would scramble to turn off the lights, lock the doors, and move away from the windows.

After one of these drills, one of his teachers felt compelled to warn the students about how to respond to an attack. "If there's a gunman in the room, here is what you have to do. Throw the heaviest object, say your book bag or desk, at him and then everyone has to charge him. That's how you avoid mass causalities," he said. He was not being paranoid. Since the Sandy Hook massacre in Newtown in 2013, there have been at least 100 school shootings, even by conservative estimates.[3]

These drills, while seemingly trivial at the time, along with the prevalence of attacks on schools, have permanently scarred the psyche of our generation. Our friend Lindsey told Jack that she knows what she would do and where she would hide if armed gunmen entered her building, because she's thought about it and planned out her moves. And our friend Maddie says she has trouble enjoying movies because she's afraid someone is going to run into the theatre and shoot.

In college, Jack remembers thinking about the optimal escape routes from his classrooms if someone were to attack our campus. Again—these are not paranoid thoughts. In 2015, some Philadelphia colleges shut down due to credible threats that a shooter would target one of the schools. Ours did not. But as we trekked from class to class, half the seats in each room were empty. Many professors canceled classes, because students simply weren't showing up.

But even these drills were not our first exposure to gun violence—not by a long shot. The Center for Media Education reports that by the time young Americans reach elementary school, they have been exposed to more than 10,000 acts of violence, including 8,000 murders on television. By the time they reach high school, those numbers double.[4]

We know that soldiers experience post-traumatic stress disorder when they come home from wars, and this seems to be the case for young people who watch their friends die in shootings. Research indicates that many such young people suffer survivor-guilt and emotional trauma later in life. After these traumatic experiences, many young people have difficulty concentrating in school and their academic performance deteriorates. Unsuccessful in school, they may turn to violence to resolve their own problems, perpetuating a cycle of violence.

Even among those who escape the fate of street violence, many young people still end their lives at the point of a gun barrel. Suicide is the third leading cause of death for young people, and half of all suicide victims use guns.

It should come as no surprise, then, that the majority of young Americans and nearly three-quarters of young minorities say gun violence may personally affect their lives.[5]

In focus groups we conducted with millennial leaders from across the country, we heard stories about a culture of gun violence. Arizonan millennial Ciana Cronin told us that there have been six gun-scares on her campus alone.

"It's pretty ghetto. I'm not going to lie. We have 2,000 kids on one campus and there's no safety there, and it's supposed to be a learning environment [but] that's not going to happen," she said. "Once there were two gangs and they had guns and then they were beating up this kid and then people started firing shots and it was madness, and we were just sitting huddled under our desks and you could hear them right outside."

Yuma, Arizona, native Anne Diaz recounted her own experience. "I remember going to Walmart one time. ... I couldn't finish even getting whatever I needed ... just because stupid people" pulled out their guns in the store, she said. Anne understands why people have guns but is nonetheless frustrated that people take out "guns in parks or public places like that."

Cronin and Diaz are among the majority of millennials who recognize the damage wrought on our communities by gun violence and worry that they will be next. Sixty percent of young people fear that gun violence will personally affect them or their communities in the future.[6] As a result, 70 percent of millennials agree that "the gun culture in our society has gotten out of control."

This doesn't mean that we want to get rid of guns altogether. Just the opposite is true, as we will see. But this context is important for understanding why gun reform is such an important priority for young people who are rising up in protest and demanding real reform from Washington.

Corrupt Politicians: How Washington Stifles Reform

Our generation is not resigned to a fate where multiple people die while you read these words. Yet today, the United States has one of the highest rates of gun violence among its developed peers.

American children and teenagers are four times more likely to die by gunfire than their counterparts in Canada, seven times more likely than young people in Israel, and 65 times more likely to be killed with a gun than children and teenagers in the United Kingdom, according to the Children's Defense Fund.[7]

But it doesn't have to be this way: there is legislation that we can pass and there are things that we can do in the United States to emulate our peers, create safer streets, and save lives, millennials say.

Part of the problem is that lawmakers would rather fight each other and promote themselves than save our children. Despite the many constituents who have died in the crossfire of gun violence, Washington legislators have not passed any significant federal gun control legislation since 1994, before some millennials were even born.

And that's not because the legislation hasn't been introduced. Since 1994, when a Federal Assault Weapon Ban (FAWB) made it illegal to purchase large capacity magazines with more than 10 bullets and banned the manufacture of semi-automatic weapons defined to be "assault weapons," multiple gun bills have failed in Congress. While Democrats and Republicans like to point fingers, both parties are to blame.

The Democrats, with their "holier-than-thou" stance of moral superiority on gun control, have fought for years to violate the constitutional rights of American voters by heavily restricting gun usage and banning weapons which they deem too lethal for civilian use, much to the chagrin of Republican and Democratic millennial voters.

Despite cries that young Americans are hippie liberals who want to abolish guns, the majority of millennials oppose outright gun control, according to Pew Research polls.[8] In fact, almost two-thirds of high school and college students have themselves considered owning a gun in the future.[9]

Though some millennials may not agree with all of Saira Blair's views, the college junior who is the youngest person ever elected to the West Virginia State Legislature does raise resonant arguments.

"I was raised in a household where we have guns and have learned to properly use them," she told *Teen Vogue*. Blair spoke for the majority of millennials when she said, "I fully support the Second Amendment. I believe in protecting the innocent and punishing the guilty. ... Firearms allow our law-abiding citizens to protect themselves and their families."

In stark contrast with these views, one of the key tenets of the Democratic Party's platforms on gun control has long been the reinstatement of the 1994 FAWB (which expired in 2004), based on the argument that the semi-automatic assault weapons banned by the bill are military-grade and without civilian uses.

One police chief said that the weapons contain "military features" that are designed "specifically to increase their lethality." Ian Michael Deutch, a National Guard staff sergeant who returned home, alive and unwounded, from Afghanistan, is an often-cited victim of semi-automatic weapons. While responding to a domestic abuse call as a deputy sheriff in Nevada, he was shot and killed by a criminal who used an assault weapon to pierce his body armor. "He was finally safe in our country. And somebody here kills him," his mother told Congress.

Sen. Diane Feinstein (D-CA), who has long been one of the bill's most vocal advocates, points to data that indicates violence falling during the Clinton-era ban. Meanwhile special-interest groups like the Brady Campaign argue that the ban caused a 6.7 percent dip in murder rates while in effect.[10] A group of NYU professors found in their research that the end of the ban "exerted an unanticipated spill-over on gun supply in Mexico, and this increase in arms has fueled rising violence south of the border." They link at least 239 deaths to the ban's expiration in 2004.[11]

But the issue is not as simple as Democrats try to paint it; the evidence on the effects of the 1994 ban is largely divided. A nonpartisan study by Christopher Koper, a criminology professor at George Mason University, among other research, has found that the ban had a negligible effect on gun violence. "We cannot credit the ban with any of the nation's recent drop in gun violence," Koper wrote. Koper argued that gun violence literature is politicized and concluded that a reinstated ban's "impact on gun violence is likely to be too small for reliable measurement."[12]

But regardless of which research is correct, many of the young people we spoke with don't think the ends justify the means when it comes to the FAWB. Millennials say that while banning all guns might hypothetically reduce violence, doing so would violate constitutional rights. Likewise, with assault weapons, the solution is not to violate rights but to place reasonable restrictions on ownership.

For this reason, polls show young people opposing the assault weapons ban by the largest margin of any demographic, with 70 percent of young Americans supporting ownership of assault weapons, compared with 51 percent of all Americans.[13]

"The right to bear arms shall not be infringed, period. That's very absolute. The U.S. Supreme Court has not nuanced that at all. Additionally, something is supposed to be a crime if it violates people's rights. Buying an assault rifle doesn't violate anyone's rights. Making it illegal does violate people's rights: their right to buy arms, their right to trade. It's a slippery slope," said Steven Adelberg, a young Republican from Arizona. "It's funny because an assault weapon ban

a) doesn't work, and b) incentivizes people to buy handguns, which are far more problematic."

Abhay Ram, a Democratic high school student leader from Chicago, agreed. "A gun is just a tool. In the hands of a soldier, it's a tool of liberty. In the hands of a criminal, it's dangerous," he said. "It's wrong for the government to have all the guns and ban them from the people."

This doesn't mean young people agree with the obstructionist, do-nothing approach of National Rifle Association-backed Republicans who stand in the way of reform. Rather, millennials think both parties are part of a broken system. Republican lawmakers highlight the importance of enforcing laws already on the books and working to put criminals behind bars. For millennials, that's a good sign—but the view that any regulation at all is the beginning of a "slippery slope" toward a ban on all guns is not persuasive.

Former Massachusetts Governor Mitt Romney explained the Republican platform on gun control in a 2012 speech. "We need to distinguish between law-abiding gun owners and criminals who use guns. Those who use a firearm during the commission of a crime must be punished severely. The key is to provide law enforcement with the resources they need and punish criminals, not burden lawful gun owners." [14]

If Romney stopped here, millennials would nod in agreement. But he went further. Romney promised not to "support adding more laws and regulations that do nothing more than burden law-abiding citizens while being ignored by criminals." But most regulations do a lot more than burden law-abiding citizens: they can help prevent the mentally ill and felons from getting weapons. In our quest for safer streets, young people seek a balance between burdening law-abiding citizens and protecting other citizens from gun violence.

Republicans often argue that Washington should prioritize increased enforcement of existing laws over passing new laws. David Lampo of the Cato Institute, for example, has said that the Columbine

High School shooters violated more than 20 existing firearms laws in the process of building their stockpile of weapons.

"So it seems rather dubious to argue that additional laws might have prevented this tragedy," he explained. Likewise, the NRA believes that it is important to protect the right to be armed, arguing that restrictions do little to actually reduce gun crime.

There is data to support this hypothesis. A 2010 National Academy of Sciences meta-study found no link between gun ownership and crime rates.[15] Analyzing 253 journal articles, 99 books, and 43 government publications, the authors learned that the overwhelming majority of the research found no correlation between rates of gun ownership and crime. Conservatives note that gun ownership today is at an all-time high, with the number of guns increasing by 90 million since 1991. Violent crime has fallen to a 35-year low, with a 49 percent decline in murders.[16]

Intransigence on the right is driven, in part, by the excessive influence of the National Rifle Association. The power of the NRA comes down to money and influence. The NRA spends 15 times as much on campaign contributions as gun-control advocates, and its annual operating budget is approximately $250 million. More importantly, NRA members are extremely invested in their cause, tying gun rights to core American principles like freedom and liberty. The NRA is able to mobilize its members to write letters to their representatives and exert their political muscle to oppose even the most reasonable of regulations.

The problem is that the NRA uses its power not just to protect against encroachments of the Second Amendment, but also to oppose any and all gun restrictions—even ones supported by the overwhelming majority of its members, like universal background checks. A full 87 percent of non-NRA gun owners and 74 percent of NRA members agree that all gun purchasers should be required to undergo a criminal background check. Yet the NRA continues to oppose this policy, calling it "ripe for abuse."[17]

It might be convenient to think that banning guns will solve our entire gun problem, but millennials say that is not just naïve—it is patently false and has been empirically disproven. Not only that, but it presents a dangerous threat to our constitutional freedoms. Ironically, millennials are simultaneously the most pro-gun and the most pro-gun reform generation in America.

The Millennial Consensus

Millennials are hardly "anti-gun." A majority of millennials opposes gun control, believing that the right of law-abiding citizens to own and carry their firearms should not be infringed. But as rational, reasonable voters, millennials believe that the federal government should impose reasonable restrictions on ownership.

Fifty-nine percent of young voters say Congress should implement reasonable restrictions on gun sales. This nuanced perspective is a sharp contrast from those of the Democratic and Republican parties. As opposed to blocking out the "other" side, our generation seeks a middle ground solution. Now.

There is a consensus among young voters that the government must act immediately. In a nationwide survey, millennials ranked gun control as a leading issue that they would consider on Election Day, second only to student loans. Millennial leader Levi McBride told us, "The Gabby Giffords and Sandy Hook shootings were the two biggest events in shaping our opinions on gun control … especially because Giffords was a government official. … The fact that a shooting like this could happen was huge." These tragedies left us demanding a government response.

At the top of our gun reform wish list are restrictions that prevent high-risk individuals such as former felons and the mentally ill from owning weapons. We see such reform as a congressional prerogative: 92 percent of 18-29-year-olds support universal background checks, a Center for American Progress poll found. This is the highest level of support among all age groups. And data seems to corroborate the view that universal background checks will reduce gun violence. A recent study in the American Medical Association's *Journal of Internal Medicine*, for example, found that states with background checks on private sales had 16 percent lower gun fatality rates.[18]

Already, 23 states prohibit violent criminals or those convicted of firearms-related offenses from owning guns. These laws should be extended to all states and expanded to those with one prior misdemeanor conviction. These criminals, research has found, are seven times as likely as those with no prior criminal history to be charged with a new offense after a handgun purchase.[19]

These laws should also be expanded to include juvenile offenders, who research indicates are likely to commit further acts of violence, as is the case in 27 states. A study analyzing a cohort of low-income, minority youth, for example, found that those who were arrested before age 18 had a 38 percent higher likelihood of a felony conviction by age 26, as compared to their peers.[20]

Those who have been arrested for driving under the influence of alcohol or have recently been entered into a rehabilitation facility should have their licenses to carry suspended as well. It is well known that alcohol abuse is linked with a person's tendency to engage in violent behavior. One trial, for example, found that alcohol consumption reduced shooting accuracy and impaired judgment about when it might be appropriate to use a gun. Such laws are already in place in 20 states.[21]

Finally, increased gun ownership restrictions should be placed on the mentally ill, millennial leaders say. In California, state laws include disqualifying factors that should be adopted nationally, including: communicating a serious threat of violence against an identifiable individual to a licensed psychotherapist during the last six months, or being held for treatment for mental illness for 72 hours within the last five years. Expanding the scope of mental illness limitations for gun ownership will do much to reduce the prevalence of gun violence and mass shootings.[22]

"I don't think it is necessarily that I want to 'infringe' on rights or take away guns by any means. I understand that firearms are used recreationally; I have friends that have gone their entire lives around rifles and have gone to shooting ranges with automatic weapons and do so recreationally. They've never been shot at, they've never had a relative shot, nor have they been around violence, and I think a lot of that is cultural," said Denny Baek, a millennial leader from California. "But if your records are having a hard time being cleared, you perhaps might not be the kind of individual that should be purchasing firearms." Denny describes what appears to be a consensus among young people—don't take away guns, but implement limits to make us safer.

Gun reform should not only revolve around who owns guns, but also how they are purchased. As of late 2015, federally licensed gun dealers were required to conduct background checks. However, private gun sales, such as those conducted at gun shows, do not require checks. A 2009 undercover sting in Nevada, Ohio, and Tennessee found that 63 percent of private sellers sold guns to buyers who admitted to being unable to pass background checks.

Online sales are problematic as well. A 2011 study found that 62 percent of online sellers sold guns to those who could not pass background checks.[23] The U.S. Department of Justice reports that "individuals prohibited by law from possessing guns can easily obtain them from private sellers and do so without any federal records of the transactions."[24]

If a bunch of professors sitting in their ivory towers know that background checks are avoidable, then certainly criminals do. A plane will crash if even one piece of the giant machine doesn't work. So too with gun control. Because criminals will choose the least restrictive avenue to purchase weapons, the effective level of regulation is the least restrictive one. It is no wonder then that a study published in the *New England Journal of Medicine* found that private-party gun sales are a leading source of guns used in crimes.[25] To be effective, background checks must extend to all methods of gun purchasing, including from gun shows and online sales, and we should crack down on black market sales.

The 92 percent of young Americans who believe in universal background checks are not alone. 74 percent of NRA households and 80 percent of gun owners believe that all potential gun buyers should be subject to a criminal background check. Reasonable regulations don't need to be controversial—everyone should be able to agree on them.

"If you aren't a criminal, why should you be worrying about background checks?" McBride said. "If you have nothing to fear, you shouldn't be afraid."

Reasonable restrictions extend beyond background checks to regulating gun manufacturing. From 2005–2010, nearly 3,800 people died and 95,000 people were injured by unintentional shootings. Almost half of these victims were under the age of 25. Safety standards for guns, like those that exist for most consumer products nowadays, would have the potential to substantially reduce the number of injuries sustained from accidental shootings. For example, many guns include a magazine disconnect mechanism, which prevents the gun from shooting when there is no magazine attached. Likewise, guns can be equipped with a "chamber-loading indicator," which makes it clear when a gun is loaded. Requiring manufacturers to build in either of these features, especially the latter, could potentially do much to reduce accidental shootings.

Regulations could be applied to make "junk guns" safer as well. These are low-quality handguns that are cheap and easily concealed, built from plastic or metals. They pose the greatest risk to users because they can accidentally fire, even when the trigger is not pulled. Ironically, the Consumer Product Safety Act, which imposes safety standards on consumer products, exempts firearms. This should end. Handguns should be required to meet safety standards and undergo professional testing before they go to market. This is not gun control—it's common sense.[26]

Finally, there is a distinction between regulating gun ownership and regulating gun sales. The first is problematic. The second should be welcomed. The federal government should do whatever it can to bust crooked dealers. Between 2004 and 2011, the Bureau of Alcohol, Tobacco, Firearms and Explosives (ATF) discovered nearly 175,000 firearms missing from dealer inventories during compliance inspections. Although gun dealers have the resources and opportunities to profit off of illegal sales, the ATF is restricted to one unannounced inspection of gun dealers each year. Take a moment to reflect on how crazy that is. Restaurants face *far* stricter inspection regulations.

Lack of regulations on dealers is due to heavy pressure by the NRA and the gun lobby. As a result, 58 percent of dealers had not been inspected within the past five years, according to a 2013 report by the U.S. Department of Justice's Office of the Inspector General. This may be due to a lack of resources—in recent years, the ATF has been underfunded and understaffed.[27] This is unfortunate because regulation of gun sales and a crackdown on crooked dealers could very well save lives. A 2009 study published in the *Journal of Urban Health* linked regulation of gun dealers with lower levels of gun trafficking. The authors found that states with increased compliance regulations had "significantly lower levels of intrastate gun trafficking."[28]

While most dealers are legitimate, the best way to stop illegal gun sales is to crack down on crooked dealers. Like most of the proposals outlined in this chapter, we believe that regulating dealers will pose little to no inconvenience to legitimate dealers while advancing the cause of reducing gun violence in the United States. Serious enforcement and regulation are important deterrents for illegal gun sales. For example, a national study found that 50 percent of high school sophomore and junior respondents believed that obtaining a gun would be "little" or "no" trouble, despite that fact that it is illegal for minors to own weapons.

But the excessive power of the NRA goes even further. The Center for Disease Control (CDC) has abided by a self-imposed ban on studying gun violence since 1996, when Congress threatened to defund the agency if it continued researching gun violence.

"The CDC's self-imposed ban dried up a powerful funding source and had a chilling effect felt far beyond the agency: Almost no one wanted to pay for gun violence studies, researchers say. Young academics were warned that joining the field was a good way to kill their careers," *The Washington Post* reported in January of 2015. This over-the-top obsession with gun rights needs to end.

CONCLUSION

The right to own guns is fundamental, so much so that it was enshrined in our Constitution as the Second Amendment, behind only freedom of speech and association. That's because our country has a long history of empowering the people. The American Revolution became necessary precisely because too much power was concentrated in the State. Pledging to never again allow the government to hold all the power, America's founders guaranteed that citizens could own their own guns. The U.S. Supreme Court has always upheld this right.

Millennials know this. So much so that we've become one of the most pro-gun generations in decades. Most millennials have contemplated owning a gun in the future, and the majority of us do not believe that it is the government's role to take away or regulate our guns—not even military-grade assault weapons. If criminals can easily get these weapons, there is no reason to restrict the rights of law-abiding citizens.

But we're reasonable people. We realize that the obsession with guns has gotten out of control. Certainly, criminals and the mentally ill should not have access to weapons. In the wrong hands, guns help criminals wreak havoc on our society; we have seen guns kill our brothers, sisters, parents, and friends. Meanwhile, Democrats and Republicans are so busy advancing their own political agendas that these criminals run free. This ends with our generation. Millennials want Congress to take a rational, reasonable approach to gun violence. We need to implement universal background checks, crack down on crooked dealers, allow inspections of any place that sells guns, and get more restrictive about who can own a gun.

The millennial consensus is clear: freedom and safety are not mutually exclusive. Choosing just safety or just freedom is the easy way out. It's what special interest groups want. But the American public—led by millennial voters—is pushing its leaders to build the courage to balance these two competing interests. We're going to fight this fight until we've won—because boys deserve to grow up with their fathers, and girls like Ciana Cronin deserve to receive an education free of gun scares.

Our generation has already begun to take action promoting gun restrictions on a local level. As more Americans die by the day and school shootings become ever more frequent, the unified consensus for a middle-ground solution to gun reform will only become more popular. This momentum will propel young voters, young elected officials, and the growing coalition of rational voters to fight against entrenched forces in Washington. We will take back our streets, restore the public safety, and protect American freedom.

Better Jobs: Solving the Millennial Unemployment Crisis

CHICAGO, ILLINOIS

I n New Haven, we learned that millennials don't follow the politically convenient path. Instead, they stake out their own territory, shaped by their unique experiences and distaste for partisan warfare.

As the year carried on, this impression would crystalize for us, nowhere more clearly than in Chicago, where having qualified to represent New York City at the Catholic Forensic League's annual Grand National Tournament, we prepared to take on some of our most formidable opponents yet.

The topic for debate was the minimum wage, and we gathered with other young people to talk about the economic issues that are troubling our generation. We knew this issue would hit close to home—not just for us and our opponents, but also for the millions of young Americans who bore the brunt of the 2008 financial crisis and the record high unemployment rates that followed.

Even so, we completely underestimated how bad the situation had gotten. In Chicago and since then, young Americans told us that even though the financial crisis was supposedly long gone, the sluggish recovery that followed has haunted them ever since.

Young people are desperate for pragmatic solutions that will put them to work. However, they disavow tax cuts and stimulus, the go-to solutions proposed by each party. Instead, millennials want their leaders to address the root cause of unemployment, starting with education reform, innovation, and free trade.

Career Malfunction: Roadblocks to Economic Recovery

Casey Ark played all his cards right. The Penn State graduate studied business and programming, pre-professional skills that would make him an ideal job candidate. He worked hard, graduated at the top of his class, and learned how to use industry software. But these efforts were to no avail, he said. When Ark graduated from college, he couldn't find a job.

"I felt like the job market was mine for the taking. I was very, very wrong. Despite diligent studying, the only real-world business skills I'd learned at college were how to write a résumé and operate three-fifths of the Microsoft Office suite," he recalled.[1]

To Ark, the culprit was in the classroom: curriculums focus on memorization and terminology rather than skills and techniques.

"At least 90 percent of my college education (and that of so many others) boiled down to pure terminology," Ark told *The Washington Post*. "My success in any given class was almost wholly based on how well I could remember the definitions of countless terms—like the precise meaning of 'computer science' or how to explain 'project management.'"

"You hear a lot of students come back from college and say 'the things we're learning in college are just as obscure as the things you're learning here [in high school].' When you actually go out into the job market, the skills you really need to learn, you don't have," explained Rohan Marwaha, a millennial leader from New Jersey. "So when they get out into the job market and they're searching, they have a hard time."

It's Never Been This Bad

Even as the U.S. economy rebounds, with the unemployment rate now at pre-recession levels, millennials continue to suffer from a jobless recovery. Half of today's college graduates will take jobs for which they are overqualified.

"It's never been this bad. ... How long we've had elevated unemployment is unprecedented," said Heidi Shierholz, a labor market economist at the Economic Policy Institute, a conservative think tank.[2]

When millennials do find jobs, they often end up in positions for which they feel overqualified. Stephen Campagnone landed gigs waiting tables and managing a hotel housekeeping office after he graduated—not exactly what he'd had in mind when he decided he wanted to get a college education.

When he landed a job working as a bank teller in his native Rhode Island, earning just $560 a week, he thought he might have found a career with upward mobility. But one year later, when he met with management to discuss a raise, he was offered just $333 more per year.

"I was just staring at my screen blankly. I wanted to rip my computer out of the wall," Campagnone told the *International Business Times*.[3] After working for another year as a teller, he moved back in with his parents and began searching for a more rewarding career. "I never really felt I was being propelled upwards, just a sense of hopelessness," he said.

Even higher degree graduates struggle to pay the bills. April Erickson earned a Ph.D. in American Cultural Studies but works as a teaching assistant.

"We are actually trying to find our way in an economy that is not made for us, isn't trying to make space for us and, as a result, I have decided I need to have a life first, and then maybe I'll move on to that job I actually wanted," she said.[4]

After graduating from Radford College, Rebecca Mersiowsky has worked at a beach club on Martha's Vineyard, as a substitute teacher in Fredericksburg, Va., and as a sales associate at a Boston boutique. "I don't think frustrated even begins to describe it," she said about the experience, in an interview with *USA Today.*[5]

We've all heard dozens of these stories—each with their own unique details but with the same message. Mersiowsky, Erickson, and Campagnone join thousands—if not millions—of young people across the country struggling to adapt to an economy that isn't ready to include them.

Crossing racial and socioeconomic lines, workers of all kinds face the same predicament; good, high-paying jobs are disappearing and all too many companies say they're not hiring.

The numbers don't lie. Between 2009 and 2013, the median income for millennials was roughly $33,883, 30 percent of millennials lived with at least one parent, compared to 23 percent in 1980, and almost 20 percent of young people were living in poverty.[6]

In her mock rejection letter to recent college graduates, *USA Today*'s Hadley Malcolm wrote: "We regret to inform you that the nation's job market continues to force college graduates to take jobs they're overqualified for, jobs outside their major, and generally delay their career to the detriment of at least a decade's worth of unearned wages. Good luck with your job search."[7]

Youth unemployment is not only costly for young people, but for society as a whole. Annually, "severely high unemployment rates" are projected to cost state and local governments $8.9 billion, according to Young Invincibles, an advocacy group.

This makes sense. On average, a year of unemployment for an 18-24-year-old costs $4,100 in forgone tax benefits and safety net benefits. As unemployed workers get older, the number increases to $9,900.[8] There are lasting impacts for the U.S. economy, too. When young Americans don't get the skills and training they need to succeed in the workforce, they make less money, leaving a "wage scar" that can persist until middle age. Each year of unemployment directly results in 16 percent lower earnings 10 years later, according to The Economist.[9]

"Even when this group eventually starts earning a paycheck, the impact of their unemployment will follow them for years," the Center for American Progress found. The advocacy group estimates the impact of the wage scar on today's young workers to be $21.4 billion in lost earnings over 10 years.

To add insult to injury, unemployment damages the confidence of young Americans, sapping our hope, and preventing us from becoming fully active members of the workforce.[10]

To turn this around, we hear the same old tropes from politicians on both sides of the aisle. Dealing with unemployment is hard, so Democrats and Republicans default to the usual bag of tricks. Democrats say jobs programs will stimulate the economy, and Republicans demand tax cuts to allow businesses to create jobs.

But millennials realize that these macroeconomic levers are only temporary solutions. Unfortunately, our unemployment isn't cyclical— it's structural. The jobs we want are long gone, so tweaks to fiscal and monetary policy have limited efficacy at best. Instead of tax cuts and stimulus, millennials across the country are demanding radical reforms to address the root causes of unemployment.

The Old Bag of Tricks: Partisan Bickering in Washington

While young people struggle to put food on the table and feed their families, Democrats and Republicans in Washington spend their time bashing their peers to promote their own reelection campaigns. The Democratic platform to solve the jobs crisis is vague at best and incompetent at worst. House Democrats have two core platforms for solving the unemployment crisis, according to their website. These platforms are labeled "Make it in America" and "When Women Succeed, America Succeeds."

Make it in America seems naïve in the face of the globalized economy. It begs the question, "how?" And a pivot towards women—which millennials certainly support—seems like a red herring in the face of our dire struggles. Yes, it's important—but it's not going to help create jobs. These catchphrases are just empty clichés. We want answers.

An important part of the Democratic agenda has always been stimulus. President Obama's American Recovery and Reinvestment Act, for example, put $787 billion into the economy.

But young Americans don't believe stimulus alone will help solve their problems. In 2010, national exit polls indicated that two-thirds of voters believed the president's stimulus package either hurt the economy or made no difference. Young voters were the least likely demographic to have supported the legislation, with only 24 percent saying the stimulus package was helpful.[11]

Opposition to stimulus stems from the realization that it is a short-term solution that does not address the deeper structural reasons for youth unemployment. In the case of the American Reinvestment and Recovery Act, there was also the valid perception that stimulus favored special interest groups, many of whom stood to collect a huge payday from massive government spending.

Stimulus may be necessary, but it is not the only answer to our unemployment crisis. Our strong dissatisfaction with stimulus is not young people saying, "Hey, this tool doesn't work." Rather, we are saying, "This is it?"

If Democrats aren't proposing pragmatic solutions that resonate with the solution-oriented millennial voter, neither are Republicans. The Heritage Foundation, a conservative think tank, gives eight policy recommendations for job creation. Four start with the word "repeal" and two involve "ending" or "cutting" current Democratic initiatives. Talk about obstructionism at its worst!

The only two actionable proposals are "advancing free trade" and "cutting the budget deficit," which are simply buzzwords—not specific policies. As a result, the Republican agenda on jobs turns away young voters who tend to be positive, optimistic, and constructive. [12]

A central tenet of the Republican platform is to "repeal Obamacare." It is understandable that Republicans believe that Obamacare might kill jobs by de-incentivizing employers from hiring new workers. But this is peripheral in that it is one of many regulations that discourage hiring; negative, in that it amounts to nothing more than attacking a Democratic platform; and unconstructive, in that it could not happen until at least 2016.

Here's the narrative we often hear from millennials: Obamacare is probably a bad bill that killed jobs, but's it the law, so let's deal with this reality and focus on job creation in the future.

So, even though a majority (57 percent) of millennials actually opposes Obamacare, young people are the least likely generation to support repealing the law. [13] Rasmussen polls indicate that just 41 percent of millennials believe Obamacare should be repealed, as compared with 53 percent of seniors. [14]

Recognizing that millennials are a largely optimistic group—four in five millennials think they will be better off than their parents, even while two-thirds say they are not earning enough money to live a good life—it makes sense that millennials are frustrated with the GOP's campaign tactics. Millennials are looking for stable paychecks and good jobs—and Obamacare feels like a distraction, not the real culprit.

A second key Republican claim is that lowering corporate tax rates will improve the economy, because tax money could be spent to hire new workers. Young people don't agree. An August 2012 XG survey among likely voters found that 34 percent of millennials thought they would be better off with a lower corporate tax rate, and only 36 percent thought it would help young people get jobs. [15]

Again, this does not mean that young people are inherently against lower corporate taxes. As with our disapproval of stimulus, it points to the fact that young people don't believe these policies will solve the root causes of unemployment and help us get jobs.

To date, we've never had a young person approach us to talk to about tax cuts and stimulus. When we conducted focus groups on this topic, millennials told us point-blank how they felt. Both parties' policies on addressing unemployment are self-serving. They are political red herrings intended to attract voters. That's why a third of young people believe their politicians' #1 priority is to help them-selves.[16] The average congressional representative is more than 50 years old—millennial employment, it seems, just isn't a top priority. They can't relate to our struggles and aren't even trying.

The root causes of unemployment are structural, millennials say. The three reasons we face high levels of unemployment are 1) slowing innovation, 2) globalization and outsourcing, and 3) a skills mismatch driven by poor education and technological change.

It makes sense that young people say these are the reasons they are unemployed, because these are directly observable phenomena. Innovative firms in developing countries, like Lenovo, are outpac-ing U.S. giants like Dell. When you go to the store, you can see that. Multinational firms are moving jobs abroad. When your friend gets laid off because his factory moves to China, you can see that. And our colleges are failing to teach us relevant skills that will help us find jobs when we graduate. Again, just take a moment to step into a college classroom, and this is obvious.

Since these symptoms of unemployment are so vivid, it is abun-dantly clear why millennials expect their leaders to start confronting these challenges—and why they're so frustrated with the rhetoric coming out of Washington.

Structural Issue #1: A Dearth of Innovation

As Jack rode towards Grand Central Station with two friends from MIT, he found himself discussing educational differences between the United States and their home countries, China and Mongolia. While both of the students discussed the inferiority of the U.S. education system—particularly in the math and sciences—they reveled at the level of innovation and creativity in the United States. "For all our advances, our system destroys creativity," one said.

For decades, America has been globally recognized as the technology capital of the world. Today more than ever, the rise of Facebook and Google, a boom in biotech, and the glow of Silicon Valley have created an impression that the United States is experiencing a technological renaissance with fast-paced innovation and change rapidly revolutionizing the way we live and do business.

But in a lot of ways, that's an illusion. Entrepreneurship is actually at an all-time low. "A broad cross-section of U.S. economists" agree that "a specific and necessary kind of risk-taking is on the decline," *The Wall Street Journal* recently reported. Between 1982 and 2011, the number of companies less than five years old dropped from 20 percent to 11 percent, census data shows.

That's problematic because innovative new firms are major job creators, accounting for the vast majority of new jobs created in the United States over the past 25 years. In terms of real wages, compensation per employee in innovation-intensive sectors of the economy grew by 50 percent between 1990 and 2007, more than twice the national average.[17]

Finally, public investments in innovation often result in revolutionary social impacts—the Defense Advanced Research Projects Agency (DARPA) is credited with inventing the Internet, and DNA sequencing research has resulted in a 14,000 percent economic return for biotech companies and has helped cure a variety of diseases.

Unfortunately, this innovation slowdown hits young millennials the hardest. While millennials are an entrepreneurial generation with dozens of technology pioneers, the number of people under the age of 30 who own businesses has reached a 24-year low.[18]

This lack of innovation can hurt the economy on a broader scale as well by making it less responsive and dynamic. "The U.S. has succeeded in part because of its dynamism, its high pace of job creation and destruction, and its high pace of churning out workers. ... The pessimistic view is we've lost our mojo," explained John Haltiwanger, a University of Maryland economist.[19]

To create new jobs, millennials are themselves working to reignite entrepreneurship, creating new companies and developing new technologies. But the government needs to play its part by investing in research and promoting innovation.

Structural Issue #2: Outsourcing and Globalized Economy

In the midst of the financial crisis in 2009, Cisco celebrated its fifth anniversary with a lavish reception in its New England Development Center. Rep. Niki Tsongas (D-MA) and representatives from the governor's office mingled with Cisco executives as they discussed the great technological advances and jobs growth that the facility had generated.

But behind the glamour and limelight lay a secret: all the while, Cisco was discreetly executing a "limited" restructuring—corporate jargon for moving jobs to India. Along with IBM, Cisco joined hundreds of companies that had begun to move operations abroad because, simply-put, the United States was no longer an attractive place to run many parts of these companies' operations.[20]

These restructurings have resulted in unemployment for American workers. China's gains in manufacturing, for example, came at the expense of 2.7 million U.S. jobs on net, according to a report published by the Economic Policy Institute, a conservative think tank. And for those lucky enough to keep their jobs, the numbers are no better. Foreign wage levels have "driven down wages for roughly 70 percent of the American workforce, or about 100 million workers," the report found.[21]

Overall, for a typical household with two earners, the annual cost of outsourcing is more than $2,500.[22] And these effects don't only impact blue-collar workers. According to Harvard professor Richard B. Freeman, a leading U.S. labor economist, "The college graduate situation has a global dimension—6 million bachelor's graduates in China that affect the U.S. market as well—which is very different than in the past."[23]

While protestors take to the streets to decry the actions of outsourcing corporations like FedEx, Nike, and Apple, the fact is that outsourcing is the result of rational incentives in a capitalist economy and is practiced by most major firms. A factory worker in the United States demands an average wage of $23.32 dollars an hour in salary and $8.47 dollars an hour in health care and benefits. In China, workers are employed at $1.36 dollars an hour. Even though U.S. workers are more productive and there are ethical issues associated with work conditions abroad, companies often make the economic choice to move jobs to the developing world.[24]

In order to succeed in the global economy, the United States needs to combat outsourcing by changing these rational incentives so that firms bring their business back to the United States. To do so, the United States will need to actively implement policies that incentivize foreign direct investment, promote trade, encourage firms to keep jobs in the United States, and support U.S. exporters. For example, instead of banning tax inversion to stop the practice, the United States should be changing tax codes to make doing business in the United States less burdensome.[25]

As a generation born into the globalized economy, millennials are less scared of foreign competition and more upset by the inaction of government leaders in making the United States more attractive.

"Globalization doesn't necessarily scare me as much as I would like to put American jobs first. Eventually, a global economy is something that we shouldn't be afraid of. I think it seems almost inevitable," Karl Meakin, a millennial from Connecticut, explained. Instead of fighting globalization, we need to harness it to our benefit.

Structural Issue #3: Solving the Skills Mismatch

Early in our debate careers, we were faced with a challenging question. We were tasked with convincing college-educated judges that a college education, on average, is not worth the cost. Surely, if society keeps telling people to go to college, it must be helpful, we assumed. The judges must have already come to a similar conclusion. But by the time we had rehearsed the case in dozens of debate rounds, we not only discovered a persuasive case against college education—we actually convinced ourselves that America is making a mistake by encouraging every student to get a college education.

Colleges are saddling young people with excessive debt without providing them the skills they need to succeed in the workforce. Just 41 percent of college graduates believe their college education helps them succeed on the job, *Harvard Business Review* found. Half of the survey's respondents said they do not know everything they need in order to do their current jobs. Employers agree; 61 percent believe there is a skills gap after graduation. One-third of surveyed workers said they missed a promotion or did not get a job because of this knowledge gap.[26]

NYU professor and renowned sociologist Richard Arum examined this topic in depth in a longitudinal study of college graduates. He found that one in three college students shows no statistically significant gains in critical thinking, complex reasoning, and writing skills by the time of graduation.

"How much are students actually learning in contemporary higher education? The answer for many undergraduates, we have concluded, is not much," wrote Arum and his co-author Josipa Roksa in their book *Academically Adrift*. For many undergraduates, "drifting through college without a clear sense of purpose is readily apparent."[27]

This is exactly what management consultants at McKinsey found in their survey exploring this topic. The firm concluded that "the 'voice of the graduate' revealed in this survey amounts to a cry for help—an urgent call to deepen the relevance of higher education to employment and entrepreneurship so that the promise of higher education is fulfilled." [28]

Just how useless is a college education today?

Apparently, today's college graduates can't even estimate if their car has enough gas to get to the station. A full 20 percent of bachelor's students and 30 percent of associate degree students had just "basic quantitative skills," Pew Charitable Trusts found. [29] 75 percent of two-year college students and more than half of bachelor's candidates could not score at the proficient level of literacy. [30] What's going on!

"If colleges aren't preparing students well enough for the job market ... it's downright scary for people like us who are going to college," said Eileen Brady, a millennial leader from Chicago. "Like, what are we going to do?"

To make matters worse, college is not even necessary or reasonable for many students in the first place. Only five of the top 25 fastest growing occupations over the next 10 years require any sort of college degree, according to Ohio University economist Richard Vedder. You don't need a college degree to work in retail, at a fast-food chain, or as a bartender. [31] So President Obama's plan to send everyone to college is not just expensive, but an "impossible dream."

A big problem with the whole college debate is that students just aren't prepared for the rigor of college in the first place. College students who graduated in the bottom 40 percent of their high school classes had only a 25 percent chance of graduating in 8.5 years, the U.S. Department of Education found. College is not an instant fix to our nation's problems. Just 13 percent of students with C or lower grade point averages in high school who enroll in college end up graduating at all. For these students, college is especially problematic; they load up on excessive debt, only to waste their time drifting through college before eventually dropping out. [32]

Finally, even in situations where a college education is appropriate, colleges are graduating students with low-demand degrees. Despite increasing demand for engineers, fewer and fewer students are pursuing degrees in engineering, technology, and computer science. In 1980, these students represented 11.1 percent of graduates; today they only represent 8.9 percent of new grads. With the advancement of technology and need for new workers in the fastest growing sectors of the U.S. economy, this is ludicrous. Graduates are instead gravitating toward the social sciences, which they believe are easier.[33]

And that's a problem, because these degrees are often not as helpful for students looking for jobs. "I have found every position to be one of the following: temporary, hourly, part-time, or volunteer. So, it's very rare to find any sort of salaried positions that pays well, but I'm not even expecting something like that," explained Caitlin Grey, a University of Chicago graduate with her Bachelor's degree in comparative human development. As of 2015, she was the temporary director of a youth employment program.[34]

Even as new graduates desperately look for work, employers can't fill openings for engineering positions. In 2014, the Manpower Group, a staffing firm, found that more than half of U.S. employers have trouble filling job openings because they cannot find qualified workers. Siemens, the U.S. arm of Germany's Siemens AG, has 3,000 available jobs all over the United States. This shortage of engineers is an ironic flipside to the millennial unemployment crisis.[35]

Together, the fact that college 1) is very expensive, 2) has a low return on investment in terms of actual skills, 3) is not necessary for many occupations, 4) is challenging for students who are not prepared in the first place, and 5) trains students in low-demand disciples, paints a shocking picture of an institution that is broken to the core. Fundamentally, it creates a skills mismatch once millennials reach the workforce—and our generation is paying the price every day.

"There's a big turnaround once you end college. If you don't have a next step laid out for you and if you don't have a plan, then you are kind of in free fall," explained Luke Siuty. He now works as an intern at Human Capital Media and as a staff writer at *Indie Game* magazine.[36] With their life plans ruined by their inability to find jobs, millennials are struggling to pay rent, and many of us are moving back in with parents.

"When I first started working I was working very odd hours and so I wasn't sure if I would have enough income to move out on my own," Nina Litoff told *Chicago Business Week*. As a result, the 24-year old public affairs assistant at the Art Institute of Chicago decided to live at home with her family.[37]

Millennials are hurting emotionally and financially. For some, things do eventually work out. Jamie Kaminsky took a job as a nanny before finding her current job, as a schoolteacher.

"Now that I do have my teaching job, I love when people ask what I do. Because I can say, I have this job, and I went to school for it and now I'm doing it. And I think people really respect that because people are so aware of how the job market is for us millennials," she said.[38]

But while we hope that things will turn around in our favor, our generation of voters will take action to promote the solutions we believe in. At home and in Washington, we are campaigning for policies that address core issues such as a lack of innovation, loss of global competitiveness, and skills mismatch.[39]

Here's what we need to do to address these issues and fight the root causes of millennial unemployment, according to young people.

Solution: Promote Research & Development

When it comes to promoting innovation, the first step for government is to increase funding for public research and development, which has been slashed across the board in recent years. Despite their increasing importance, NASA and the National Institutes of Health, for example, have seen their budgets repeatedly cut. Only 20 percent of the public supports these cuts, with the plurality of voters, 40 percent, pushing for budget increases.[40]

R&D funding is especially important to millennials, who are the most educated generation ever and see science as a "source of awe and a means for innovation."[41] Take a look at the widely popular Facebook Page "I F***ing Love Science," which has 18 million likes—more than three times *Scientific American* and *Popular Science* combined—and you'll understand why. This generation "came of age watching Bill Nye the Science Guy" and grew up with the likes of Larry Page, Steve Jobs, and Mark Zuckerberg as role models.[42]

For millennials, who view the world as positive and see current events ultimately leading toward a better future, science and technology investments are a way to cure disease, level the economic playing field, and do good. And because this young generation of do-gooders is optimistic and forward thinking, they are willing to make short-term sacrifices in return for long-run gains in terms of economic growth and job creation.

This pragmatic approach is appropriate given that investments in research can have an incredibly high return of between 20 and 60 percent annually.[43] Investment in R&D has a so-called spending multiplier, meaning each dollar spent generates more than a dollar for the economy, not to mention the health benefits that ensue. It is estimated that every $1 in National Institutes of Health funding generates upwards of $2.13 in pharmaceutical sales, stimulating economic growth. The U.S. investment of $4 billion the Human Genome Project is estimated to have generated $965 billion in economic growth alone.[44]

"We're really advanced in technology right now and that's going to create a lot more jobs. A lot of the jobs of the future are going to have to do with the sciences," explained Ajay Singh, a Democratic millennial leader from Texas.

Nonetheless, the U.S. budget in the sciences has shrunk from 0.25 percent of GDP 40 years ago to just 0.13 percent today. Meanwhile, many of our peer countries in the developed and developing world have taken the opposite approach, increasing their spending in the sciences. R&D funding is therefore not just a question of innovation, but it is also a question of global competitiveness—both of which are important to keeping jobs in the United States.

Congress should make the Research and Development Tax Credit, which allows companies to take unlimited tax deductions for research spending, permanent as well. Doing so will incentivize companies to increase research spending to socially optimal levels, rather than re-allocating funding toward immediate investor returns. Promoting R&D will help create jobs and propel our economy forward from its place as the 27th out of 42 countries for R&D.[45]

Think science doesn't make for sexy stump speeches? Think again. No one can visibly see the impact of a "shovel-ready" jobs programs or a tax cut. Everyone can visualize the tangible benefits of investing in innovation. And science is a cool way to motivate and energize millennials. "I F***cking Love Science" has 18 million likes on Facebook. Do you?

Solution: Reduce Regulation and Protect Small Business

Andrea and Zoey Green were 8 and 7 years old when they decided to open a lemonade stand so that they could earn the $100 needed to take their dad to Splash Kingdom for Father's Day. Like many enterprising young kids before them, the Texas sisters made some lemonade and kettle corn, set out a table, and began to raise money for the cause.[46] But 60 minutes and $25 in profit later, the girls ran into trouble with the authorities. The girls were shut down because they didn't have a "peddler's permit," which would have cost $150, or approval from the Dept. of Health.[47]

As you might imagine, these absurd regulations have millennials up in arms. "A Florida law requires vending-machine labels to urge the public to file a report if the label is not there. The Federal Railroad Administration insists that all trains must be painted with an

"F" at the front, so you can tell which end is which. Bureaucratic busy-bodies in Bethesda, Maryland, have shut down children's lemonade stands because the enterprising young moppets did not have trading licenses. The list goes hilariously on," reported *The Economist*.[48]

Michael Sinensky is one small business owner who has been a victim of regulation. Before he could start a bar, he spent a year parsing through regulations involving 10 city agencies, 30 permits, and more than 20 inspections. And even if he were to pass all of these regulatory hurdles, new health-care regulations would require Sinensky to treat managers and regular employees equally. This, he said, would force him to cut subsidies for managers who would otherwise have received extra benefits. "In my industry, regulations have caused me to adjust the way I operate to cause overall more harm to my employees then the owners," Sinensky lamented. [49]

Bars are far from the only companies stifled by regulation. In the tech industry, proposed restrictions on Uber and Amazon could prevent thousands of Americans from finding work and slow the pace at which we adopt game-changing innovations. And in biotech, many start-ups lack access to public markets due to onerous regulatory compliance requirements that can cost upwards of $2.5 million. Those projects that are funded can have such long approval periods that patient advocacy groups are left to fight the FDA for access to life-saving technologies.

Even President Obama, a champion of big government, acknowledged the problem. "Rules have gotten out of balance, placing unreasonable burdens on business—burdens that have stifled innovation and have had a chilling effect on growth and jobs," he wrote for *The Wall Street Journal* in 2014. With 36 new regulations passed every day, our government seems to be exacerbating—not solving—its regulatory woes. Neither party is taking sufficient steps to address this issue.

And millennials are both personally affected and upset by small business regulation. "My dad started a small business at the height of the recession and he was ultimately not successful in that endeavor because not only of the recession but the taxes and the regulations that he faced," Roberto Ruiz, a millennial leader in New Jersey, said. "The taxes that he faced, especially in the state of New Jersey, were at levels that if he would have started the company in the State of Florida he wouldn't have had to deal with. On top of that, New Jersey has some of the highest income taxes in the nation, so not only was the corporation being taxed but the income he earned from that corporation was being taxed, so you had almost triple taxation."

Ruiz said that reducing the regulatory burden on small business is his top priority, and he is not alone. Samantha Paul works at a small business in southern California and she says that the growth of small businesses is key to our country's economic success. "You have to consider the value of smaller business and start-ups that provide opportunity to people," she said. "When you are innovating and when you are investing, that is going to create so many new opportunities."

Ashley Rinner, a conservative millennial from Ohio, agreed that the effects of regulation and taxes on small business resonate strongly with her. "My neighbors actually have a small business. They have a Chinese restaurant. They came from China, they immigrated and slowly the rest of their family is coming over. And they almost lost their small business because more taxes were raised, and it's just not a good situation," she said.

Deregulation of small business is an election-winning issue for presidential candidates and city council contenders alike. The issue drives at the core of what it means to be an entrepreneur in America. Making it easier for small business owners to create new jobs is a great way to help solve the millennial unemployment crisis in America.

With politicians catering to corporate donors, small businesses never seem to get the attention they deserve in the halls of power. In government procurement, where the government must select its own contractors, for example, small businesses get the short end of the stick, losing out to corporations with deeper pockets.

Ruiz, who was a "hilltern" this past summer in the office of Rep. Carlos Curbelo (R-FLA), described the procurement process as unfairly favoring large businesses. Say you have a car factory that sells bulletproof cars. Ruiz said that the pre-approval process for a small business could take up to three years and that existing contractors could protest the new vendor. These roadblocks make little sense for a country already struggling to create new jobs for millennials.

"About a third of government contracts should really come from small businesses or really emerging businesses," Ruiz said. "When I was in D.C., I met some people that worked for a small business that did cyber security and were trying to get contracts with the federal government, but were constantly being beaten out by huge cyber security companies that had tons of power with lobbyists and what not. But they held certain attributes, they held patents for certain software that other companies could not get, so our government wasn't getting the latest and greatest technology because of our ridiculous procurement process."

It doesn't have to be this way. To start, the Securities and Exchange Commission (SEC) and Government Accounting Office (GAO) should be required to conduct surveys to understand which regulations are most burdensome, and then remove these. Instead of assuming regulations always need to be renewed and extended, all regulations should have predetermined sunset dates so that bureaucrats must receive explicit approval to continue enforcing regulations. The default needs to be toward less regulation, not more. Likewise, an independent watchdog should audit regulatory agencies and publish information on compliance costs.

Not only should legislatures end the regulatory madness, but to win millennial support they must actively deregulate small businesses. For example, the Entrepreneur Access to Capital Act would have made it legal for entrepreneurs to crowdfund for their businesses online by selling equity stakes in their firms, giving them a new source of cash. Though the bill passed with an overwhelming bipartisan majority in the House, it was never passed in the Senate.[50]

Solution: Encourage High Skilled Immigration

Walk through the halls of any engineering school and you'll see thousands of first- and second-generation Americans striving to contribute to the U.S. economy. You'll find them in robotics groups winning national competitions and science labs raking up awards for their research. Walk up to one of these students and introduce yourself. Ask what they want to do when they graduate. The answer is most likely medicine, engineering, or software development. Some have permanent visas, but others do not. These are the people building America's economy—inventing technology that help give our workers a competitive edge.

But not all these students will stay in America. Not because they don't love our country—they do—but because we're kicking them out.

"I once was interviewing for a not-so-big firm, and I passed the first round. Yet when the HR [human resources] person asked me if I was an international student and I said yes, the recruiter immediately said I wasn't eligible for the position anymore because the company doesn't sponsor the H-1B visa application," said Ying Yuan, a UPenn graduate who now works at the accounting firm Ernest & Young in Philadelphia.

Foreign students are real people who have much to contribute to our economy. We're the ones sending them away. As a friend of ours recently joked, "Hey, I need a job more than you do, because if I don't find one, they're sending me home."

The reality is that many high skilled workers are not as lucky as Yuan, whose H-1B visa application was sponsored by EY. Every year, thousands of students are forced out of the United States. Take Sadhak Sengupta, for example. The Indian immigrant is a medical research scientist working at the Roger Williams Medical Center in Rhode Island. He had been working on H1-B visas for years as part of a team developing a treatment for brain cancer using immunotherapy techniques. But in October of 2015, *The New York Times* reported that Dr. Sengupta's H-1B visa "unexpectedly failed to renew."

"I am so disappointed, I don't have words to describe," Sengupta said. "Instead of hiring workers here, shall I bundle up my research for a cure for brain tumors and take it back to India? Is that what America wants?"

"We have been here years, we have kids here, we bought houses," said Vikram Desai, an electrical engineer in a similar predicament. "We consider ourselves future Americans, not temporary workers."

Driving this point home for millennials is Mike Krieger, co-founder of the iconic social networking app Instagram. The Brazilian native and Stanford graduate told *Bloomberg* that it took him longer to get a visa than it did to actually build the web application, which he later sold to Facebook for $1 billion.

"It was approaching the point of hard conversations," he said. "I had moments where I was like, 'Maybe I should just tell Kevin [his co-founder] to forget about it and find somebody who is easier to hire.'"[51] Now, of course, millennials upload thousands of photos to Krieger's app every day.

This is crazy. Researchers believe that every foreign-born engineer in the United States creates an average of 2.6 jobs for American workers.[52] A full 26 percent of U.S.-based Nobel laureates are foreign-born. This isn't charity—it is in our self-interest to bring talented foreign workers to America. But we're doing the opposite.

"Because our current immigration system is outdated and inefficient, many high-skilled immigrants who want to stay in America are forced to leave because they are unable to obtain permanent visas. Some do not bother to come in the first place," a letter penned by Facebook CEO Mark Zuckerberg reads. This is often due to visa shortages, long waits for green cards, and lack of mobility."

Congress needs to turn this issue around immediately. It can start by actually passing the "staple a green card act," a bill that would give every STEM student at a U.S. university a green card upon graduation. This is a very popular bill in stump speeches. Politicians love to talk about it. But it never gets passed. The United States should dramatically expand EB-5 "entrepreneur" visas, which allow foreign investors to attain green cards if they invest at least $500,000 into economically disadvantaged areas to sponsor job-creating projects. EB-5 visas by definition promote economic activity. America has a shortage of engineers, scientists, and entrepreneurs. We can change that.

Comprehensive immigration reform would be nice. We'll get to that later. But that's more controversial and there's room for reasonable people to differ on how that should be implemented. Not so with highly skilled foreign workers. We need them. The only question we should be asking is how fast can we get them and how long can we keep them.

Solution: Increase Foreign Direct Investment

As winter turned to spring in Massachusetts, former governor Deval Patrick boarded his first flight to Ben Gurion International Airport in Israel. The governor was not on a delegation with fellow politicians or on vacation with family. Flanking him were the state's most prominent business leaders looking to court Israeli investment in their businesses.

The trip came towards the end of 2011; over the previous four years, foreign direct investment from Israel—the country with the second largest concentration of NASDAQ companies in the clean energy and water technology, medicine, and software spaces—had grown by 79 percent. Patrick's model, which is now being reviewed by state governments across the country, provides a lens into how foreign direct investment can invigorate the American economy— and how politicians can play an important role in developing these mutually beneficial relationships.

Foreign direct investment is a powerful tool for job creation, and globalization has opened the floodgates. The bipartisan consensus on foreign direct investment is a breath of fresh air. In 2011, value-added by U.S. affiliates of foreign-owned companies accounted for 4.7 percent of U.S. private output and 5.6 million jobs. In 2011, the federal government established SelectUSA, a federal program to increase foreign direct investment in the USA. These programs indicate that America is headed in the right direction. But we want more.

"We're in the 21st century, we are a globalized society. Instead of working against other countries, if we work with other countries to create some type of international businesses, our domestic economy will benefit," said Stephanie Brito, a millennial leader from Florida.

First, the United States must create an environment that is conducive to foreign investment. "To get the companies and industries we want, we not only need to make the first move, we need to be the prettiest girl at the ball," opined Anne Kim of *Washington Monthly*.[53]

Instead, we're standing in the corner, wearing a worn-out dress and not even talking to potential courters. It's time to clean up. That means investment in infrastructure, especially freight, port, and air transportation, which are the pillars of international trade. Unfortunately, infrastructure projects are notoriously inefficient and slow; an investment in infrastructure needs more than just money, it requires a commitment to results and a strong public-private sector partnership.

Next, we need to start exploring the ballroom, talking to the most attractive men and women on the dance floor. Multilateral trade negotiations are a time-tested tool that will allow the United States to boost investment and exports. Already, we have a competitive cost structure, an economy with strong exports and superior services that will allow our country to benefit immensely from free trade agreements.

As recently as 2015, polls show that 69 percent of millennials said free trade agreements are good for the United States, as compared with just 51 percent of seniors and 60 percent of Americans 30-49. We're the most pro-trade generation out there. Rather than fearing foreign competition, we embrace it. After all, there's no point in denying reality, right?

A focus of multilateral trade agreements should be taxation, which has been an obstacle to Foreign Direct Investment (FDI) in the past. Protectionism is politically convenient, and helps win union support, but is often a major sticking point for trading partners, especially in Asia. The economic consensus on free trade is that it benefits all parties involved.

Leaders of the President's Council of Economic Advisors, from the days of Gerald Ford to today, all agree that free trade helps the economy.[54] It is ironic, then, that Democrats in Congress turned against free trade, recently blocking the Trans-Pacific Partnership (TPP) before it eventually passed. 65 percent of young people and 49 percent of Americans overall said the TPP would improve the economy, according to Pew Research.[55]

Who were these Democrats serving? Their constituents? Certainly not, since voters tend to favor free trade and the evidence is very clear that free trade is good for the economy. Their party? Not at all. President Obama desperately hoped the TPP would pass, and Hillary Clinton called it the "gold standard" before flip-flopping on the issue.

No, as is becoming all too common in politics today, elected officials were serving their own interests, hoping to galvanize the populist segment of the Democratic base and maybe protect themselves from potential primary challengers. The politics of free trade demonstrates an important point: millennials are fighting against self-interested politicians, not against a specific political ideology. We're fighting for common sense.

Finally, America needs to make the first move. The American government needs to unleash the potential of SelectUSA, which is the arm of the federal government that encourages foreign investment. Congress must allow SelectUSA to act to encourage FDI in specific regions of the country. Current constraints say that it must only promote national FDI.

This is absurd. Farmers in Iowa need to export their crops; programmers in Silicon Valley want to export software. It's just a different ball game. Regional industries—like West Virginia coal and

California biotech—need a regional focus. At the same time, Congress should increase SelectUSA's budget from its meager $7 million to create value for our economy.

Solution: Encourage Exports by Small Firms

With exports supporting 11.3 million jobs in the United States, it is increasingly important that we create policies that give U.S. firms a competitive edge in the global marketplace.[56] The Department of Commerce has played an important role in supporting U.S. firms, coordinating 77 trade missions to 38 countries, which resulted in $1.25 billion in export sales, and coordinating foreign trade shows, which resulted in $11 billion in exports.[57]

"The strong correlation between exports and U.S. jobs is why the Department of Commerce is focused on helping American companies sell their goods and services all over the globe," said U.S. Secretary of Commerce Penny Pritzker. "The fact is, 95 percent of worldwide consumers live outside U.S. borders, and for our businesses to grow and create jobs, we have to make it possible for them to reach new markets. As an Administration, we are committed to setting the conditions that promote trade and investment, and ensuring that exports continue to drive local, state, and national economies and create jobs."

Future administrations should support export financing, taking tougher stances on foreign currency manipulation and supporting aggregators, which help small businesses gain international visibility.

Solution: Promoting the Insourcing of Jobs

Americans keep telling their favorite brands to "bring jobs back home." Companies are responding. GM, Ford, Starbucks, Caterpillar, Google, and GE are among the U.S. firms that have begun to insource jobs, bringing capacity back to the United States.

Publically, the companies say that being in the United States improves time-to-market, ensures intellectual property protection, and leads to better product quality. As cynical millennials, we think their motivations are less pure: they realize that the money they lose on the margins when insourcing can be recouped by the improved brand imaging that comes with bringing manufacturing home.

But that's okay, because it's true. Millennials, who have been largely categorized as civically minded, are among many Americans who say that they would rather buy from companies that keep jobs in America. Survey data shows that millennials would be willing to pay more for American-made products, more than any other demographic.[58]

The federal government should use its influence to accelerate this trend, directly intervening to provide additional benefits to companies that insource through tax benefits. On a more basic level, companies should not face tax penalties for bringing jobs back to the United States. Businesses also expect long-term certainty about the U.S. economy, especially when it comes to tax liabilities. America needs to fix its tax code and clarify the responsibilities of U.S.-based and international companies.

Finally, the United States should "shamelessly court" companies to bring jobs to America. Already, foreign countries are offering huge incentives for companies to move abroad. China, for example, often requires firms to bring their manufacturing operations to China as a precondition for doing business there. Singapore and South Korea offer firms free land and tax holidays. Israel offered Intel real cash to bring operations to the small country, subsiding $1.2 billion of Intel's initial investment there. At the very least, the United States should be actively talking to companies about the benefits of staying in the United States and directly asking them to keep operations here, a proposal championed by Economic Strategy Institute President Clyde Prestowitz.[59]

If the U.S. president were to ask for pledges from CEOs to keep jobs in the United States, this would provide the country with a cost-free way of saving jobs. By playing to the patriotism of CEOs as individuals and by making "the ask," the president has everything to gain and nothing to lose. It would be really neat if a candidate began asking for these pledges on the campaign trail—what a way to show the American people that s/he is committed to jobs!

Solution: Help College Graduates Become Job-Ready

At York College in Pennsylvania, the auditorium is filled to the brim with dozens of students in shorts and flip-flops. This is no Beyoncé concert, no Bill Gates lecture or other celebrity gathering. At the front of the room stands Laura Wand, in her short cut blonde hair and suit, talking to students about one of the many things they won't learn in school: professionalism.

"Dude, dress up. This isn't the mall," Wand, now the vice president of business development for Johnson Controls, a local employer, told the crowd. "Multitasking is a myth," she said. "You got a great job. Turn off the cell phone. Stop texting." While these tips seem like common sense, for many millennials in the audience, the suggestions were unheard of.

"I will be hitting the job market in less than a month now," Evan Smrek, a college senior who attended the talk, told NPR at the time. "They mentioned some aspects of interviews, or just how to conduct yourself. I was kind of like, 'OK, I wish I had known that a month ago, when I had my interview.' But it's definitely something to take away for following interviews." [60]

Professionalism is one of many work-related areas in which many college graduates are unprepared. McKinsey's report on the "Voice of the Graduate" revealed that colleges often treat work-readiness as a low priority, to the detriment of their students. Universities must re-envision their roles as pre-career institutions rather than simply places of higher learning—a wholesale rebranding of the college experience. How can colleges achieve this goal?

They should start by hiring career counselors. The median student-academic advisor ratio is approximately 1:300, though it ranges widely among schools.[61] Because there is little data available on student satisfaction rates with career advisors, we surveyed a few hundred students at 28 universities. While our sample was by no means representative, its results are telling. Seventy-nine percent of students said that they rarely or never see their career advisors, and 92 percent said they would like more support in setting and accomplishing career goals. Colleges need to fill this gap.

Moreover, every student should have an internship in college. No exceptions. If universities are meant to introduce students to the workforce, then students ought to have an experience actually working. In many universities, students are on their own when finding internship opportunities. Today, one out of every four students does not have an internship by the time s/he graduates from college, *Bloomberg BusinessWeek* found. These students disproportionately do not have jobs at graduation. Whereas 61 percent of students who had internships received job offers by the winter of their senior years, only 28 percent of students without internship experience had offers. So we need to help students get internships if they want to find jobs.[62]

Schools should be encouraging STEM education as another tool to promote job creation, and young people believe the federal government should incentivize these programs through low-interest loans. Making it cheaper to get a STEM education is important, and creates a strong incentive for students to go into these fields—and with this earnings boost comes a greater likelihood that the loans will be paid off. College should not shelter students from the impact of their career choices. Instead of leaving students to figure this out for themselves, universities should release statistics on employment rates for graduates of different majors.

In order to get students interested in STEM, the government should invest in STEM education at the secondary and elementary school levels. In the Pathways in Technology Early College High

School (P-TECH) program, for example, every student gets an internship and has the opportunity to graduate with an associate's degree in computer information systems and electromechanical engineering technology. The curriculum for the school was developed with IBM.

Reynoldsburg High School in Ohio, by contrast, is divided into various pre-professional "academies" that have relationships with nearby institutions. Loving High School in New Mexico gives students hands-on training by teaching them to build houses in an effort to prepare them for careers in architecture and construction. Local governments should fund and promote these creative, pre-professional initiatives.[63]

There are other places where the government can play a role. The federal government should grade universities on the "work-readiness" of their students, creating a competitive incentive for universities to train their students for the workforce. This metric can be publicized, just as traditional rankings play into the college selection process. The federal government's funding of universities should be contingent on their ability to produce students ready for the workforce. Universities (public and private) should only be re-certified if they can demonstrate that greater than 25 percent of their students demonstrate gains in critical thinking and verbal skills. This percentage should be gradually increased over time.

State governments must take an active role in reforming public colleges as well. University presidents should be appointed on the basis of their ability to create a pre-professional atmosphere, and governors should be assessed on the ability of their public universities to meet federal standards for workplace preparedness.

There is no excuse for public colleges, which the government directly controls, to continue to stagnate. If public colleges can improve the work-readiness, they will either win students from private institutions or force private institutions to make changes.

Solution: Encourage Vocational Training and Apprenticeships

Unlike many millennials his age, William Fuller graduated with much more than just a high school diploma. In 2014, he brought home a carpentry certification and a full-time offer from a cabinetmaker in Lester, Pennsylvania. Fuller, who began working in construction with his uncle at a young age, was pushed to become job-ready at Philadelphia's Mercy Vocational High School, "which aims to ensure that students leave not only with the basics they need to earn a high school diploma in the state, but also an industry certification."

"I always liked taking apart things and putting them back together," Fuller says. That's why the career-training programs at Mercy were appealing to him. "It shows you how the world is, and what to expect when you're going to be going out there to work."

Anna Prisco, a New Jersey resident and millennial leader, believes job programs like Fuller's are crucial to putting our generation back to work. "I think education can fix things, such as people being over-prepared or underprepared for the job market, which is a huge problem. A lot of people go into college now and get degrees, and we have a workforce that is far overeducated for the jobs that we have because our generation places such an overemphasis on college," she said.

"Having vocational school instead of college for some people may be more efficient because people are coming out of college with thousands and thousands of dollars of debt and they still can't get a good job. And they'll resort to a job that they could have gotten from a vocational school with much less in debt. I think some emphasis on vocational school, or a lot of emphasis, would help," she added.

"We've done a disservice in this country by suggesting that there's only one path to success, which is to get a bachelor's degree," Mark Edwards, executive director of Opportunity Nation, a millennial advocacy group, told *U.S. News & World Report*. "There are many good-paying jobs available today that, quite candidly, a four-year Bachelor of Arts degree does not prepare them for."[64]

Millennial workers in the trades tend to earn good wages— between $50,000 and $100,000 a year. Jennifer Yost, who has worked as a carpenter apprentice for the past three years, earns $35.77 an hour, with vacation pay and a pension.

"I came into the apprenticeship when I was 33. And I wish I would have known about it right out of school, you know? Just so I could have taken advantage of it then and had all these years reinvested," she said.

Yost said she's happy to finally be self-sustaining, saying that she no longer needs to ask others for help. Over the course of their careers, workers who complete apprenticeships tend to earn $240,000 more than their peers who don't. And 87 percent of apprentices receive jobs upon graduation, according to the World Economic Forum. Apprenticeships give young people the opportunity to learn real skills that they will be able to use in the workforce.[65]

Though most Americans associate the trades with World War II era factories, it turns out there's a shortage of workers with these "middle skills." According to the National Skills Coalition, there's a 10 percent gap between the 44 percent of workers with these skills— such as woodworking, welding, and carpentry—and the number of jobs available, which are 54 percent of total jobs in the United States.[66]

"I want 23-, 24-year-olds that can buy a house, because they have a living-wage career, and I think this field of advanced manufacturing has those opportunities," explained John Niebergall, an advanced engineering teacher at Sherwood High School in Oregon.

The unions are on board, actively recruiting new workers to join the trades. The Pacific Northwest Regional Council of Carpenters, for example, estimates that 40 percent of its carpenters will retire in the next decade. With these boomers gone, there's a growing need for young people to fill the ranks.

Recognizing this opportunity to spur economic growth while creating jobs for young people, states are investing in improving technical education in their high schools. In Oregon, Governor Kate Brown said that when she talks to companies, their number one concern is "having a talented, diverse work pool to hire from." As this need becomes more acute, the governor recently added $35 million to the state's technical education budget, nearly doubling it.

"The industrial worker of today that sort of looks nearly extinct in the United States may be one of the most prized assets we have in a very short period of time," explained Frank Foti, CEO of Vigor Industrial, a shipbuilding firm with more than 1,000 employees, in an interview on *PBS NewsHour*. With growth in "middle-skilled" industries, he said, we are going to see increased competition for talented workers.

"Everyone's thoughts at least in high school is, 'I'm going to go out there. I'm going to work my ass off. And I'm going to make nothing doing it. I might as well go flip a burger instead of swing a hammer; much easier, for the same price,'" explained Zac Clayville, a high school graduate who now works as a tool room attendant. "But not many people realize that there are really well-paying jobs down here," he said.

Solution: Reforming Job Training

Job retraining programs are another area where the federal government can implement substantial changes, because it exerts the most control on the programs. There are currently 44 federal employment retraining programs, and navigating them can be time-consuming and inefficient. "Though well-intentioned, the current array of programs causes confusion for job seekers as well as employers who might otherwise want to engage in federally funded job training services," wrote Kendra Kosko, a former vice president for government relations at the HR Policy Association who now works for the U.S. Senate Pensions Counsel.

The federal government should unify job-retraining programs and encourage states to create a simplified online application process for their programs. Congressional Republicans recently proposed a bill that would give states the ability to appoint a greater number of employers to job-retraining boards. The bill, the Supporting Knowledge and Investing in Lifelong Skills Act, would also streamline or eliminate 35 inefficient job retraining programs, including 26 programs identified in a 2011 GAO report.

Millennials don't buy into the Democratic argument that every demographic group from Native Americans to veterans requires its own special job-retraining program. In fact, creating a diverse talent pool of workers will allow state governments to develop more effective and comprehensive programs. Cost savings from streamlining job retraining programs should be reinvested to expand the capacity and quality of such programs. In addition to sponsoring state job retraining programs, the federal government should sponsor the creation of unique content—videos about job retraining—for websites like KhanAcademy.com. A set of online career videos would give unemployed workers a resource to lean on and create great value at a low cost.

CONCLUSION

The job situation for young people may be worse than ever before, but it's not all gloom and doom. Young people are smart and resilient, and they know what it takes to get our economy working again. That's why the dialogue they are having amongst themselves is so radically different from the conversations that are happening in the halls of Washington.

While our leaders worry about tweaking fiscal and monetary policy, millennials worry about the facts on the ground: a lack of innovation, globalization, and a broken education system. By solving these issues, millennials are optimistic that they'll have prosperous futures. 88 percent of millennials say they expect to earn enough to live a good life in the future, even while two-thirds say that is not the case today.

"It's hard to imagine a time when there was this level of optimism among a group so hard-hit by economic conditions," said Kim Parker, associate director of the Pew Research Center's Social and Demographic Trends project. "In the face of the Great Recession, it's pretty phenomenal."

To combat structurally high unemployment, millennials expect their leaders to invest in tangible solutions to this problem; that's why millennials are the most pro-R&D generation in America, the most pro-trade generation in America, and believe globalization should be harnessed as a force for good. Millennials are widely supportive of small business, support deregulation, and expect their leaders to "shamelessly court" foreign direct investment.

To solve the skills mismatch, which millennials identify as root cause of their unemployment, millennials want public colleges to face greater accountability and want their states to invest in vocational training programs and apprenticeships. These policies represent a positive, constructive and optimistic approach to dealing with an issue that has haunted millennials for the past decade.

Like they did with gun control, millennials have carved out a unique stance on this public policy issue, which is phenomenally important to their future. Choosing neither the Republican approach, nor the Democratic approach, millennials have developed their own consensus that offers a realistic path toward economic prosperity. This consensus transcends partisan, economic and racial lines—it is a pragmatic effort by millennials to create a better future for themselves and their families.

Food for thought: the rise of anti-establishment leaders in politics today is a natural consequence of this interest in practical solutions.

Young people don't believe that traditional politicians are speaking their language or even talking about the issues that make a difference in their lives. So when they find candidates who champion these practical ideas—who speak their language—they swoon.

Thus, widespread support for anti-establishment candidates is not so surprising—at least these people are talking about outsourcing instead of the tax code and about why colleges aren't working, instead of Obamacare. This is something to keep in mind as we delve deeper into the important policy questions facing the millennial generation. We'll explore this attraction to authentic, anti-establishment candidates in greater detail soon.

Less Debt: Make College Affordable

NEW YORK, NEW YORK

Today, too many college students find themselves "academically adrift," wandering through college and then graduating without the skills they need to succeed in the workforce. This was the case we made at Columbia University in New York City, which was a breakout performance for us early in our careers as debaters.

We chose to argue the less popular case: that going to college is a bad idea, and ended up convincing ourselves—and a panel of college educated judges—that this was true. When we were eventually eliminated from the tournament, it was by a team that also believed college education is a bad investment, and forced us to defend the expensive institution!

Of course, for all our sarcasm about college, we are college students and we recognize that in a rapidly changing economy, the U.S. will need millions of college-educated workers. And we know that young people want to go to college, because it's an important tool for socioeconomic mobility. You can come from any background and rise through college to achieve a place in the middle class.

So instead of simply shunning college education as a waste of time, our generation is looking to figure out how to simultaneously improve outcomes for college students and make college more affordable. For young people looking to achieve financial security, fulfilling the promise of higher education is a crucial step on the road toward achieving the American dream.

The College Debt Trap

Today, colleges hardly achieve their goals of being socioeconomic equalizers; instead, many of these institutions of higher education epitomize—if not exacerbate—economic inequality. While wealthy students can afford the trappings of a traditional college education—an on-campus apartment, spring break trips to Florida, and expensive fraternity fees—less fortunate students graduate with tens of thousands of dollars of debt, which helps shape their future career opportunities.

In 2015, Jack explored the stark contrast between college life for the wealthy elite and middle-class students in "A Tale of Two Winter Breaks," a feature story for the *Daily Pennsylvanian*. He compared the experiences of two college freshmen—let's call them John and Mary—who lived in the same building and experienced for the first time the sharp contrast between their lifestyles.

John spent his winter break partying in Aspen. Mary worked an eight-hour shift at Chick-fil-A to earn extra money and help pay for college. John ate expensive restaurant diners; Mary ate in the dining hall with her friends. In America, we admire success and appreciate the wealthy. But colleges should be working to level the playing field; instead, they continue to raise prices and burden students with an average of $28,000 in debt, making it even more difficult for Mary to catch up.

By now, many readers are probably acquainted with the well-trodden statistics. 70 percent of college graduates leave school with debt, and over the past decade, the price of a college education has nearly doubled.[1] Today, Americans are liable for $1.2 trillion in outstanding college debt, and soaring tuition is a national crisis. The rising cost of college tuition is driven by inefficient managers seeking to maximize their revenue without cutting costs. It costs roughly $8,000 a year to educate an undergraduate at an average residential college, according to the Cato Institute. Yet the average bill charged at a public university is $16,000. Private universities, on average, charge $37,000 in tuition.[2]

Millennials—of all political and economic stripes—recognize that high levels of debt have adverse effects on college students, first while they're in school and then again after they graduate. Debt pigeonholes students into "profitable" majors and changes their career trajectory. "It really impacts how you look at future careers because you're not only trying to be financially secure but you have all this debt you're graduating with that you have to handle," said Leigh Ann Eisenhauer, who didn't receive financial aid to attend the University of Pennsylvania. "I pay for everything here and so I'm limited in what I can do. ... I think a lot of people are excluded because of that."

Leigh Ann is not alone. As a freshman at Harvard College, Nancy Ko asked the humanities faculty how low-income students or otherwise disadvantaged students could find a path into academia. "I had to leave the dinner early for a meeting, but before I left, an employee of [the Office of Career Services] grabbed me aside and told me with a pitying look, 'Your parents were grocery store owners. So maybe it's your turn to do something more like law or medicine, and later on it can be your kids' turn to do academia,'" Ko recounted on Facebook.

These days, most of Ko's classmates will be compelled to choose a course of study that aligns with their socioeconomic status. A Credit Sesame poll found that more than twice as many millennials—33 percent compared with 14 percent of Gen X—said salary was an important factor in selecting a major. It's no wonder that the mean household income of students who study English is close to $100,000. Everyone else is scared away into more "secure" majors.

And while many of Leigh Ann's friends are stressing over boyfriends and homework, she has to think about paying the bills. "Cumulative student loans were significantly and inversely associated with better psychological functioning," a University of South Carolina study found. This can be particularly harmful for the third of college students who already report feeling so stressed it is difficult to function.[3]

"I am not rich, my family is not well off at all, the people around me aren't struggling with the same issues as me. I have to worry about whether my parents are going to be able to pay the rent, whereas the people around me are complaining about studying for a test," Brito said. "I didn't realize what a disadvantage that put me at."

Many of these students take out debt in the hopes that after just a few years in the workforce, they will be able to pay off their loans and return to a sense of normality. Unfortunately, this is frequently not the case. All too often, post-collegiate decisions are marred by student loans. Take marriage, for example. Ashley Matusz and her boyfriend Joe Fisher told *USA Today* that they have struggled to balance their romantic relationship with financial concerns. "Ever since the beginning, I was like, 'You know I'm going to have a lot of debt,' " Matusz said. "I see it as both of our debt, not just hers," Fisher explained. One financial advisor went so far as to suggest that couples plan "money dates in addition to movie dates," to discuss financial obligations and keep their marriages on track.[4]

Despite their best intentions, 7 percent of adults with college debt delay tying the knot, according to a Pew survey. Similarly, home ownership rates in the 25-34-year-old age bracket dropped 8 percent between 2004 and 2013, no doubt due in part to debt and tightening credit after the financial crisis.[5] "My generation, especially, has been given mixed signals by society," explained Duke graduate Camille Noe Pagan, author of the novel *The Art of Forgetting*. "We're told to attend the best schools we possibly can—but then we're punished when we can't afford it."

It's for these reasons and more that millennials consistently rank student debt as one of the most important issues for Washington to address.[6] Allstate polls show that 30 percent of millennials who define themselves as "just started out" cited student loans as their biggest financial challenge. Unlike jobs and guns, which are broader issues that affect all Americans, college debt uniquely affects young voters. One Facebook "meme" pokes fun at this difference, imagining a young girl's grandfather criticizing her for "whining" about the exorbitant price of college. She reminds him that back in his day, even after adjusting for inflation, college tuition was a fraction of its current price.

For some young people, the cost of debt is becoming so high that they are choosing to avoid it—either by not enrolling in college, or by choosing their colleges based on price.[7] For no one was this tradeoff clearer than for Ronald Nelson, a Tennessee student who made national headlines when he was admitted to all eight Ivy League schools, and again when he rejected all of them. "It's an experience that I'll absolutely never forget, being able to open up eight different letters and then seeing, 'Congratulations, welcome to our class of 2019,'" he said. Feeling he couldn't afford these schools' tuitions, Nelson accepted a full-ride to the University of Alabama.

Today, the issue of college debt has rapidly climbed in importance, now ranking as one of the most important priorities for millennial voters. Young people are going to continue fighting until reform is implemented at a local, state and federal level—not because we're entitled to "free" college, but rather because ensuring universal access to education is important to making sure that the American dream remains achievable. While there are many who would like the government to wave a magic wand and forgive their debt, most young people support a number of realistic solutions to fix the underlying issue.[8]

Fixing a Broken System

Andrew Kelly, Senior Fellow at the American Enterprise Institute, diagnosed the college debt problem as having two underlying causes, in an interview with *The Wall Street Journal.* First, "Existing federal-aid programs give colleges every incentive to enroll students and less reason to worry about whether they are successful," he said. Meanwhile, students choose their colleges without good data indicating the costs and quality of the different options available to them, and lenient federal lending standards "make it easy to amass debt at bad colleges."[9]

Elite universities have for the longest time competed in a race to the bottom: whoever spent more money building facilities and offering new classes won the most students. That needs to change. With costs soaring out of control, governments have an opportunity—and a responsibility—to change incentive structures so that colleges will finally be pressured to adapt. Today, 79 percent of millennials say the government should be more involved in making college affordable. By focusing on market-oriented reforms to bust up noncompetitive and monopolistic university systems, the federal government can help millennials achieve our goals.[10]

To start, the federal government needs to pair funding with incentives to cap tuition hikes and improve the quality of education being delivered to students. "Risk sharing" is one option that's being thrown around a lot these days. It refers to incentives that penalize schools when students don't graduate. Since graduation is the best predictor of student loan default, the idea is that schools should be held accountable for their educational outcomes. If many students aren't graduating, the school is fined, creating a financial incentive to invest in student success.

This would be a great start. Since schools are wasting money largely on perks—like nicer dining halls, new cultural awareness houses, and extra bureaucrats—cutting this waste is a big part of the solution. Derek Bok, a former Harvard president, once acknowledged that "universities share one characteristic with compulsive gamblers and exiled royalty: there is never enough money to satisfy their desires." Vance Fried, an Oklahoma State economist, suggests that colleges separate funding of teaching and research, expand class sizes, eliminate unpopular majors and programs, and fire administrators. A shocking amount of money is wasted on administrative support, costing $7,000 a year per student. For all the talk of tough choices, there's plenty of fat to cut.[11]

Certainly, the federal government needs to publish credible data quantifying the value of a college education. *The Economist*, for example, argued that America's top colleges are Washington and Lee University, Babson, and Villanova—not Harvard, Princeton, and Yale—since these schools empirically boost student earnings by the largest amount. The Department of Education should prioritize publicizing its own rankings—with detailed analysis of where tuition dollars are going, a measure of average student debt loads, and how tuition correlates with educational outcomes. This may be unpopular with the institutions that don't get ranked at the top, but it's important to improving outcomes for young Americans.

Two of the most common questions to the federal government's loan ombudsmen—the office that works with students to resolve issues with student loans—are "Who is my loan servicer?" and "How much do I owe?" according to the Center for American Progress. In other words, college students have no clue how to use the government's repayment system. To facilitate better communication, the federal government should make the loan repayment system for federal loans clear and easy to use. With unambiguous information, students can pay down their debt, make more informed choices about debt instruments, and pressure colleges to deliver better value. [12]

But reformed incentives are not enough. Young people today want the federal government to invest in making college education accessible to all American citizens.

Free Community College

When Jonah sat down to watch the State of the Union in 2015, he was already excited.[13] Two weeks earlier, while sitting on the edge of his desk on an Air Force One flight from Detroit to Phoenix, President

Obama announced that during his State of the Union address, he would be introducing a plan to make college education more affordable.[14] Later, in Tennessee, home of one of the most successful free community college initiatives in the nation, the president fleshed out his proposal: free tuition for the first two years of community college.[15]

"Forty percent of our college students choose community college," President Obama said in his SOTU speech. "Some are young and starting out. Some are older and looking for a better job. Some are veterans and single parents trying to transition back into the job market. Whoever you are, this plan is your chance to graduate ready for the new economy, without a load of debt."[16]

The president's words struck a chord with Jonah and fellow millennials who wish college was more affordable. "Millennials know all too well the necessity of a college education and the costs that come with it. Many have said that completing at least some college is as important as obtaining a high school diploma. If that's the case ... two years of college should be as free as K-12 education. We're all helped when more of us have better, higher-paying jobs," he said.

While fiscal conservatives decried the President's overreach and questioned the federal government's ability to pay for the program, millennials rallied behind it. The proposed legislation would guarantee that families who earn less than $200,000 per year could send their children to college for free, assuming the students maintained a 2.5 GPA. The proposal is expensive, costing $80 billion over 10 years, and the remainder of the tab—approximately 25 percent of the tuition bill—would fall on the shoulders of state governments.[17]

Even with this expense, a majority of young Americans said the proposal was worth the cost. Overall, 58 percent of high school graduates said they would have taken advantage of the program, including 65 percent of adults without a college education. Support was highest in low-income (60 percent), Hispanic (76 percent) and black (59 percent) households.[18] A more educated workforce has tremendous economy-wide benefits. Workforce development "produce[s] widespread benefits for employers and society as a whole, likely leading to sustained increases in productivity and economic growth," a University of Texas study found.[19]

With such widespread support, it's no wonder that free college is the talk of the town. But with little action coming out of Washington, millennials are turning up the heat. "Given the current mood in Washington, the potential for any proposal of such magnitude becoming reality is quite low," explained Ramin Sedehi of the Berkeley Research Group. "It faces hurdles not just in Washington, but in many of the states." Millennials aren't afraid of the challenge: 76 percent of young people said college is worth the costs. This generation of trailblazers is going to fight to make their dream of free and public college education a reality.[20]

Seeing how crucial college tuition plans are to winning millennial votes, party leaders on the left and right have amped up their support for the proposal. Democrats Hillary Clinton, Martin O'Malley, Elizabeth Warren, and Bernie Sanders all came out in favor of so-called debt-free college programs. While the specifics of each plan were slightly different, the general concept was met with widespread support, not just from millennials, but also from the general public. Overall, 62 percent of Americans support some type of debt-free college tuition program.[21]

"Bernie Sanders Is Saying What Millennials Have Been Thinking All Along," reported Elite Daily, a millennial news website. Mic News said Sanders' plan was "Definitive Proof That Bernie Sanders Is the Candidate Young People Need."

The Vermont Senator, whose Feel the Bern t-shirts are ubiquitous these days on college campuses from New York to Portland, has long been a champion for solving the student debt crisis. His "College for All Act" would make all college education free, not just two-year community college. This structure would be similar to public, four-year education offered by many countries. Sanders would fund the plan with a Robin Hood tax, a financial transaction fee on some stock and bond trades. His plan is projected to cost $70 billion annually, with two-thirds funded at the federal level and the remainder by the states.

"At a time of massive income and wealth inequality, at a time when trillions of dollars in wealth have been shifted from the middle class and working families of this country to the top one-tenth of one percent, at a time when the wealthiest people in this country have made huge amounts of money from risky derivative transactions and the soaring value of the stock market, this legislation would impose a speculation fee on Wall Street," Sanders said. And considering that 76 percent of millennials said that "college has become harder to afford," and that 73 percent said "graduates have more student debt than they can manage," it's no surprise that Sanders is considered by many to be a millennial darling (his social media savvy doesn't hurt).[22]

Sanders' plan does not come without its downsides. In "Why Free College Is Really Expensive," *The Daily Beast* explains: "The proposal will cut the economic legs out from underneath innovations such as open online courses, which may be on the cusp of delivering low-cost, high-quality college education for all. Organizations trying to deliver radical new models will now have to compete against a $70 billion subsidy for the old system." Second, plans like Sanders' create a vicious cycle where increases in federal aid allow colleges to raise tuition.

In a recent study, the New York Federal Reserve found that federal policies often enable "college institutions to aggressively raise tuitions." Quantifying this "pass-through effect," the New York Federal Reserve found that every dollar in Pell Grants leads to a 55-cent increase in tuition price. Each dollar in subsidized loans leads to a 70-cent tuition hike. The idea is quite simple. If the average college student is willing to pay $20,000 to go to college, and the federal government subsidizes $10,000, then instead of charging students the remaining $10,000, I charge $15,000. Since college is still a business, companies are able to exploit the "willingness to pay" of their customers by raising prices. In technical terms, colleges, particularly elite private institutions, are well modeled as monopolistic companies extracting rent from consumers.

It's on this basis that former Maryland Governor Martin O'Malley has criticized the Sanders' plan. "If you simply cut a check for tuition, you're going to see tuitions go up and up and up, and eventually we all foot that bill. So we have to do two things at the same time," O'Malley said. "We have to increase degree attainment and bring down costs." And when it comes to college affordability, O'Malley is a man with credibility. He froze tuition for four years during his tenure as governor, before limiting state university tuition increases at 3 percent.[23]

O'Malley calls for "debt-free college" in contrast to free college. He calls for immediately freezing tuition rates and then capping tuition at 10 percent of the median income for any given state. For students who still couldn't pay for school, he would subsidize their loans at low interest rates. Today, private lenders often charge a relatively high rate of more than 6 percent interest because of high default rates. Though O'Malley calls it a debt-free plan, he is really focused on protecting prices from skyrocketing through intervention. For fiscal conservatives, it looks like an achievable compromise.[24]

Hillary Clinton's New College Compact, by contrast, is a hodgepodge of policies that creates incentives for public colleges to keep students debt-free, cuts interest rates, and makes the refinancing of loans easier. Her plan has been met with far less enthusiasm than Obama's or Sanders'. "Leverage and incentives are not a mandate," NPR reported. "States under budget pressure could say 'no thanks' to Clinton's proposed incentive grants, and so could individual universities." Clinton's funding sources have drawn far more criticism than has Sanders' Bill Gates-endorsed Robin Hood tax. She plans to cut tax deductions for the wealthy.[25]

Largely missing from the debate on making college more affordable is the Republican Party. "If college graduates are going to reap the greater economic rewards and opportunities of earning a degree, then it seems fair for them to support the cost of the education they're receiving," said New Jersey Governor Chris Christie, a Republican. When viewed as an entitlement, free college tuition appears like a Democratic issue. But eliminating government waste and championing efficiency has always been a core Republican ideal. Conservatives should acknowledge that public colleges are a racket—charging exorbitant fees and delivering subpar value—and commit to making them cheaper, better, and more sustainable. This can and should be a Republican issue.

This is exactly the mind-set that ended up convincing Tennessee Governor Bill Haslam, a Republican, to pioneer free community college. The governor, long an advocate of tying state funds to community college performance, recognized that he could kill two birds with one stone. First, he could invest in the job-readiness of new college graduates, and second, he could reform community colleges by tying new grants to strict reforms. "Republicans believe in outcomes and accountability. [Reforming college] should fall right into our sweet spot," he said. "The challenge is always going to be, are you willing to put your dollars where your mouth is." [26]

The plan, named Tennessee Promise, funded the "last dollar" of community college tuition, once federal funding sources had been exhausted. Acknowledging just how far behind students are on the road toward a college education, it covered a fifth semester for students to receive remedial education. Soon, the governor found 70 percent of incoming community college students in the state require remedial education. *Scientific American*, hardly a political magazine, commended Tennessee for taking the "national spotlight as an educational innovator."

Haslam's goal, however, was not education reform. The corporate CEO in him said his primary goal is workforce development. "We are not coming anywhere close to having the trained level of workforce that we need here," said Haslam, "either in quantity or quality of workers." Haslam argued that investing in education pays for itself because it mitigates the "cycle of poverty" and reduces state spending on other entitlement programs. "He's not doing education reform just for the sake of it," explained Richard Laine, the education director for the National Governors Association. "He's doing it for the workforce and the state economy." And that's what we want.

If Republicans want to be "the jobs party," investing in public education is a way to get there. Marco Rubio was the only 2016 Republican contender to come out with a plan on this issue. The Florida Senator's Dynamic Repayment Act would enroll federal borrowers into a program in which they paid 10 percent of their income each month toward loan repayment. "Our current loan repayment system often turns what should be reasonable debts into crippling payments," Rubio told *Bloomberg*. "Some graduates find they are forced to work multiple jobs, often in fields they didn't train for, simply to avoid defaulting on student loans. ... No one should be forced to go broke because they choose to go to college." This is a decent start for the party-of-no.

Young people will not give up easily in their battle for a more affordable college education because this is an issue that ripples through their lives, sometimes with disastrous effects. Both parties must join millennials in their campaign for reform. For Democrats, this means less stump speeches and more actual legislation, and for Republicans, this means making college reform an issue of cutting out waste in public colleges and improving the job-readiness of graduates.

Colleges are Not Off the Hook!

Colleges love to point fingers at other people for rising costs. As the financial reporter for *The Daily Pennsylvanian*, Jack had the opportunity to speak with the University of Pennsylvania's financial aid office on a regular basis. The school consistently refused to take responsibility for student debt. Instead, they pathetically implied that students take out loans "by choice."

"The fact that we have an all-grant aid policy that doesn't require them to borrow means that it's now a long-term debt instrument that the family can use to help pay their cost. It's not that the family can't afford what we've determined, it's that they have alternative methods they can use to pay that cost," said Penn Director of Financial Aid Joel Carstens. "I think what we see most often ... is that they're borrowing because it's available to them, not because it's required."

Talk about being out of touch with reality: students of all backgrounds beg to differ. "It's out of necessity," Eisenhauer said. "It's not like I'm taking out loans just because they're available to me. My parents shouldn't have to work 10 more years to put me through college," she said. The indifferent, almost passive aggressive tone of university administrators indicates a huge divide between how students and universities perceive the student debt crisis. Far from a "long-term debt instrument," students take out loans because they simply don't have the cash flow to pay college tuition, which often exceeds a household's entire income. "My total [loan amount] is $3,500," Rita Wegner told *The Daily Pennsylvanian.* "My parents took out the rest of what Penn didn't give me"—a total of $15,000—"because we felt we couldn't pay anything."

For all their finger-pointing, college administrators hold as much responsibility as the government, if not more, for solving the student loan crisis: after all, they are the ones who have raised tuitions 150 percent in recent years. Millennial leaders are looking towards colleges to reduce, or at least contain, the exorbitant and rising costs of a college education. And there isn't any shortage of ideas for doing so. McKinsey consultants Adam Cota, Andre Dua, and Martha Laboissiere, for example, propose a few ways to make college more affordable.[27]

First and foremost, colleges need to do a better job making sure their students graduate—and do so in two to four years. Today, only 60 percent of bachelor's candidates complete their degrees within six years, according to the National Center for Education Statistics, and just 30 percent of those seeking associate's degrees graduate in three years. With college tuition already really expensive, colleges need to recognize the importance of helping students graduate in a timely manner so that they don't waste an enormous amount of personal and government-sponsored money.

To understand why so many students aren't completing their degrees, we need to address poor K-12 education. "Only 25 percent of [high school] students are proficient in all four subjects [English, math, reading, and science on the ACT]. 60 percent came up short in two of the four subject areas, while more than 25 percent failed to demonstrate proficiency in any subject at all," reported *U.S. News & World Report*. With this in mind, it's no wonder college students don't graduate—they weren't prepared to be there in the first place! If all undergraduates were college-ready, the country would add 300,000 college graduates per year, according *The Atlantic*.[28] Part of the solution, then, is to fix the education system, which we discuss later.

Colleges should take into account learning that happens outside of the classroom to minimize the number of credits students need to graduate. Forty percent of undergraduates are older than 25. By recognizing their experiences and granting academic credit, schools could shorten graduation times by as much as 10 months for a bachelor's degree and 4.5 months for an associate degree. Veterans such as medics and mechanics who gained skills on the battlefield would benefit.

Southern New Hampshire University and Brigham Young University–Idaho are examples of colleges moving in the right direction. Both schools have reshaped their transfer credit requirements to make sure students are getting the most bang for their buck. They are also helping students manage their course work, to ensure that they graduate as quickly as possible and with the fewest credits (because often, students pay per credit). Instead of milking students for extra dollars, they want to help make education more affordable. And they're no doubt attracting students with their lower price tags.

Colleges need to transform their educational methods to create more value for students while also cutting costs and reducing tuition. Course redesign makes school more engaging, and according to the National Center for Academic Transformation, is profitable for colleges, improves attendance, grades, course competition, and overall course retention.[29] Redesign can involve the use of technology in the classroom as well as online tutorials and teaching best practices. Rio Salado College and Western Governors University, for example, used self-paced online instruction and flexible adjunct faculty and student mentors to deliver instruction. Colleges should also begin to implement experiential and project-based learning approaches. Sixty-eight percent of millennials have stated that experiential learning is their most preferred method of developing new skills, and research indicates that these methods help students develop important critical thinking skills and create a more proactive learning environment.[30]

Free college is not a magic bullet—and millennials know it. But today's student debt crisis is as unsustainable for America as it is unmanageable for millennials. Young people are looking for our leaders in Washington to join us in our fight and to have the courage to implement new ideas. And we're also asking our colleges to look inwards and begin a long journey toward reform—by cutting costs to lower tuition, holding themselves accountable to performance metrics, and working with students to help them become career-ready. But we're not holding our breath.

Young People Innovate Their Way Toward Affordability

While Washington fails to solve the college affordability crisis, young people are innovating and inventing market reforms that we think will drive down the costs of a college education. Some young leaders envision low-cost alternatives to the traditional college experience. These young leaders are rolling up their sleeves to get the job done in their efforts to win the war for reform.

The idea behind Ben Nelson's "Minerva Project," for example, is quite simple: kill dining halls, facilities, sports fields—essentially anything non-instructional—to create a cheaper college experience. Minerva is an accredited university with offices and a dorm in San Francisco, but here's the catch: it costs roughly $10,000 a year. How does Minerva achieve these cost savings? Seminar courses are offered online in classes that are capped at 19 students. Each year, they study remotely from a different country, living in dorms with other Minerva students, in order to provide a truly global experience. Minerva will open Berlin and Buenos Aires campuses in 2016 and plans to open campuses in Mumbai, Hong Kong, New York, and London in the future.

"Lectures, gone. Tenure, gone. Gothic architecture, football, ivy crawling up the walls—gone, gone, gone. What's left will be leaner and cheaper," writes *The Atlantic*. "If it succeeds, it could inspire a legion of entrepreneurs, and a whole category of legacy institutions might have to liquidate. One imagines tumbleweeds rolling through abandoned quads and wrecking balls smashing through the windows of classrooms left empty by students who have plugged into new online platforms." Dear Ben Nelson, thank you and good luck. We hope you succeed.

Dale Stephens, a member of the first class of Thiel Fellows, a program that pays college students $100,000 to drop out of college and work on a new idea, is another young American applying his unconventional thinking to reforming the college process. His "UnCollege" initiative encourages students to pursue their own projects in a self-driven learning project, arguing that the opportunity costs of college, in terms of tuition and lost wages, are too damn high.

"The future of education is self-directed. We are at a point where individuals have more power than institutions. Right now you can go and take courses from Ivy League schools, for free, online. And you can even get credit for those courses. That means that the value of going to college has nothing to do with the content—it must be about more. We believe that the value of college is in creating communities of like-minded people, and we want UnCollege to be one community of people who value self-directed learning," Stephens told *Forbes*.

Outside of these niche programs, students are increasingly looking for new pathways toward an affordable college education. A common approach is to replace the four-year bachelor's degree with two years of community college, followed by two years at a four-year institution. "It's less expensive to start in this way. For many people it feels more egalitarian; it's a much broader range of people," explained Josh Wyner of the Aspen Institute. Today, this option is a popular route to a bachelor's degree, if not already the primary choice. National Student Clearinghouse Research Center found that as of 2014, 46 percent of all students who completed a four-year degree had been enrolled at a two-year institution at some point in the past 10 years.[31]

CONCLUSION

Millennials are willing to invest in our own futures. College debt is not "evil." What is evil is a system that exploits young people and their families, telling them day after day that a college education is the key to a better life—and then milking them for every last penny once they're in the system. With $1.2 trillion in outstanding student debt and 50 percent of young people underemployed once they graduate, there's a clear mismatch between the value we're getting and the price we're paying for college.

Millennials appreciate market forces. That's why *Reason* called us "hipster capitalists." "The hipster ideal today is neither a commune nor a life of rugged individualism. It's the small, socially conscious business. Millennials are obliterating divisions between corporate and bohemian values, between old and new employment models," wrote Elizabeth Nolan Brown. But while millennials are happy to accept and play by the rules of a capitalist society, we realize that today, colleges are an unregulated monopoly. Instead of competing against each other to bring down costs—as businesses ought to—colleges continue to raise prices and pass this cost on to the government.

Politicians, either too old to commiserate with us or too focused on "more important" legislative priorities, have ignored this trend for decades. The situation only got this dire because governors kept raising their public college tuitions and the federal government has subsidized private colleges, enabling them to charge exorbitant fees. All the while, free-flowing money has created a debt-bubble that threatens to burst more than just our pocketbooks, but our dreams too. Our government has been complicit in a grand-con that has robbed millennials of their efficacy and forced them to put their lives on hold.

Now, as we come to power, we're making our politicians—on both sides of the aisle—finally address this concern. On the left, Democrats have finally begun to step up to the plate. But talk is cheap, so millennials aren't going to stand down until the debt-free college tuition plans of President Obama, Bernie Sanders, and Martin O'Malley are the law of the land. Meanwhile, on the right, so-called good government reformers have their work cut out for them. If Republicans are to be the party that eliminates government waste, then public college is a bonanza.

As we come to power, college debt will be a top millennial platform. But we're not keeping our fingers crossed. In the meantime, we'll celebrate moves towards online education as new tools are implemented to raise the quality of education, and we'll root for Ben Nelson, Dale Stephens, and other educational disrupters until the day comes when "no-loan" policies are more than public relations stunts and our peers can graduate having paid a fair price for a good education. These young leaders, at least, are already taking the world by storm with their entrepreneurial spirit and creativity.

"A fair price for a good education." Is that really so much to ask for?

Environmental Protection: Hipster Capitalists Save the Planet

LEXINGTON, KENTUCKY

I n the fight for an affordable college education, we saw young people stepping up to elevate a "millennial problem" into a defining issue in the 2016 presidential race. Elsewhere on the political map, a similar battle is emerging, but with much more immediate consequences: millennials are elevating the conservationist movement from a niche concern for tree huggers and vegans into a prominent part of political discourse.

To explore this issue with young Americans, we traveled to Lexington, Kentucky, where—just weeks before the Kentucky Derby— organizers of the Tournament of Champions, which is the national championship for our debate event, asked millennial leaders to consider how we ought to balance environmental protection against the need for economic development.

Here, in our last stand before graduating high school, we heard dozens of young people—including the eventual champions—make the ultimate millennial argument, that environmental protection and economic development are not mutually exclusive. Just the opposite, they are co-dependent.

Young people say that environmentalism is a uniquely millennial issue; as the planet's next guarantors, we feel an obligation to protect the environment. But as hipster capitalists, the methods we use are strongly market-oriented. These beliefs have led to a significant generation gap in terms of our generation's feelings toward the problem and potential solutions.

As a result, young people have begun to take to the streets, as we will see, to push those in power to adopt our platforms and save the planet from the imminent dangers that lie ahead.

In Paris, We Fight: A Generation of Activists

There were screams and pleas as riot police fired tear gas, and angry protestors, some of whom wore masks, fired back with projectiles. As the images went viral online, chants that "a state of emergency is a police state" could still be heard.

This was only the beginning. Around the world, 570,000 people marched in 175 countries. From the streets of London to Madrid to Berlin, music and speeches were accompanied with an array of placards, some with images of polar bears with the words "Save Me" and others with the phrase "Stop Global Warming." All united under a common mission: to call on the 30,000 world leaders who would soon descend on Paris for the UN Climate Change Conference (COP21) to work together on solving what actress Emma Thompson called "the issue of the 21st century."[1]

In the days and weeks leading up to the conference, the protests continued. At the opening of Solutions 21, an "exhibition for businesses to showcase their proposals for tackling climate change," police were seen carrying protesters, according to *The Guardian*.[2] One week later, as negotiators put final touches on the COP21 agreement, 10 protestors dressed as a "polar bear army" in a legal demonstration for climate justice near the Eiffel Tower. Elsewhere in Paris, "indigenous peoples—Amazonian Indians, Eskimos from Greenland, tribal chiefs from Papua New Guinea—started the day with drums and song," *The Irish Times* reported.[3]

At the center of these protests and the climate activism that rippled through Europe in December 2015 were young millennial leaders such as Youtube darling and youth director of the nonprofit Earth Guardians Xiuhtezcatl Roske-Martinez. The indigenous climate activist raised in Boulder, Colorado, in the Aztec tradition first made national headlines as a six-year-old. "When I was five years old I wanted to go to all the factories and shut them down with my little brother, but once I turned six I realized that it was us who was buying from the factories. We're supporting them," he said then, amid cheers. "Every choice we make is for or against our future."[4]

Dubbed the "anti-Bieber," Roske-Martinez has since spoken on international stages and addressed the UN General Assembly in 2016 at COP21. "Everywhere, young people are rising up and taking action to solve the issues that will be left to our generation," he said. "Youth are suing their state and federal governments across the United States, demanding action on climate change from our elected officials. We are flooding the streets and now we are flooding the courts to get the world to see there is a movement on the rise and we are at the forefront."

Roske-Martinez was just one of more than 5,000 millennial leaders who went to Paris to attend COP21 and the Conference of Youth (COY) that has been held in parallel with COP since 2005. By his side was 18-year-old Zambian native Andozile Simwinga, who attended the conferences as a UNICEF youth ambassador. "[The effect of climate change] has really made me feel low—I go out of my house every day and I look at the environment," he said. "People have cut down trees, there's deforestation everywhere. I want to do environmental studies but what am I going to address? What am I going to talk about? What am I going to tell [...] my children and also the future generations? We had trees here; we had different types of animals."[5]

Simwinga and his peers shared success stories in the movement toward environmental justice. "You people [are] integrating sustainability into kindergarten curricula in Canada, recycling cell phones to eliminate e-waste in Africa, and mapping resources for climate adaptation in Samoa," reported *Scientific American.*[6] To promote environmental reform, these young people are breaking down ethnic, geographic, and political barriers. They are unifying for change.

At the end of the day, the millennial activism at COP21 was monumental, and helped usher in a groundbreaking international agreement to mitigating climate change. Global leaders from 195 nations agreed on "legally binding" limits to carbon emissions.[7] "In the light of a collapsing world, what better time to be alive than now, because our generation gets to change the course of history," Roske-Martinez said. "Humans have created the greatest problem we face today, but the greater the challenge, the higher we will rise to meet it."

The Millennial Consensus

Millennials say climate justice is an issue divided along generational, rather than political lines. Three in four of us recognize that global warming is real, as compared with 61 percent of Americans. Meanwhile, 55 percent of millennials believe that rising temperatures are caused by humans, compared with just 40 percent of American citizens.[8] And these beliefs affect the way we vote. Two-thirds of young Americans say they plan to vote for a candidate who supports cutting greenhouse gasses and increasing financial incentives for adopting renewable energy. Just half of seniors agree.

It's no wonder then that 75 percent of millennials believe that millennials care more about the environment than our parents. Millennials see climate change as a war to be won, not a passing fad. Ashley Reid and Iris Morrell, environmental activists and California leaders, believe climate change is America's No. 1 national security priority. Reid and Morrell see climate change as a local issue that brings young liberals and conservatives together. In their hometowns, the process of rationing water has already begun, impacting their daily lives—from when they can bathe, to flushing the toilet, and caring for their lawns.[9]

Millennials believe that the government should intervene to mitigate the effects of climate change. "If you believe in global warming, climate change is going to affect all of the citizens of the world and all the generations to come, so therefore I feel like it's the State's responsibility" to address the issue, Morrell explained in an interview. Texas millennial Ajay Singh summarized the millennial sentiment, describing climate change as "something that affects everyone," "equally devastating to everyone," and our "utmost priority."

So we're taking action. "Because climate change is such a long-term problem, and because millennials are tomorrow's policy makers, our generation must know the importance of stopping it," Grayson Sussman-Squires told *The Huffington Post*. "Unless the grassroots campaigns gather a vast new following, policy changes ... [will] wait until one of the Koch brothers' beach houses is ruined by a superstorm."

Millennials are not just talk—56 percent of millennials say they would pay higher prices to protect the environment as compared with 20 percent of seniors. "We're seeing a widening gulf among older and younger Americans," said Sheril Kirshenbaum, director of the University of Texas Energy Poll. Not only are they willing to make sacrifices to ensure a cleaner environment, but they want to take action immediately. Fifty-seven percent would support cutting coal use, 62 percent want utility companies to obtain a percentage of their electricity from renewables, and 43 percent support a carbon tax, making them almost twice as likely to support these policies, as compared with seniors.10

"Of course, it is going to be important to find an alternative energy source. First of all, fossil fuels are nonrenewable resources and are not completely sustainable, especially at the rate at which we're using them," Denny Baek said in an interview. "However, what exactly is the preferable alternative fuel source has obviously yet to be determined. Based on where you are, it's hard to be able to find a way to create a dam in Arizona at the same scale as if you were closer to the ocean."

What's at Stake?

In the 2009 British film *The Age of Stupid*, the year is 2055 and the world has been ravaged by environmental disasters. Las Vegas is swallowed up by desert. The Amazon has burned. London is flooded. The Alps have been stripped of snow. India is a nuclear wasteland. In one of the film's most powerful scenes, the protagonist, an archivist tasked with reviewing footage from before the disasters, asks: "why didn't we save ourselves when we had the chance?"[11]

The fictional movie has many parallels with today's reality. Glaciers in the Alps are melting.[12] Deforestation is destroying the Amazon and Himalayas, where unfettered economic development is projected to reduce forest cover from 84.9 percent to 52.8 percent.[13] Dwindling natural resources have sparked conflict between India and Pakistan, and the Pentagon has warned that climate change will be a "threat multiplier" potentially resulting in full-scale resource wars.[14] Already, the Global Humanitarian Forum attributes 300,000 deaths annually to climate change and reports that climate change "seriously impacts" 325 million people worldwide.[15]

"The sea is already swallowing villages and eroding shorelines; where permafrost thaws and the tundra burns; where glaciers are melting at a pace unprecedented," President Obama said on a recent trip to Alaska. "And it was a preview of one possible future—a glimpse of our children's fate if the climate keeps changing faster than our efforts to address it. Submerged countries. Abandoned cities. Fields that no longer grow. Political disruptions that trigger new conflict, and even more floods of desperate peoples seeking the sanctuary of nations not their own."

Death tolls attributed to climate change are projected to reach 500,000 by 2030, with vulnerable populations in developing nations hit hardest.[16] The result will be "unprecedented reversals in poverty reduction, nutrition, health, and education," the UN projects, because as the climate deteriorates, limited resources will be used to combat stressors like droughts and flood, rather than for social needs. Developed nations like the United States will be next up on nature's chopping block.

With the environment will go thousands upon thousands of jobs. Nicholas Stern, a former chief economist for the World Bank, released a 700-page report, sponsored by the British government, entitled "The Stern Review on the Economics of Climate Change." In it, he argues that the costs associated with climate change will be equivalent to losing 5 percent of global GDP. In the worst-case scenario, that could climb to 20 percent. Protection, by contrast, would cost just 1 percent of global GDP.

While Stern addresses climate change exclusively, other problems could be equally catastrophic. An unprecedented level of pollution has dirtied our air and water supply, with big cities like Bakersfield, California, Phoenix, Fresno, Pittsburgh, Louisville and Cincinnati worst affected. Meanwhile, toxic chemicals are being spilled into our drinking water and poisoning our families. In 2015, for example, the Gold King Mine near Silverton, Colorado, spilled 3 million gallons of contaminated water, and the EPA was faulted with poor regulation. Of course, abroad, the problem is even worse: in China, people have to wear masks to avoid inhaling too many pollutants, and in India, 75 percent of rivers and lakes are so polluted by industrial projects they cannot be used for drinking or bathing.

So what's at stake? The better question is: what isn't?

The Republican Establishment Just Doesn't Get It

Despite these dire outcomes, politicians on the right belittle environmental threats, with some going so far as to blame climate change on dinosaur flatulence (whatever that means) and rain dances. "The idea that carbon dioxide is a carcinogen that is harmful to our environment is almost comical. Every time we exhale, we exhale carbon dioxide," said former Speaker of the House John Boehner. Beware of "environmental jihad," joked Sen. Ron Johnson (R-WI).[17]

But millennials are not laughing. In a recent poll, the majority of both young Democrats and Republicans chose "ignorant," "out of touch," or "crazy" to describe climate deniers.[18] Roberto Ruiz, a Republican millennial from New Jersey, says his party needs to sober up and address climate issues head-on. "This is like Alcoholics Anonymous. The first step in this recovery process is acknowledging that global warming is an issue," Ruiz said. "We need to stop with the pseudo-science and stop with the 'global warming doesn't exist,' because yeah, it's an issue."

For millennials like Ruiz, climate justice is a critical issue that affects how they vote. Recent polling data indicate that "an over-whelming margin of millennial voters—including Republicans—say climate change denial would make them less likely to support a candidate—with more than 41 percent saying it would disqualify that candidate regardless of their other positions. With such strong senti-ments, it is not surprising that millennial voters prefer a candidate who backs climate action over one who denies climate science by nearly 50 points."[19]

Still, while some conservative leaders and even the Pope call for action, many Republicans, including 2016 presidential hopefuls, remain in the dark. "I'm a skeptic. I'm not a scientist. I think the science has been politicized. … I think we need to be very cautious before we dramatically alter who we are as a nation because of it," said former presidential candidate and Florida governor Jeb Bush. Yes, Jeb. You're definitely not a scientist. So why don't you listen to 97 percent of actively publishing scientists who all agree that climate change is real and human-caused?[20]

Sen. Ted Cruz (R-TX), whose fiery conservative stances have made him a Tea Party favorite, offers an even more absurd and uniquely non-responsive argument. "Climate change, as they have defined it, can never be disproved, because whether it gets hotter or whether it gets colder, whatever happens, they'll say, well, it's changing, so it proves our theory," he said. Cruz refuses to discuss the legitimacy of climate science—instead, he makes a roundabout argument attacking his opponents. In doing so, he does a disservice to the American public, which expects our leaders to inform themselves about the important issues facing our country and to engage in a proactive dialogue about solving them.

To put it simply, much of Republican climate denial is based on very flimsy ground. "If you listen to the hysterics ... you would think that the Statue of Liberty will shortly be under water and the polar bears are all drowning, and that we're dying from pollution. It's absolutely and utterly untrue," Sen. Rand Paul (R-KY) told supporters. Talk about a straw man argument!

We recognize that many well-intentioned people don't believe in climate change. As one of our early readers wrote, "I am a skeptic as I have reviewed credible scientific evidence to the contrary that is ignored and considered heresy by all whom disagree." It is the prerogative of every American to choose their own belief system. We respect an informed opposition and readily acknowledge that the evidence on climate change in not unanimous. But while everyday Americans may believe whatever they wish, our representatives must be held to a higher standard. If they are to act in good faith, then our leaders cannot ignore overwhelming scientific evidence.

Unfortunately, not all climate change deniers do so for the right reasons. Much of the opposition to environmental reform is the result of a conscious effort to court campaign contributions from Exxon, Shell, and other companies reliant on the fossil-fuel economy. The Koch Brothers, for example, have funneled more than $79 million towards climate deniers in recent years to protect their oil empire, and Republicans have scrambled to pick up these funds.[21]

Overall, between 2003 and 2010, 140 foundations funneled $558 million to 100 climate denial organizations, according to a Drexel University study by Robert Brulle. This "dark money" financing has become increasingly covert, with financers using third-party pass-through organizations to conceal the funder.[22] "The climate change counter-movement has had a real political and ecological impact on the failure of the world to act on global warming," Brulle reported.

Like a play on Broadway, the countermovement has stars in the spotlight—often prominent contrarian scientists or conservative politicians—but behind the stars is an organizational structure of directors, scriptwriters, and producers," he said. "If you want to understand what's driving this movement, you have to look at what's going on behind the scenes."

Beyond the surface of these petty politics and implicit corruption, an obstructionist movement has grown that stops environmental regulations in their footsteps, often regardless of merit. Take the Clean Water Rule, a relatively benign regulation, which Obama introduced in 2015, that protects streams and wetlands from pollution. To say the Republicans, who called the move "a raw and tyrannical power grab that will crush jobs," responded in outrage would be an understatement.

"The rule is being shoved down the throats of hardworking people with no input, and places landowners, small businesses, farmers, and manufacturers on the road to a regulatory and economic hell," said John Boehner, a Republican Party moderate. Boehner's visceral words indicate just how exaggerated the rhetoric on both sides of the aisle has become. This rule is literally a nonissue: pollution of drinking water is Americans' No. 1 environmental concern, with 84 percent worrying a great or fair deal about it. So why are Republicans picking a fight?

Republicans are not alone; as we will note, Democrats have been obstructionist on environmental policy too, not that this excuses Republicans. Millennials are tired of the Republican Party's inability to innovate and adapt to the new environmental reality. "I'm tired of the GOP saying, 'Oh, we have to keep coal and oil and these things,'" Ruiz said. "Before us you didn't have lead-certified buildings; before us you didn't have the green revolution to recycle every single thing. ... At the bottom of emails, how many times have you seen, 'give a hoot, don't pollute, keep this on your screen.' ... That's an entirely different mind-set from generations ago."

There's a reason that Republican millennials like Ruiz tend to view the Republican Party negatively on environmental issues. So far, the topic has received no focus from Republican candidates, none of whom include new ideas in their 2016 policy planks. When we asked John Guarco, then the Executive Vice President of Duke's student government, why he was no longer a Republican, he named the environment as one of three issues that caused him to switch. Guarco's perspective is typical. While Republicans see the environment as a fringe issue to ignore, we don't.

The irony of it all is that when we asked millennials what policies they do support, most talked about free-market principles—a conservative talking point—and advocated what has been dubbed free-market environmentalism. "Environmental policies based on markets, incentives, and entrepreneurship offer Republicans a chance to win them [the millennials] over," wrote Terry Anderson, author of *Free Market Environmentalism for the Next Generation.* But as long as Republicans remain the "party of no," they will remain on a surefire path to disaster.

In the beginning of this chapter, we noted that our final conclusion is that millennials believe in a nuanced and balanced approach to environmental conservation. With all of our attacks on Republicans, you're probably thinking all millennials are about to start voting for Democrats. Let's make two notes, then. Being balanced doesn't necessarily mean being centrist. According to millennials, the balanced and pragmatic thing to do is to acknowledge and mitigate the effects of climate change. So yes, let's be explicit here: Democrats are way ahead of Republicans on the issue of climate change, because at least the party is not in denial. But Democrats aren't off the hook. You see, the biggest problem with Democrats is that they're all talk and no game. And when they do decide to get tough on the environment, they tend to pick the wrong battles.

Democratic Policies Don't Work

For all his eloquent speeches, until recently it was unclear whether President Obama understood the magnitude of global warming or sought to mitigate its effects. By the time he reached the fourth quarter of his presidency, however, the "lame duck" president began to make notable progress. In 2015, President Obama signed an international accord, named the Paris Agreement after the city where it was negotiated, on carbon emission limits with the Chinese, and signed executive orders creating new clean air and water regulations. Even so, the party still has a long way to go.

In a recent negotiation with China, the United States committed to reducing its carbon emissions by 26-28 percent below 2005 levels by 2025, nearly twice the existing target—without imposing new restrictions on power plants or vehicles. Meanwhile, China set 2030 as a target for its carbon emissions to peak. In 2016, President Xi and President Obama met in China to finalize their agreement. The negotiation is the first time such talks have occurred at the presidential level.

"This is clearly a sign of the seriousness and the importance the Chinese government is giving to this issue," said Barbara Finamore, senior attorney and Asia director for the Natural Resources Defense Council, an environmental advocacy group. "The relationship [between the United States and China] is tricky, but climate has been one of the areas where the two sides can and are finding common ground."

At home, President Obama ushered in the Clean Water Rule, which was finalized by the EPA and the U.S. Army in June of 2015. The new rule—which will apply to 60 percent of the nation's water and benefit the one in three Americans who gets drinking water from streams that are vulnerable to pollution—will allow the president to leave a legacy. "For the water in the rivers and lakes in our communities that flow to our drinking water to be clean, the streams and wetlands that feed them need to be clean too," EPA Administrator Gina McCarthy said of the rule.

Finally, the president led the way in the 2015 climate talks that culminated in a global climate agreement. All these actions were positive developments that advanced climate justice. Some fear, however, that Obama's actions were too little too late. Obama's election "was accompanied by intense hope that many things in need of change would change," lamented Al Gore. "Some things have, but others have not. Climate policy, unfortunately, is in the second category."[23]

Instead of focusing on real reform—like significant investments in renewable energy subsidies or incentives for nuclear power development—the Democrats have focused on regulations, which today cost the economy $216 billion.[24] But while slapping on red tape might be a politically expedient way to demonstrate environmentalist credentials, millennials are looking for real reform. "Command and control regulations, the Clean Air Act, the Clean Water Act, and the Endangered Species Act, to name a few, from Nixon-era Republicans, may have played with boomers. But millennials want results, not regulations," explained Terry Anderson.

Worse, Democrats have been as obstructionist as Republicans, using environmental excuses to shut down legitimate, job-creating projects like the Keystone XL Pipeline, which would have facilitated the flow of oil from Canada to U.S. refineries. While Democrats argued that the pipeline was dangerous, given the risk of a leak and increased emissions, both these assertions were rooted in fear and partisan politics rather than fact. Even EPA data indicated that emissions would increase by less than 1 percent. That's why even though we are tree-huggers, the majority of millennials on the left and right supported the Keystone Pipeline, which would have created an estimated 42,000 jobs[25] and reduced U.S. dependence on foreign oil by 40 percent.[26]

Millennial Elephants, a conservative blog, captured this sentiment after President Obama vetoed the Keystone Pipeline, calling it a "wedge issue" for millennials. "Millennials may in fact be more environmentally liberal but through two environmental analyses, State Department experts determined that the pipeline's impact probably would be minimal, even on climate change-inducing carbon dioxide emissions," the blog wrote. "Moreover, millennials are tired of high unemployment and living at home; this means they are ripe to be won over with an economic growth/job creation argument. The economic rewards of extracting Canadian oil are too attractive and the options for getting it out of the country are too numerous."

Never have either of us heard such a persuasive condemnation of the liberal approach to climate reform than during the weekend we spent in Kentucky. During our stay, we were impressed but not shocked by the efficiency and tact with which our peers tore through liberal regulations, indicting and thoroughly convicting our leaders of playing politics with environmental policy—and having little to no impact on the safety of the planet, which matters most. Young people across the country recognize that they have foundation to work with on either the Democratic or Republican side of the aisle. As a result, millennials have created their own new form of environmentalism.

Green Everything

Lisa Curtis started her high school's recycling club, traveled to Copenhagen to observe international climate talks, and compulsively composts her food. But she's not an environmentalist, she said. "It's starting to be used in more of a derogatory way. 'Oh, you're such an environmentalist, oh you are not in touch with the real world,'" she explained on NPR.

Curtis is one of a new breed of millennial environmentalists who reject the label. Just 32 percent of millennials see themselves as environmentalists, compared with 42 percent of Gen X and 44 percent of boomers. Instead of replacing light bulbs or driving hybrids, sustainability is an approach to everyday life, from recycling to national defense and manufacturing.[27]

"Millennials reenvision environmentalism as a value that broadly underpins equally important issues like economic growth, national security, energy, poverty, public health, and climate adaptation. In many ways, the traditional environmental movement is too constricting for the globally connected and complex policy issues millennials are looking to solve. While environmental groups aren't going extinct, they're certainly in need of reform and innovation to keep up," said Matthew Stepp, formerly executive director of the Center for Clean Energy Innovation who is now a policy director at PennFuture.[28]

Sustainable development is already one of the most popular topics among millennials. As millennials come to power, we are going to embed sustainable policies into every law—from highway reform and new infrastructure, to agriculture bills and automobile regulation. While not yet in political power, millennials have already begun to act—using rational financing incentives to drive change.

Solution: Innovation + Subsidies = Development

At the top of the list of millennial reforms is renewable energy subsidies. Millennials have long supported the renewable energy movement because they believe it is the energy of the future. Solar and wind power sources will create jobs and reduce carbon emissions. Seventy percent of millennials believe subsidies are an important step to get the engine of renewable energy turning, a *Reason* poll found. This is in stark contrast to 51 percent of seniors who support the subsidies.[29]

Millennials are inspired by science and believe that renewable energy research is their top priority when it comes to environmental protection. Many of the most important challenges in renewable technologies are still ahead of us. For example, there is no existing solution to the problem of storing solar/wind power. Investment in research could dramatically speed up the pace of change, because it could lead to findings that would make wind/solar financially prudent energy sources for consumers. Government intervention and incentives are appropriate here, because companies tend to prioritize short-term profit over longer-term investments, especially when the return on the investment is uncertain.

The government has already invested $34 billion in green technology. While time will tell if these investments are profitable, millennials appear to think they are a great idea, realizing that only with new technologies will renewable energy become economically feasible and widely implemented. "Millennials see the development of strong, domestic, renewable energy as essential for the long-term health of our environment," explained the Roosevelt Institute in a report based on interviews with 3,000 millennials.[30]

Even conservative millennials, like Anna Prisco, want to see more government involvement in renewable energy development. "I think that the role of the government here should be to provide subsidies and incentives to companies that research into renewable energies," she said.

Solution: Let's Go Nuclear!

The nuclear power industry seemed to be booming in the United States—until 1979, that is. Just 12 days after the release of the film *The China Syndrome*, which depicted a near nuclear meltdown in Pennsylvania, the United States experienced its worst-ever nuclear accident at Three Mile Island in Pennsylvania, and fear broke loose.

But millennials don't remember the accident or the fear. That's because none were born until at least one year later. After the accident, as the first set of millennials grew up, nuclear reactor construction fell annually until 1998, despite the fact that no new accidents arose. Because we have never experienced a nuclear meltdown and recognize that a magical solution to the issue isn't about to come out of thin air, the majority of millennials support nuclear power.

Seventy percent of millennials want to prioritize available alternative energy sources, with 53 percent explicitly supporting nuclear energy and 57 percent saying that nuclear energy is safe, according to recent Pew and Gallop polls. This makes millennials more likely to favor nuclear energy than the average Democrat but less nuclear-friendly than Republicans.[31]

An even higher percentage of millennials support nuclear energy in practice, saying they would prefer alternative energy but will take what they can get. "Nuclear is better than fossil fuels, but personally I'd prefer things like solar and wind," said Karl Meakin, a Connecticut millennial. "I think hopefully over the next three years or so [solar power] will be adopted more widely."

Where millennials don't fear accidental nuclear shutdowns, they do fear the intentional shutdown of facilities that has been promoted by anti-nuclear activists. In California, for example, only one nuclear power plant remains: Diablo Canyon. Research indicates that if the nuclear plant were replaced by renewable energy, it would cost $15 billion. That's why the most recent nuclear power plant to be closed—San Onofre—was replaced almost entirely by natural gas. So nuclear fuel may not be perfect—but the alternatives appear to be worse.

Likewise, the environmental impact of eliminating the Diablo reactors would be equivalent to eliminating all wind turbines and solar panels in the state of California. Not exactly ideal to millennials, already concerned by the current state of fossil fuel emissions. It's facts like these that have led millennials to believe that as long as solar power is not commercially plausible, nuclear energy will be the cleanest energy we can get.[32]

Millennials Jesse Jenkins and Sara Mansur captured the millennial sentiment quite accurately in their article for *Forbes*. "What?! Global warming is the intergenerational threat today, not nuclear power. With coal and other fossil-fuels driving carbon dioxide emissions to their highest levels in history, ours is a generation preparing for a world that will be deeply and irrevocably impacted by climate change—a world plagued by severe heat waves, floods, droughts, and record wildfires, and the potential displacement of millions of people," they wrote.

But even if millennials get their wish list of policy reforms, we want our government to be working on environmental protection with our neighbors as well. One of the biggest criticisms millennials have of our government's environmental policies is that we "go at it alone." Given the magnitude of climate change and its global impact, millennials expect Congress to cooperate with India, China, and the rest of the world to develop a set of uniform policies.

Solution: Global Environmental Cooperation

Mia Zhou grew up in Maoming, a coastal city in China dominated by the petrochemical industry, which generates 60 percent of the city's GDP. Like many of her millennial counterparts in the United States, Zhou studied hard so that she could go to college and find her place in the burgeoning Chinese economy. But unlike most young people in the United States, Zhou resigned herself to live with the "pungent air" that came with growing up in one of China's fast-growing industrial hubs.

Things changed for Zhou in 2011. She was a senior in high school, preparing to head off to college, when Maoming's mayor was found to have taken 70 million Yuan in bribes ($11 million USD). Zhou realized that if the Chinese people could stop corruption, maybe one day they would have the potential to save the environment. Three years later, while Zhou studied international politics at Sun Yat-sen University, that potential was realized: for the first time in Maoming's history, the people left the safety of their homes to protest an unsafe Paraxylene development. Zhou became emboldened in her mission to mobilize Chinese youth and fight for reform.[33]

Caroline Engle, by contrast, grew up in western Kentucky, where she learned to love fishing and farming. While her upbringing was as different as could be from Zhou's, Engle fell in love with nature as well. The seventh-generation Kentuckian became an environmental leader at the University of Kentucky, where she works with the student group UK Greenthumb, and the Sierra Student Coalition, a student arm of the Sierra Club, an environmental group.[34]

Against all odds, the duo crossed paths in 2015, drawn together by their common passion. Zhou and Engle both belonged to millennial groups—the China Youth Climate Action Network and Sierra Student Coalition, respectively—that wanted to promote global collaboration towards mitigating climate change. And so the groups decided to join forces. Together, they co-authored a letter calling for the United States and China to collaborate on passing environmental reform.

"We, as youth leaders of the environmental movements in the United States and China, come together to express our shared desire for collective action to improve our economies, public health, and infrastructure domestically while also taking cooperative and equitable action to mitigate the shared crisis of climate change," they wrote to President Xi and President Obama. "We cannot solve this problem alone, and so we look to you as our nations' leaders to strengthen the U.S.-China partnership by committing to these requests that will ensure our safe and just future through an equitable climate agreement in 2015."

As a generation that has grown up in many ways without the geographic barriers of the past, thanks to technological innovations, we recognize more than ever the importance to collaborate with other nations in our quest towards achieving a more sustainable planet. As Denny Baek of California told us, climate justice is not an issue for one nation—it's an issue for humanity.

"We are the only species on the planet that wastes resources at the rate that we do. When we migrate to a specific area, it becomes desolate and dead and we move on. We are destroying the land faster than we can let it heal," Baek said. "This is humanity's problem; we as people have to be conscious of that, and if we want to start working together ... there are so many hurdles we have to cross. It is up to the coming generation to be accepting and open-minded and get past political, sexual, religious, intellectual, economic, religious differences and barriers before we can consider coming under one united partnership."

That's why millennials were excited when President Obama came home in 2015 with an international agreement to combat climate change. The Paris Agreement included commitments from developed and developing nations to reduce carbon emissions. While the treaty used vague language to describe exactly how much emissions would be reduced, the idea behind the accord was to trigger domestic changes in each of the signatory nations. It's a good start.[35]

At a 2011 U.N. Climate Change Conference, a Middlebury College student interrupted negotiators and announced her support for a global agreement, before being removed (because, of course, she did not really represent the United States). "I am speaking on behalf of the United States of America because my negotiators cannot. The obstructionist Congress has shackled justice and delayed ambition for far too long. I am scared for my future. 2020 is too late to wait. We need an urgent path to a fair, ambitious, and legally-binding treaty," she declared.

Many millennials are coming to believe that we shouldn't only work with other countries, we should also learn from them. California millennial Henri Stern, for example, says China is way ahead of us. "We do a decent job, though actually China does a much better job than we do, in terms of fostering nuclear, wind, solar, geothermal," he said. "We can learn from them that they have realized that they have a problem, a serious problem, and they're actively doing things to fix them."

Stern says that China is cleaning its water, reducing its reliance on coal and fighting desertification—all with greater impact than the United States. "China's water sources are polluted. China is desertifying and they are too heavily reliant on coal. So what they are doing is they are upping water standards, they are creating what's called the great green wall of China between the desert in the west and fertile lands in the east, to stop the spread of the desert—which is happening in large part in China, which is also happening in the U.S. in California," he said. "They are being much more proactive then we are."

Solution: Divestment from Fossil Fuels

"Calling for Divestment, Protesters Blockade Mass. Hall," reported *The Harvard Crimson*.[36] "Stanford students begin 'indefinite' sit-in over fossil fuel divestment," wrote *The Guardian*.[37]

From the halls of Swarthmore College, where protestors sat-in at administrative offices for three weeks, to the University of Mary Washington, where police ended a sit-in by removing protestors, and to Harvard, where a blockade of administrative offices forced administrators to relocate to a nearby Au Bon Pain, students across the country have been pushing their universities to divest from fossil fuels.[38] So far, 16 schools have divested.[39]

"We will be here until we see meaningful action from our administration," Emma Walker-Silverman, a Stanford undergraduate, told *The Guardian*. "Dramatic climate change isn't an issue that you can just hope goes away. ... We want to send a strong message that this model of business is no longer acceptable." Some activists have taken a different approach from Walker-Silverman and her peers, holding referendums, where millennials have turned out in record high numbers to vote to divest their schools' endowment funds from fossil fuels.

Even outside of the "college bubble," divestment has become a tool of choice for activists. Today, Barclays and other global investment banks offer their clients access to sustainable investment options, and mutual funds offer their investors the opportunity to opt-out of unclean investments. Green bonds—which are sustainable investment vehicles—now trade at a premium, and investors care about whether their dollars are being spent in environmentally friendly ways.

CONCLUSION: IT'S ON US

"The largest mobilization against climate change in the history of the planet" happened in New York City on September 21, 2015. Four hundred thousand marchers—representing 300 universities—gathered together to raise awareness about the importance of protecting our environment.

These young people came together because they recognized that as the last generation with the capability of making a difference, it's our responsibility to save the planet. And that's no easy task—especially with Washington insiders sacrificing the environment in favor of politically expedient decisions. As millennials ascend to power, we are making the fight for climate justice a top priority. By creating a global regime to fight carbon emissions, we are working toward a better future. So someday, young people can commend us, not ask the fatal question: "why didn't we save ourselves when we had the chance?"

Bill Nye ("The Science Guy"), a millennial hero, called our generation to action in a 2015 speech at Rutgers University. "The oncoming trouble is climate change: it is going to affect you all in the same way the Second World War consumed people of my parents' generation. They rose to the challenge, and so will you. They came to be called the 'Greatest Generation.' I want you all to preserve our world in the face of climate change and carry on as the 'Next Great Generation,'" he said.

Challenge accepted.

Entitlement Reform: What is the Role of Government?

SAN JOSE, CALIFORNIA

Former House Speaker Tip O'Neil is famous for having called Social Security the "third rail" of American politics, warning that any politician who dared engage on the subject would suffer politically as a result.

Today, with Social Security on the verge of bankruptcy, politicians are heeding O'Neil's warning and ignoring the issue entirely. For young people—a group that stands to lose the most if our entitlements become insolvent—this bodes poorly for the future. Today, more than half of millennials believe that Social Security will not exist at all when they retire, and just 6 percent believe they will receive benefits at today's levels.

Entitlements are divisive; by definition, they involve a Ponzi scheme where the young subsidize the old. Generally, this is a good thing—we know we'll pay in now, and we'll get the benefits later. But these days it looks like young people are paying the bill—for everything from Social Security to health care—and it's not as clear we're getting commensurate benefits. Because most entitlements rarely receive popular attention, especially among young people, we need to dig a bit deeper to understand where millennials are going to lead the welfare state—and how they feel about the role of government in our society, more generally.

To get better insights on these questions, the next stop on our journey is San Jose, where young leaders from every region in the country have come together to talk about pressing issues facing our country. These leaders are focused on civic engagement, hoping to motivate their peers to stand up and fight for America's future.

In San Jose, we organized focus groups on a wide variety of issues—but the one we were most keen to learn more about was entitlements, mostly because it's an issue no one is really talking about.

What is the Role of Government?

Millennials hate theoretical questions. After all, we believe in pragmatic politics, not ideology. But to understand what millennials are going to do to the welfare state, it's important to explore how millennials think about the role that government should play in our lives. If we take polling at face value, the answer is simple: millennials want a small government. Young people favor "smaller government, providing fewer services, with low taxes" over "larger government, providing more services, with high taxes" by a margin of 57 to 41. The American public overall favors small government by a similar margin.[1] At the same time, 58 percent of millennials believe that the government should "spend more on financial assistance to the poor, even if it leads to higher taxes." This view clearly comes in conflict with our intention to limit the role of government. Clearly, government intervention is a careful balancing act.[2]

"It's a competence issue. I can't trust this federal government, this Congress, this President [Obama], to do things in a way that are actually going to positively affect me when they are so far-flung," Ian Baucke explained. "I'm from here in California. We spend the most on education and the most on welfare, and we're dead last for education and No. 1 in poverty, essentially. And I think that it's really a noble idea and I agree that we as a society are responsible to help other people, but I feel more that society and the government are not necessarily the same thing and shouldn't necessarily be conflated."

Baucke, a conservative from southern California, wants to preserve opportunity and believes that large government hampers innovation, instead opting for a more entrepreneurial attitude. "My dad, he grew up like in Raytown, Missouri [a suburb of Kansas City], with a $50,000 house, which is all he had tied to his name. And he's worked his way up, he paid for college himself, and he has his own self-employed small business for development planning … and I think that we need to have a system in place that allows people to be innovative, and we're straying away from that.

"My philosophy is, I don't want my daily life to have me come into contact with the federal government. … I agree that health care is too expensive, college is too expensive, day care is too expensive, but that doesn't justify arguments that they should be free. There should be changes to the system we have that we know will make it more cost-effective," Baucke added.

On the other side of the spectrum sits Alsan Diouf, a New Jersey Democrat and millennial leader whose primary concern is ensuring a better quality of life for Americans. "We have a responsibility to take care of the people who need help. Everyone has a different reason for why they are poor and it's not always so simple, like, 'Oh, go get a job.' There are a lot of reasons that play into why you may be unemployed, why you may be poor, that are systematic. I think we definitely as a society have a responsibility to help the poor, I think we shouldn't just say, 'You're on your own, go solve it yourself.' "

Diouf would pay for these policies with higher taxes. "Rich people can afford to give and definitely shouldn't be paying less and still have a great quality of life. For people who earn less money, the percentage probably impacts them much more," she said.

But Ashley Rinner, an Ohio native, worries that higher taxes on corporations affect small businesses too. She's learned that the hard way, watching her neighbors struggle to make ends meet with their Chinese restaurant. Instead, Rinner believes that charities should help the poor. "I think the millennials need to realize that we need to help people; it's not the government's job, it's ours," she said.

In practice, millennial support for small government but desire to help the poor means that millennials tend to support individual freedom but will opt for government intervention when they believe it will create a fairer society. Either way, small government conservatives and big government liberals can agree on one thing: the welfare state is broken and needs fixing. Washington doesn't have the courage to make hard decisions—millennials are taking the lead in exploring and advocating for real change.

The Millennial War on Poverty

The lights cut out and the refrigerator was near empty as Ruby returned home from a long exhausting day of school and work. On the outside, the Texas millennial was the perfect role model of a high-achieving millennial leader. Exams were a breeze and Ruby was more than college-ready. Outside of the classroom, she was a leader in extra-curricular activities. But while her friends left school to brush up on their SAT vocabulary, or coordinate spring break trips to volunteer in Africa, Ruby began the second phase of her day: going to work.

This was nothing new. Ruby had been working since she was in elementary school to help pay the bills. But things had never been this bad. Throughout her childhood, Ruby's mom often worked two jobs. And with additional income from welfare, things usually turned out all right. But now the year was 2008, the Great Recession had hit, and welfare benefits had ceased. Poverty became something more than an exam topic to study—it became personal.

"Poverty isn't talked about enough and when it is, it's usually by people that have good backgrounds. And I think welfare helps a lot because my mom and dad used to get it and they stopped getting it, and after that I saw changes in our house," Ruby said. "My mom works two jobs and we still struggle. Yeah, it's really hard. There was less food in the house sometimes and lights would get cut off sometimes. It kind of sucks."

For the 15 percent of Americans living below the poverty line, Ruby's story is resonant; hunger and distress are top of mind. Poverty among young people is accelerating. In 1980, one in eight young Americans was below the poverty line. Today, that's climbed to one in five.[3]

"In Fairfield ... I go shopping to Walmart, or I go with my friends to grab a pizza at the plaza. But then when we're driving out and exiting the plaza, I see a mother and a father and their two kids with a poster saying, 'Can you please help,' " said Arsh Sharma, a millennial who worries about income inequality in America. "Public education is free but you can't send your child to school in the same clothes every day getting no water, no nourishment, not taking a shower."

And while discussions of poverty are ripe with stereotyping, poverty does not discriminate. When Hanna Brooks Olsen sought help from a local job training company, she was told, "You don't look poor enough to be here."[4] Olsen was shocked and saddened.

"Of course, at that exact moment, I had, yes, a college degree and a coveted unpaid (because of course, it was unpaid) internship at a public radio station. But I also had a minimum wage job to support myself, $17 in my bank account, $65,000 in debt to my name, and $800 in rent due in 24 days. I was extremely hungry, worried about my utilities being shut off, and 100 percent planning to hit up the dumpster at the nearby Starbucks when I was done there," Olsen wrote in a blog post.

Olsen is among the many college students who struggle with poverty every day. As she notes, "More college students live in poverty—actual poverty, not just 'can't-afford-pizza-better-call-the-parents' brokenness—than the overall population." And this reality is rooted in facts. College towns like State College, Pennsylvania, are in some of the poorest counties in the United States.

Partially because they are disproportionally affected by poverty and partially because they are the civic-minded generation, millennials tend to be dedicated to community service, fighting on the front lines of the war on poverty to help low-income families make ends meet. Hence, the rise of the "service fraternity" whose "brothers" (male and female) dedicate their time to helping others in need. Overall, millennials are more likely than any other generation to say that that citizens have a very important obligation to volunteer, an Associated Press-GfK poll found.[5]

But millennials want help in their fight, and generally think that the government should be playing a bigger, more substantial role in fighting poverty. In fact, 58 percent of millennials say the government should spend more money assisting the poor even if it means higher taxes, according to a Reason poll. Almost three-quarters say government has a responsibility to guarantee that every citizen has a place to sleep at night and enough food to put on the table.[6]

But that doesn't mean millennials are necessarily welfare-lovers or free health-care fanatics. When it comes to addressing government entitlements, millennials recognize that there are distinctions to be drawn among different types of government aid.

"I think that there is a difference between cash assistance and housing assistance and the food stamp program," explained Ariel Soldatenko, a millennial leader from New York. "The government in a developed country has at least the responsibility to ensure that people have food to feed their children and a place to live that's warm and to have access to clothing and basic necessities. It's not right in a country like America, where the top 1 percent has so much wealth, that people should be living in the streets," she said.

The majority of millennials agree that the federal government is not doing enough to help Ruby, her family, and others in need. But as a generation, millennials are divided on how to navigate the complex road toward reforming entitlement spending.

Welfare is the Worst

Since he was a little kid, Levy always wondered why his aunt and uncle weren't married. It seemed strange. The two lived together for years, had never separated, had children, and seemed to be in love. Levy forgot the issue until a few years ago, when the Arizona millennial learned the real reason the two were still unmarried.

"My uncle didn't marry his wife so that he could work and she could get welfare for her and her three kids. It's disgusting that that can happen," Levy said. "It's a tough issue because there are people that actually do need it. And those people feel attacked ... but in reality, we're just trying to stop the abuse. They tried drug testing but only found a handful out of something like 70,000 in Arizona. So that's obviously not it." Levy's distrust of cash-based assistance is not uncommon among millennials, many of whom would send the program to face the chopping block if they had the choice. In fact, millennials today often refer to cash assistance as the "most corrupted" government welfare program.

This is nothing new. Americans have long disdained welfare more than nearly all other anti-poverty initiatives because it provides cash assistance to able-bodied, working-age adults. "Americans are attracted to that notion that people should be responsible for themselves, turn to government as a last resort, and that voluntary assistance and communities are preferable to government when individuals need help," said Princeton University professor Martin Gilens.[7]

"There has always been a certain degree of cynicism and concern about welfare benefits—about government programs—especially those that provide cash to the poor," Gilens said. "Even in the 1930s, when FDR was initiating the first federal relief and assistance programs, he characterized welfare as a narcotic and a subtle destroyer of the human spirit."

But millennial opposition towards cash-based welfare programs is taking a new form. For millennials, the focus today is on modification and reform, not simply reducing welfare funding. Likewise, criticism tends to be less racially motivated than in the past and more directed at commonsense solutions to making the system more efficient.

Millennials reject both the Democratic and Republican approaches to welfare reform. Republicans—who repeatedly insist on defunding welfare, food stamps and other entitlement programs—are viewed as being at best naïve and at worst malicious. Indeed, even the Cato Institute, a conservative think tank, has acknowledged that states with the lowest welfare benefits—like Mississippi—also have the highest poverty rates in America. At the same time, millennial voters are quick to criticize Democrats for being slow to make necessary changes.[8]

Work requirements top the list of millennial reforms because they incentivize poor families to look for work, help lift them out of poverty, and guarantee that tax dollars are spent on people looking to contribute to the economy. Already, 83 percent of Americans support work requirements for welfare recipients—so the political capital exists to begin immediate reforms.[9] "If not giving it entirely to the states, putting in welfare requirements or educational requirements" is necessary, argued Ian Baucke.

"There's no reason why the government should be providing welfare to people who can work but choose not to," said John Guarco. "I'm not sure if we should be defunding welfare programs. But we should be creating systems where it is in people's best interest to get a job, and if it turns out that people are not getting a job when they can and are able to, in that respect I would call for lowering the amount of funds for welfare."

But millennials want more than just work-search requirements to prevent abuse—they want welfare programs that are more efficient. "I don't think we should increase welfare or decrease welfare; we need to fundamentally rethink welfare," explained Justin Wittekind, a millennial leader from southern California. "People definitely need help, but at the same time, you're not going to help people with an entitlement culture that doesn't encourage responsibility." How do we make welfare more efficient? This, of course, is a much more divisive question.

There has been a push toward removing penalties for two-parent poor families to encourage couples like Levy's aunt and uncle to marry. Such a program would incentivize families to stay together, which is one of the strongest anti-poverty measures. "In the partisan minefield of American welfare policy, a powerful consensus has emerged in recent years. ... It sees single-parent families as the dismal foundries that produced decades of child poverty, delinquency, and crime," reported *The New York Times.*[10]

Existing welfare programs need to be consolidated. These programs tend to be widely spread out and hard to navigate. Reducing the number of points-of-access for families on welfare on the local, state, and federal level would make the process easier for them and reduce administrative costs. The entire application process, from the mountains of paperwork to slow processing, should be replaced. Payments for work-related costs for transportation, clothing, and hygiene should be prioritized to help welfare recipients get back on their feet.

For millennials, these straightforward, rational policies are always the first place to start. They allow us to develop "a better solution," explained Illinois millennial Shruti Baxi.

Millennials are the broke generation—and we want to help the poor. But right now, cash-based assistance programs are some of the most broken in the country. Millennials are expecting Washington to take a serious look at the inefficiencies of the welfare system, reduce welfare abuse, and make sure that those who do deserve assistance get it in a timely manner.

Health Care for All

Let's con the millennials. If we go on national television and speak on their favorite shows, maybe they'll agree to subsidize our health care.

This was the logic of the Affordable Care Act (ACA) and its backers. "The mission of the Affordable Care Act was to get healthier and younger people into the system to help offset the premiums," Parker Beauchamp, CEO of INGUARD, a national risk management and health insurance firm, told *The Street*.

But Obamacare's millennial marketing was a flop. "In a desperate attempt to connect with the young audience, liberal message-makers unapologetically use sex, alcohol, and corny jokes to sell the program," wrote *The Daily Beast*.

Despite the president's appearances on young peoples' favorite TV shows, less than one-third of uninsured young Americans said they would sign up for Obamacare, according to a Harvard study. This wasn't because they disagreed with the idea behind Obamacare. On the contrary, a vast majority of millennials, 69 percent, agrees with the fundamental principle behind the Affordable Care Act—that everyone has a right to health care. Sarah, a Texas millennial whose parents immigrated to the United States from Colombia, explains that millennials believe in the "whole ideal of everyone deserves good health and quality care."

What millennials don't like are the practical results of the law. Forty percent of young Americans believe Obamacare will bring worse care, and 51 percent say it will bring higher costs.[11] Generation Opportunity, a millennial advocacy organization, reported that health care premiums rose on average by 91 percent for young men and 44 percent for women after the law was passed. These estimates sound inflated, but they capture the overall effect: Obamacare cost millennials in the wallets.[12]

"Millennials think the U.S. health care system is fundamentally flawed. They believe it is purposely geared toward the sickest and oldest, and structured to profit from their treatment," wrote Paul Keckley, a former managing director of the Navigant Center for Healthcare Research and Policy Analysis. "They want a system of health that balances resources for the young and healthy with compassionate care for the elderly and sick."[13]

Millennials recognize the importance of all Americans receiving health care, including young people, who are usually the ones to opt out. "Over the past year I had to get surgery, and then I had to go get physical therapy. My surgery was $20,000, so if I didn't have health care, my family would be like broke," Alsan Diouf explained. "And then the physical therapy itself over the course that I was doing it was close to $15,000, of just therapy. So if we didn't have any help with that, it would be very bad. Now imagine another catastrophe." Ashley Rinner is another one of those young people who definitely needed her insurance. "I've put my doctors through the ringer. I've broken nine bones. Three years I've had to get CAT scans on my head. I've definitely hit the insurance top," she said.

Millennials are looking at a system that will balance their economic concerns with the health needs of the elderly. Millennials believe this balance is tipped heavily in favor of the elderly—hence, exorbitant costs for young people, who tend to use their insurance less than older Americans, on average. Overall, 57 percent of millennials disapprove of the law, Harvard reports.[14] Buzzfeed Editor-in-Chief Ben Smith doesn't hold back. He says outright that Obamacare "screwed" young people.

"President Obama's enemies often accuse him, in the starkest political terms, of crudely acting to shift resources toward his political base: green-energy donors, single women, Latinos, African Americans," Smith wrote. "But the next 12 months are likely to reveal the opposite. Imminent elements of Obama's grandest policy move, the health-care overhaul known as ObamaCare, are calculated to screw his most passionate supporters and to transfer wealth to his worst enemies."[15]

Millennial concern about cost hikes should not come as a surprise. Already, millennials are twice as likely to challenge the cost of their medical care, Price Waterhouse Cooper reports. Nineteen percent of 25-to-34-year-olds have asked for a discount on medical care, compared with 8 percent of the general population—so we are price-sensitive. Millennials want everyone to have health care—we just don't want to foot the bill.[16] Smith describes Obamacare as a "vast transfer of resources from young to old."

Millennials may not be the most informed demographic when it comes to health—only 22 percent of young people report that they know "a lot" about the bill—but many young people feel strongly that they are getting the short end of the stick.[17] For example, before Obamacare kicked in, many states had laws in place that guaranteed that seniors' health care premiums should be capped at five times the premium paid by younger Americans. Obamacare changed that ratio to one: three.

With Obamacare here to stay, many millennials are capitulating to the program, while others are simply paying the mandated fine for remaining uninsured because they can't afford insurance. "At least taking the penalty, it's just something I have to deal with once, at the end of the year," Assante, a millennial from New York, told *The Guardian*. "Since I don't make a lot of money, the cheapest plan that I was able to get was probably $75 a month, but my deductible was about $6,000. By the time I would reach my deductible, it would be a couple of years."

So while millennials in theory support universal health care, in practice they appear to be voting in the exact opposite direction—both with their dollars, and at the polls.

Social Security and Medicare are Going Bankrupt

Paula Dromi is a 75-year-old social worker living in Los Angeles with one of her sons and a friend. Despite her age, Dromi has no plans to retire. "I'll be working another 20 years, assuming I can," Dromi told *Time*. Dromi joins millions of older Americans who are prolonging retirement because they don't have the financial means to stop working. Thirty percent of middle-class Americans say they will need to work until age 80 to live comfortably in retirement, according to a

Wells Fargo study, and three-quarters expect to work in their retirement years to make ends meet.[18]

In other words, the end of retirement is coming sooner than you think. For decades, older Americans have been supported by the tax dollars stored into Social Security. Retirement meant a time to relax, spend time with family, and sometimes even travel. But that's all changing now. By 2030, the baby boomers will have spent what's left of the Social Security Trust Funds—and the Gen Xers and millennials will be left out to dry.

"I think most people in our generation have almost come to think that the generation that is currently in power is going to almost fail us," Ian Baucke worries. "Social Security is going to go bankrupt and then no one is going to get it, and whenever someone tries to change it, they get crucified, which I think is ridiculous."

More than half of millennials today don't think that Social Security will exist when we're ready to retire, and of those who do think it will exist, only 6 percent think it will exist at the same level it does today. This won't only mean lower standards of living for the elderly; it will mean older millennials working until they quite literally can work no more.[19]

Retirement funds aren't the only things drying up—the government is running out of funds to pay for Medicare, which provides medical care to the elderly. Need a heart transplant? That might be too bad if the government doesn't get its act together. Medicare will be "effectively bankrupt" by 2021. Today, its unfunded liability—the difference between expected revenues and outflows—is expected to total $30 trillion. And with it goes subsidized health-care benefits that allow the elderly to live longer, healthier lives.[20]

"At the current rate of payroll tax collections, Medicare would be able to pay about 86 percent of costs in 2030, declining to 80 percent by 2050," *Reuters* reported. Politicians on both sides of the aisle have scrambled to solve this problem, which would have a dramatic effect on seniors, a key voting demographic that spends roughly 90 percent of their disposable income on health care costs.[21]

Insolvency is ugly. It sounds theoretical, but when it happens, it's the most vulnerable people in America who feel the pain. As early as 2016, the Disability Insurance Trust Fund will go bankrupt and payouts will be cut by 19 percent. The fund will use current payroll-tax revenue to pay for the remainder of the benefits. So we're in for an unfortunate preview of the damage wrought by our broken entitlement regime.[22]

Why is Washington Failing to Act?

With Social Security and Medicare going bankrupt, we'd expect to hear Washington politicians actively debating and discussing solutions to this crisis. ... Right?

You guessed it. Washington is silent on entitlement reform. Neither Democrats nor Republicans have passed any serious reform in decades, even as we get closer and closer to insolvency. Both parties fear they'll lose votes from seniors, a demographic that turns out to vote in disproportionate numbers, so they avoid passing serious changes.

The debate usually goes like this. Republican candidates—like 2012 presidential candidate Mitt Romney—announce that Medicare and Social Security are going bankrupt. They declare their support for raising the retirement age and cutting benefits. Democrats run a series of fear-mongering advertisements telling seniors that Republicans want them dead (okay, maybe not so literally, but that's really what they are trying to say). Republicans backtrack. Rinse, repeat.

Bloated entitlements threaten to undermine the welfare system that millions of Americans have come to expect. To implement entitlement reform—and prevent a multitrillion dollar catastrophe—Washington will need to unite in true bipartisan cooperation. It's going to require cuts to benefits—not politically popular among any generation—and reforms. Privatization will need to be seriously considered, if not adopted. Incremental change is nearly impossible; the only way to fix our entitlements will be via a "grand bargain" of sorts between the two parties. Whatever reform is passed, it will likely be unpopular.

Given the level of polarization in politics today, a grand bargain seems unlikely. The interests of young voters—actually having a solvent welfare state—fall to the back burner. The average congressperson is 57 and the average senator is 63, so our leaders don't have the same level of urgency as we do. For them, kicking the can down the road is a viable option. For us, it's a guarantee that by the time we try to collect Social Security, we'll receive an error message saying "sorry, account overdrawn." [23]

Lobbyists are part of the problem. Millennials don't have a central lobbying organ. Seniors have the AARP. This means that seniors are better able to project their political might. They're using that power to stand in the way of reform. Congressional representatives acknowledge that AARP plays a major role in shaping new legislation. For example, the organization has all but vetoed private accounts for Social Security. "AARP adamantly opposes replacing any part of Social Security with individual accounts," said Marie F. Smith, formerly the organization's president.

Millennials can't solve this one alone. Protests won't work. The free market won't work. Even local grassroots movements won't work. Entitlements are uniquely the realm of the federal government—the big, lethargic bureaucracy that we all find so difficult to understand, let alone navigate. So for millennials, the only viable course of action will be to vote for politicians who support entitlement reform. We need to pray—against all odds—that America's leaders have the courage to fix the problem before it's too late.

Making Hard Choices: The Millennial Approach to Social Security

As the retirement bubble comes closer and closer to bursting, young people have begun to advocate for radical changes to Social Security.

Today, the most popular policy proposal championed by millennial voters is the move toward privatized retirement accounts, which has gained the support of 73 percent of millennials. In practice, privatization of Social Security would mean that millennials and future generations would be able to control their retirement funds and invest them in the stock market at their own discretion.[24] Likewise, two-thirds of young Americans believe that federal payroll taxes should be increased for high-income earners to support the Social Security program.[25]

"Give people options to do private investment accounts and those kind of reforms; maybe a slight reduction in benefits just because it's not sustainable," Baucke suggested. "[Social Security is] built the same way since it was when it started and America is in a very different place."

"Younger people think private accounts make sense," acknowledged Martis Davis, formerly an AARP spokesman. "Polls by some organizations suggest that young people believe in flying saucers more than in Social Security. We have a problem with that. We don't want to end up being perceived as dinosaurs," he told *The New York Times*.

Millennials are looking toward innovative proposals spearheaded and tested by individual states as possible models for a new federal system. The California Secure Choice Retirement Savings Program, for example, is a new proposal for solving the Social Security crisis that went into effect in California in 2016. Under that program, employers who do not offer retirement plans would be required to deduct pay from employees for their contributions to a low-risk retirement savings plan. Today, just 64 percent of private sector workers have access to a formal retirement plan, and fewer than half sign up for one.[26]

A third proposal is the USA Retirement Funds Act, sponsored by former Sen. Tom Harkin (D-IA). Harkin's plan would make it difficult for Americans to borrow from the 401(k)s before they retire, a source of "leakage" which results in the depletion of many retirees' savings.

Harkin's plan would also mandate that employers with more than 10 employees enroll their workers in a retirement fund and ensure that employees have a steady income stream in retirement. This federal proposal would scale up the California plan to give retirees income later in life.

For millennials, the concern is less on the precise details of any of these plans, or others, but rather on finding some way to salvage Social Security so that it is sustainable. A full 95 percent of millennials agree that "reforms are needed to the current retirement system" and 90 percent say "lawmakers need to make this a high priority," according to the National Institute on Retirement Security (NIRS). Whether via comprehensive reform—as proposed by Speaker of the House Paul Ryan (R-WI) and Harkin—or through more incremental changes, like reducing benefits or adding means testing for benefits, we definitely need reform soon.[27]

Not all changes are equally popular. Millennials are the least likely to support raising the eligibility age of Social Security. Just one-third of millennials support the change. This should come as no surprise, since the only people who would be affected by raising the age for Social Security eligibility are those younger than 55. It is just another case of our generation paying the bill, but not receiving the benefits.[28]

But this cynical generation isn't about to wait for the government. We're preparing for the storm to come. Eighty-two percent of millennials feel it is important to save for retirement and 63 percent of millennials started saving for retirement at or before age 25. Whereas Social Security is the primary source of income for 58 percent of the Silent Generation, more than 72 percent of millennials do not expect Social Security to be their main source of retirement income and 42 percent think they will get no retirement income from Social Security when they retire.[29]

It is clear that as the retirement ages climb and concerns over the solvency of Social Security grow, Americans will grow increasingly concerned over the future of retirement. But if millennials have anything to say about it, new programs will be implemented to replace the failing Social Security program that exists today. These changes need to happen soon—we're cutting very close to bankruptcy.

Healing Medicare

Solving the Medicare shortfall is as challenging as it is critical; thousands of lives are at stake if the program fails. That's why less mainstream ideas, like the Medicare voucher program first authored by Sen. Ron Wyden (D-OR) and Rep. Ryan in 2011, are gaining traction among millennial voters—at least they deal with the problem. The proposal would allow seniors to use their Medicare benefits to purchase approved private health-care plans and would cap cost growth at 1 percent of GDP plus inflation. 46 percent of millennials said they support this proposal, compared to just 25 percent of Americans 65 and older.

Democrats strongly oppose what's been dubbed the Ryan Medicare platform. "The Republican plan to kill Medicare is a plan that tries to balance the budget literally on the backs of America's seniors," Senate Minority Leader Harry Reid (D-NV) said. But this hyper-partisan rhetoric, which doesn't actually address the program's strengths and faults, only further turns off millennials. "There's nothing there. [The Democratic platform on Medicare is] just, 'We'll protect it.' Well, great, thanks. How?" Jonathan Assink, a lifelong Democrat and Barack Obama supporter who works as a barista in Seattle, told *The Seattle Times*. "At least the other side talks about it.[30]

Behind opposition to a Medicare voucher program is a fear that private insurers will not be able to fully meet the needs of seniors. But millennials think this fear is unfounded—only vetted programs would be included in the marketplace created by Ryan's Medicare reform. Chetan Chandrashekhar, a University of Washington student studying urban planning, agrees. "The attack ads that we've seen against

Paul Ryan about ending Medicare as we know it, they seem cheap," he said. "We need to have a real discussion."

For one thing, millennial support for Ryan's program is based on their affinity for free-market solutions (and Ryan's personal brand of fiscal conservatism). But more importantly, millennials simply crave innovative plans to solve the Medicare crisis—and Ryan's is a particularly well-developed solution that will reduce Medicare costs. With no magic wand to solve our budgetary problems, many millennials are satisfied accepting a new solution, albeit imperfect, if it moves us closer to a solvent Medicare system that will support us in old age.

Incremental changes are important too. Chandrashekhar wants to "reduce overlap by integrating Medicare and Medicaid (which provides health care to the poor) and programs for veterans and government employees." On both sides of the aisle, proposals to raise the eligibility age for Medicare, means-test benefits, increase taxes, reduce coverage, raise premiums, and pay physicians less for their services, are being discussed. The problem is a) none of these solutions alone will make Medicare solvent, and b) all of these solutions violate this basic premise that we can somehow fix Medicare easily, without harming benefits.[31]

Medicare is widely heralded by millennials as an important part of the social safety net. Unless Washington can take action to ensure the program is solvent, our generation will never reap its benefits. So we're calling for wholesale reforms, and the polls we've cited indicate millennials are the generation most open to stomaching big changes to the system. The issue definitely needs to be addressed, and our generation is leading the way to providing our leaders with the support and political capital to make these changes before it's too late.

Minimum Wage

Debbra Alexis was fed up. After three years working in Victoria's Secret's flagship store in New York City, the college graduate was paid a meager $9.93/hour, passed up for promotions, and had her hours changed anywhere from 10 to 30 hours per week at a moment's notice. In June 2013, things changed. Alexis and three of her colleagues sent their manager a letter demanding better hours and higher wages, enlisting the public for support.

"The company saw the workers as people who were invested in the brand and so they took them seriously," Terasia Bradford, Retail Action's lead organizer with Victoria's Secret, said. "Victoria's Secret is invested in its image and so it should be invested in its employees, as well."

Alexis is one of the many millennial activists who have risen up to demand higher wages in recent years. Two-thirds of young Americans favor raising the federal minimum wage to $10.10 an hour, according to a *Reason* poll.[32] One primary reason young people support the minimum wage is that we are its primary recipients—61 percent of those earning the minimum wage are millennials living in poverty.[33]

Overall, millennials think it's important for low-wage workers to earn living wages. And millennial advocates are winning this battle, backed by the Democratic base and President Obama. Today, 29 states and Washington, D.C., have minimum wages that are higher than the federal rate. In the past two years, 17 states have increased their minimum wages.[34]

Not everyone agrees that a higher minimum wage will improve the economy. Mario Espinosa, a millennial leader from California, said that the minimum wage benefits the Democratic base at the expense of our economy. His mom works a minimum wage job, and he says that while she appreciates the extra money, he still doesn't believe it's a rational policy. Talk about adamant opposition.

Espinosa is not alone in this belief. Conservative economists argue that higher wages force companies to cut costs, often by firing employees. Roberto Ruiz, a New Jersey millennial, says he's seen these negative effects in his community. "We had a pizzeria in my town and when New Jersey raised the minimum wage a couple years ago, they had to lay off workers. And guess what, those workers were high school students," he said.

Texas millennial Cole Harper thinks the benefits of the minimum wage may be oversold. "I think it may be overplayed how much good it would do because I think it rallies up the base a lot," Harper said.

But Ruiz understands the appeal of the minimum wage and thinks it's a tough debate for our generation. "It is a double-edged sword because you have a generation that's being constantly told that we can't hire you because we can't afford to hire you. At the same time, we're a generation that when we do get hired gets paid nothing." This moral argument—that it is wrong for workers to make below a living wage—is the basis for much support of the minimum wage.

Moral arguments aren't the only ones used to condemn McDonald's and laud Starbucks. Liberal economists argue that because the labor market is noncompetitive, firms wield disproportionate power and are therefore able to exploit workers. Since labor-demand is inelastic (McDonald's needs someone to flip burgers, no matter the cost), firms will have to keep the same number of employees and pay for their higher wages by reducing their own profits. Therefore, with higher minimum wages, employees can expect higher wages with no significant job cuts.

Economists Hristos Doucouliagos and T.D. Stanley analyzed 64 minimum wage studies and found that the most precise estimates were heavily clustered at or near zero employment effects. Their results "find ... an insignificant employment effect from minimum wage raises." Likewise, economists Paul Wolfson and Dale Belman identified 27 minimum wage studies, revealing no statistically significant negative employment effects of the minimum wage. Finally, Arindrajit Dube, T. William Lester and Michael Reich in 2010 used a large sample of U.S. counties on either side of a state border over a 16-year period and found "strong earnings effects and no employment effects of minimum wage increases" on one side of the border.[35]

Conservative data scientists who purportedly crunch the same numbers come to opposite conclusions! A meta-analysis of 102 minimum wage studies conducted by the National Bureau of Economic Research found that 67 percent of studies found negative employment effects, 25 percent found no effect, and only 8 percent found a positive employment effect. Of the 33 most robust studies, 85 percent point to negative employment effects.[36]

Surveys of businesses tell the same story. According to *The Wall Street Journal*, a $10 minimum wage would cause 54 percent of employers to reduce hiring and 34 percent to begin immediate layoffs. Overall, the Congressional Budget Office (CBO) finds that this would cost the United States between 500,000 and 1 million existing jobs, while the American Action Forum estimates it would cost the United States 2.3 million new jobs per year. It's no wonder then that economists David Newmark, Mark Schweitzer and William Wascher found that a higher minimum wage results in a net increase in the proportion of poor families, with the "losers" outnumbering the "winners."[37]

Despite the lack of consensus in academic communities, millennials are in agreement. Guaranteeing that employees receive a living wage should be an important government priority. As millennials take over as politicians and CEOs, our generation will continue to fight for higher wages for workers. After all, 68 percent of millennials say government should ensure everyone makes a living wage and three-quarters of us think the government has a responsibility to guarantee every citizen has a place to sleep and enough to eat.

CONCLUSION

Even though young Americans are divided on the role of government, they agree that the welfare state needs to be reformed. Congress lacks the will to make tough choices. The result will be devastating— as our generation matures, we'll find there's no social safety net to fall back on. So millennials will need to take the lead. By fixing welfare, overhauling Social Security and Medicare, raising the minimum wage, and influencing the health-care debate, millennials help create a country that is not only more considerate of those in need—but also more proactive in creating a sustainable future.

There's no denying that the political will necessary to ensure the sustainability of entitlements is unprecedented for modern times. Reforming Medicare and Social Security will require a "grand bargain" between Democrats and Republicans. No matter what the agreement is, it will be unpopular. Neither party will be willing to act alone. Compromise will be unavoidable. Our best hope is that millennials take their consensus to Washington and through their representatives—or by running for office—unify around a reformist agenda to save the welfare state.

Though lobbyists often try to paint entitlements as a battle between the young against the old, the opposite seems true. Millennials are the last hope our parents and grandparents have of saving Social Security and maintaining the safety net that Americans of all stripes support.

Immigrant Opportunity: Eliminating the Shadow Class

BOSTON, MASSACHUSETTS

America has a permanent underclass. 11 million shadow workers live paycheck to paycheck, hoping to put food on their tables and set aside enough money to send back home to their families. Technically, they don't exist: meet America's undocumented immigrants.

Today, millennials are immigrant champions. The millennial consensus is driven by demographics. Today, U.S. public schools are "majority minority," according to the Department of Education. One in four millennials come from immigrant backgrounds, and 73 percent think it's great to have people from other countries come live in America.[1] Overall, 65 percent of millennials believe immigrants strengthen American society, compared with 49 percent of Americans.[2] Millennials grew up in a very different country than our parents did.

Millennials believe in border security and want to enforce the rule of law—they are not about to open the borders to everyone—but they want to face reality. There are 11 million illegal immigrants in our country and they are not going anywhere. These are also good, working people who don't deserve to be vilified. That's why the next stop on our personal journey is to Harvard in the middle of winter, where it is below freezing temperature after a long night of snowfall. David has food poisoning and Jack is half asleep after a grueling weekend. But we've trekked out to Harvard Yard early in the morning to watch the top four teams—and what we see leaves a lasting impression.

The topic for the tournament was a controversial one—illegal immigration and whether birthright citizenship ought to be abolished. In the early rounds of the tournament, all of the debates ended up boiling down to one question and one question only: are illegal immigrants good for the economy? All teams were able to successfully argue that given our country's economic climate, that should be Congress' top priority. But the teams that were winning—and making it farther into the tournament—were doing something different. They refused to oppose immigration. Instead, teams forced to oppose birthright citizenship started to argue that illegal immigrants are *even better* for our economy than even regular, legal immigrants.

Creative debate arguments are commonplace, but sitting in a large auditorium watching the final round of the Harvard Debate Tournament, nobody was expecting what they saw. One team argued in favor of birthright citizenship, while the other argued that America was better off with a population of illegal immigrants. Two of the best teams in the country were both making pro-immigrant arguments—effectively refusing to engage in the debate to which they were assigned—because neither wanted to defend the *unwinnable* argument against immigrant reform. Talk about a different mind-set!

Today, three in four millennials believe that anyone born on U.S. soil should be a citizen, as compared with just 57 percent of Americans. 81 percent of millennials support a pathway to citizenship (or "amnesty," according to GOP rhetoric), as compared with 72 percent of Americans (still a large majority). Sixty-six percent of millennials supported the DREAM Act, which would help send the children of illegal immigrants to college, as compared with 54 percent of Americans. On just about every major indicator, young people are the most supportive of immigrants in the United States. [3]

At the same time, millennials take a pragmatic and centrist approach, nuancing their opinions with realistic proposals. Millennials believe immigrants are good for our country, but they also believe in tougher border security to enforce the rule of law. A sizable majority—62 percent of young people—believes that stronger border protection should either be America's top immigration priority, or an equal priority to creating a "path to citizenship." In their calls for reasonable solutions to our country's immigration mess, young people face a tough challenge. They must overcome the visceral political nature of immigration politics and the bigotry that has fueled a resurgent xenophobic movement in the United States. They must also address the widening generational and demographic divide that has made immigration such a divisive topic.

The Plight of Undocumented Immigrants

America's 11 million undocumented immigrants hail from all across the world and include young children and adults. While young Latin Americans make up the majority of new illegal immigrants, our country's shadow class is not a new phenomenon. The majority of undocumented immigrants have lived in America for more than a decade and 4 million have children born in America who are U.S. citizens.[4]

Certainly, undocumented immigrants violated the law by entering the country. But once they arrive in the United States, these immigrants not only commit fewer crimes than the average American citizen but also often add more to government coffers in taxes than they use in services. The Immigration Policy Center notes that fear of deportation creates added incentives for young, male immigrants to stay off the streets. That's why in California, for example, foreign-born people represent just 17 percent of prison inmates even though they are 35 percent of the population.[5]

Meanwhile, undocumented immigrants often pay taxes, either in the form of automatic paycheck withdrawals, or using special tax

ID numbers. But while they pay taxes, they are ineligible for state benefits. That's why the American Immigration Council reports that undocumented immigrants may add between $20 billion and $85 billion in net taxes to government coffers.[6]

"Immigrants also add to the workforce, they add to the taxes we collect, and they add to the consumerism in the U.S," explained Mario Espinosa, a California millennial. "There's a certain concern for immigrants that might bring in drugs or other illegal substances or anyone affiliated with things such as the cartels, but the majority of people came over for jobs."

With all the time spent demonizing Mexicans and other illegals, many undocumented immigrants contribute to society. And they face unprecedented abuse. They are often overworked and underpaid. With no legal recourse and daily fear of deportation, undocumented immigrants have no alternative but to succumb to this abuse. For undocumented workers, the United States offers access to a life that would never have been possible at home. Violence and poverty force migrants—often children and teenagers—to seek a better life. Undocumented immigrants risk death, traveling on the roofs of trains, and crossing the desert with dangerous "coyotes"—smugglers—all in hopes of reaching the United States

And this goal is as elusive as ever: border security has gotten tighter every year and deportations have reached an all-time high. It's never been so hard to cross into the United States.

In her groundbreaking documentary, *Which Way Home*, Director Rebecca Cammisa, with HBO Documentary Films, follows unaccompanied child migrants from their hometowns in Central America to the Mexican border. Juan Carlos is one of the migrants she follows, a chubby boy from Guatemala who is 14. When Carlos left for Los Angeles, to send money back home, he left the following card for his mother: "Mommy, I hope this letter finds you well. The purpose of this letter is to let you know that I love you and I don't like to see you suffer with so many problems. Therefore, I decided to leave and work in the United States so that you and my brothers are well, and are not lacking in anything."

Through the horrifying stories of the child migrants Cammisa follows—from rape, to death, to starvation and mutilation—she tells the collective story of child migrants in South and Central America. We desperately want them to succeed—but deep down we know that more than 80 percent of them will never reach the United States.

If only legal immigration options worked, cry out both parties. Sympathetic Democrats say they would then be able to rescue more immigrants from poverty and allow them to help grow our economy. Republicans argue that this would allow us to control the spigot of immigration, helping attract highly skilled workers while preventing an influx of inexpensive immigrants from Mexico who will drive down U.S. wages and collect entitlements. But despite their hopes, legal immigration options are broken and navigating the immigration system is nearly impossible.

The Millennial Consensus

Talking heads in Washington would have you thinking immigration was somehow a partisan debate. Republicans want to toss out illegal immigrants and save our economy. Democrats want to give everyone amnesty and open borders. The partisan rhetoric in Washington hasn't always been so dramatic—or as severe. In a video that has gone viral since it was posted in early 2016, the *Houston Chronicle* takes us back to 1980, when Ronald Reagan and George H.W. Bush first debated this topic in the GOP primary.

David Grossberg, a young man who must have been in his 20s at the time, stands up and asks if the children of illegal immigrants should get free public education. Bush says yes, but we need to address the fundamental problem. "We're creating a whole society of really honorable, decent, family-loving people that are in violation of the law. ... These are good people, strong people," he said, to applause from the audience. Reagan follows. "Rather than talking about putting up a fence, why don't we work out some recognition of our mutual problems, make it possible for them to come here legally with a work permit," he said.[7]

Wow. Here's two old-school Republicans debating this issue, before we were even born, and they're finally talking like reasonable people. No wonder the GOP used to actually win national elections! When President Reagan said Latinos should all be Republicans, he wasn't being facetious; there was actually a reasonable case to be made for Republican candidates. Now compare that with today's rhetoric. When I turn on the TV, or rather instant streaming on my computer—because who watches TV these days—I see GOP insiders fighting viscerally over how tall to build the wall that will protect us from "those evil Mexicans." The tone and poise of our leaders has changed since the days of Ronald Reagan—and not in a way we should be proud of.

Jokes aside, the Reagan-Bush style dialogue around immigration reform resonates with millennial voters, who tend to be tolerant of undocumented immigrants. Millennials are not leftists who want open borders. Rather, millennials tend to believe that we must accept the cards we've been dealt—11 million good, honest people living undocumented in our country. We should first figure out how to enfranchise these people and then tighten our borders and fix the legal immigration process to restore the rule of law.

When young people think about immigration, what comes to mind are actual people; the guy who graduated from high school with us but couldn't get college loans, and the gal who needed a ride to graduation, because her parents couldn't take off from their two jobs. "There was this student in my school, his name was John Carlos, and he was a senior last year, and he recently graduated, and he was super, super intelligent and really motivated. And he got accepted to NYU and the University of Florida. But because he's not a legal citizen, he did not qualify for any type of financial aid whatsoever," explained Stephanie Brito, a millennial leader from Florida and the daughter of Cuban immigrants.

"And that kind of brings to light, what are we going to do about these immigrants, which are called dreamers; how are we going to make our country a better place for people like this, who contribute to the classrooms, who are an integral part of my school experience? This kid helped me with math. If he had been deported, I would have struggled so much with math," Brito said.

Like Brito, we graduated from a predominantly immigrant high school that was majority Chinese, Korean, and Russian. We view immigrants as hard-working people who contribute to society. Some of our closest friends still don't have U.S. citizenship. Their parents work low-wage jobs so that their kids—our friends—can have the opportunity to succeed. And they do. Sit in on one of our computer science classes and you'll quickly notice that America's next generation of engineers include many immigrants. Immigration has always been an engine of economic growth in America; our melting pot is a competitive advantage.

When you go to school with immigrants, you learn to respect and admire, rather than demonize them. "If they managed to come over here already, I don't see why you would throw away all of their work getting here. ... That's probably all some people have to live by," explained Anne Diaz. David is reminded most distinctly of a recent conversation with a close friend. They were talking about politics and she mentioned that it didn't really matter anyways, because she can't vote. He asked when she thought she'd get a green card. "Maybe by 2070," she joked.

Despite all the talk about Mexican immigrants, it's not just Latinos who are affected by our country's archaic immigration system. Samantha Paul, for example, worries about her friend Babaka, an immigrant from Africa. "She is absolutely one of the most intellectual people I know. She is incredibly intelligent, and she's very open-minded, and she's outspoken, and she doesn't have citizenship yet. But just imagining her not being able to obtain citizenship for whatever reason bothers me. And I worry about that all the time," Paul said.

And with changing demographics, millennials are experiencing the impact of our failed immigration policies personally. Anne Diaz, a first-generation immigrant, said that her father was deported when she was very young. Diaz, who is a young leader, said she spends time helping the children of illegal immigrants in her community find scholarships and raise money for college. Often, she said, her peers don't know how to apply for federal aid and don't believe they can afford to get an education. Diaz said that she is a conservative and describes herself as a Republican, but on this issue, she could not disagree more strongly with her party.

Ciana Cronin tells a similar story—but she describes herself as leaning Democratic. Cronin is a Vietnamese immigrant and was adopted by a couple that illegally emigrated from Europe, she said. Her parents later received U.S. citizenship and Cronin is now a young entrepreneur in Arizona. She believes that most millennials of all backgrounds can relate with the immigrant struggle. "My mom married my dad because it was easier to get citizenship that way. They were also together for like 15 something years, so it's not that nefarious," she said. Her dad, she said, came here with just $200, and her mom worked four jobs to make ends meet when she got here.

What these millennial experiences have in common is a tolerance for diversity driven by personal interactions. Nine in 10 millennials describe themselves as being tolerant. We approach the world with what philosopher John Rawls described as a "veil of ignorance." Rawls said that when designing the rules for a society, you should be ignorant of what social position you yourself will occupy. Millennials derive their sensitivity for diversity—for transgenders, gays, blacks, whites, immigrants, and the poor—from a view that they themselves could be in that position, and many have friends who are.

Despite their tolerance for and appreciation of immigrants, millennials are not diehard liberals who want to open the borders to everyone. As Cronin explained, "I don't think blanket amnesty is even a good idea in any way, shape, sense, or form. If you bring people in and they say, boom, citizenships, then other people will come in and just wait it out until another blanket amnesty is granted." Millennials want to see a balance between helping immigrants and protecting the rule of law. "There would be screening and ... making sure that anyone coming into our country isn't bringing anything bad in," explained Paul. "People are so blindsided by the fact that someone's an immigrant, they don't speak English, they're not from here."

Given our experiences, millennials will not tolerate the game of "kick the can down the road" that dominates the immigration debate. Our generation is already lobbying Congress to pass immigration reform. For politicians, this issue is a golden opportunity to win millennials and Latino votes. But so far, neither party has taken substantial action. Instead, the political machine has obstructed immigration reform, even though the majority of Americans—and the vast majority of millennials—agrees on this issue.[8]

For Republicans, Immigration is a Liability and Opportunity

In 2013, Republicans had the chance to pass a bill that would have endeared the party to millennials and Hispanics and done wonders for the party's image. Instead, they failed to pass a comprehensive immigration reform bill and offered no alternative. Proposed by the Gang of Eight, a bipartisan group of senators, "The Border Security, Economic Opportunity, and Immigration Modernization Act of 2013" passed the Senate, only to be defeated in the House. On the right, heavyweights including John McCain, Lindsay Graham, David Brooks, and Karl Rove went to bat to advocate for the legislation.[9]

Taking a moderate approach, the bill's authors would have created a path to citizenship for undocumented immigrants, added 40,000 patrol agents to the U.S. border, created a points-based immigrant system to help talented immigrants get priority, and increased the number of H-1B visas granted to foreigners who receive STEM diplomas from U.S. colleges. This is exactly the type of legislation that young people are looking for from Congress. It was balanced, moderate, and fair.

The bill would have been a huge step in the right direction. It would have created jobs. For millennials who were struggling to make ends meet, that's huge. The nonpartisan Congressional Budget Office estimates that the law would have saved $700 billion by 2033, while lowering U.S. wages by only 0.5 percent. The bill passed the Senate by a vote of 68-32. House Republicans refused to conference on the bill, despite strong support from party insiders.[10]

House GOP leadership stated, "Border security and interior enforcement must come first." Republicans decried the bill as amnesty for criminals, but refused to propose an alternative. Now, senators who supported the legislation in 2013 are coming under fire from the more conservative elements of the party. Instead of embracing immigration reform, Republicans trounced it.

When Republicans talk about the importance of border security, they often raise an economic argument, that undocumented immigrants will drive down wages and take American jobs. Harvard professor George Borjas found that the influx of unskilled workers from 1980 to 2000 accounted for a 3.7 percent average wage loss for the American worker. But while less than half of undocumented immigrants pay taxes, all their children receive education, at a cost of $1.7 billion per year. So it is an economic imperative to increase border security, they say.[11]

But Republican opposition to immigration reform is not just economic; it appears to be racial. Fear of immigrants is a major source of Republican hesitation on immigration reform. The party establishment has come to grips with this issue. "There's nothing new going on today that's gone on before," explained Sen. Lindsay Graham (R-SC). "This isn't the first time that there's been some ugliness around the issue of immigration."

Republicans have a stark choice to make—they cannot win both the nativist wing of their party and millennials/Latinos who buy into conservative values and policies.

"On overall policy, polling has consistently shown that while a sizable portion of Republicans - including many, but not all, conservatives - take a hard line on illegal immigration, another of roughly the same size or larger sees things differently; they're accepting of a potential path to citizenship or some form of legalization," CBS News elections director Anthony Salvanto explained. Republicans must choose that latter group. Minorities will form 75 percent of new households in the next decade, and millennials are the biggest voting bloc in America. It is unsustainable for the GOP to alienate the two most demographic groups that will have the greatest influence in the 21st century.

Republicans can appeal to millennials without abandoning their hard-liner approach. They should couple immigration reform with strong border patrol by funding drones and other technology that will help keep the border safe. The only alternative is to support xenophobic policies and encourage stagnation. If Republicans choose to do this, they will relegate themselves to political obscurity. "If Republicans are to draw their votes primarily from the pool of white voters in America, they are simply on an unsustainable path," acknowledged Republican pollster Kristen Soltis Anderson in her book, *The Selfie Vote*.

The irony is that Republicans are not lacking when it comes to good ideas.

In his book, *Immigration Wars*, Jeb Bush proposes that America reduce the number of family-based visas granted every year and instead double the number of work-based visas granted. He argues that it is unfair and inefficient for distant family members or parents of immigrants to "step over" millions of other people waiting patiently for citizenship. Work-based visas, by contrast, prioritize immigrants who will materially contribute to our economy by working hard and promoting innovation. This is good, conservative, jobs-oriented public policy that we support.

Bush would use immigration to stimulate the economy. He would staple a green card to the diplomas of all foreign-born STEM students to stimulate the U.S. economy. He would expand student visas and EB-5 investor visas, which are given to foreigners who create jobs in underserved communities with their investments. In order to increase fairness in the immigration process, Bush would abolish the visa lottery, which favors potential immigrants from small countries over larger countries like India and China. He would replace it with a first-come-first-serve immigration process. In his position on immigration reform, Bush shows his willingness to compromise and a level of positivity that is missing from the Republican discourse today. His ideas resonate strongly with millennials because they are new, different, and pragmatic.

The former Florida governor supports legal status for undocumented immigrants currently residing in America, but not a right to citizenship. Bush would pass the DREAM Act to help undocumented immigrants—who were brought to this country as minors and either graduated from college or served in the military—get citizenship. Finally, Bush would increase security on the Mexican border and proposes a system such as E-Verify to crack down on the hiring of undocumented immigrants. At least that is what the Bush of 2013 advocated.

Since then he has backtracked. Bush has disavowed many of the ideas in his 2013 book for fear that they will not bode well with the Republican base. That's unfortunate, because even conservative millennials support immigration reform. Pew Research shows that 57 percent of conservative millennials believe that immigrants strengthen our country compared with 39 percent of boomers. Seventy-eight percent of Democratic millennials agreed with the statement.[12]

Immigration is in the same league as gay marriage and the environment in terms of its sharp age-based delineation in views. Millennials are fighting for serious reform.[13] Republicans have to make a choice: are they going to keep alienating large portions of the electorate, or are they willing to compromise in order to appeal to America's two most important new demographics?

Democrats Should Capitalize on Immigration Reform

While in most areas Democrats are as guilty as Republicans of incompetence, immigration is an exception. A recent Fusion poll of likely millennial voters found that 49 percent support the Democratic Party's immigration reform position compared with 30 percent who support the Republicans'. Meanwhile, 12 percent of millennials blame Democrats, 15 percent blame President Obama, 30 percent blame both parties and 33 percent blame Republicans in Congress for America's broken immigration system.[14]

Democrats may be perceived as being too dovish on border security for millennial tastes, but in other ways they are successfully appealing to our sensibilities. Democrats have championed immigration reform, speaking positively about immigrants as an engine for growth in the United States. For starters, at least, the tone of this conversation is correct.

Democrats have constantly opened the door to compromise, specifically including 40,000 additional border patrol agents in their most recent proposal. In fact, under President Obama's leadership, deportations have climbed to an all-time high. In 2013, 438,000 immigrants were deported to their home countries. (*The Los Angeles Times* reports that this number may be inflated, because U.S. Immigration and Customs Enforcement changed the definition of a deportation, which is a fair point.)[15]

Democrats have long supported a pathway to citizenship or residency for undocumented immigrants—a plank supported by three-quarters of American voters, a majority of Republicans, and 81 percent of millennials. But Democratic failure to execute these policies has led to dismay among their base. A majority of Americans and a plurality of Hispanics disapprove of President Obama's handling of immigration, likely wanting to see even more aggressive action on the issue.

When the House failed to pass comprehensive immigration reform, President Obama unilaterally granted temporary legal status and work permits to 5 million undocumented immigrants in 2014. "Are we a nation that tolerates the hypocrisy of a system where workers who pick our fruit and make our beds never have a chance to get right with the law?" announced Obama. "Whether our forebears were strangers who crossed the Atlantic, or the Pacific, or the Rio Grande, we are here only because this country welcomed them in," he said. A full 67 percent of millennials support outright amnesty; so, among Latinos and millennials, this was a popular move.[16]

After the pathway to citizenship, the DREAM Act is a core staple of Democratic immigration policy. The bill would help undocumented immigrants who were brought to America before they turned 18 qualify for citizenship if they completed a college education or served in the U.S. military. The bill never passed, despite the support of 64 percent of millennials and 54 percent of Americans.

"The problem, of course, is that it's not college that's their dream. It's a life with a real job, perhaps in medicine, law, education, science, the arts, and so much more. Those are the real dreams," said DePaul University President the Rev. Dennis Holtschneider. "And those are the dreams we are deferring or killing. It breaks our hearts."[17]

Democrats should make an economic argument for immigration. Whereas immigrants may create an influx of labor in the United States, the evidence is overwhelming that immigrants are a key driver of U.S. economic growth. Immigration induced a net 4 percent real wage increase for the average native worker due to the influx of spending immigrants promoted, according to The Public Policy Institute. During their working life, immigrants will pay approximately $80,000 more in taxes per capita than they use in government services because they are not eligible to take advantage of many of the social service programs.[18]

Three in four economists say immigration has a "very positive impact on the economy." In fact, 40 percent of the Fortune 500 CEOs are immigrants, and immigrant-led businesses stimulate the economy.[19] Elon Musk, CEO of SpaceX and Tesla, for example, is literally changing the world, by revolutionizing space exploration and electric cars. He emigrated from South Africa to Canada, before eventually moving to the United States.

Immigrant-led businesses stimulate their local economies. "[There] are immigrants who came from Cuba who were able to bring their culture to Miami, and because of that they were able to open a successful business and improve our economy," Brito said. "Immigration, instead of taking away our jobs—I think it does create new jobs."

Republicans, who are generally very pro-military, are often surprised to learn that the U.S. citizen children of illegal immigrants are more likely to join the U.S. Army than native-born citizens. Margaret Stock, a retired Army Reserves lieutenant colonel, estimates that children born to illegal immigrants represent 8-10 percent of Army recruits. "What happens is, if you take all these people out of the (recruiting) pool, it's going to have a huge impact on the military," she said. Recent proposals have even considered allowing "Dreamers"—illegal immigrants brought to the United States as minors—to join the army. "If Dreamers want to put their life on the line for this nation, we should ... honor their willingness to serve," said Mike Coffman, a Marine veteran.[20]

For Democrats, like Republicans, immigration reform is a compelling opportunity. If Democrats can take their proposals to the next step—making them palatable enough to get them through Congress—they will come out as heroes. Democrats can help lock in the millennial and Latino demographic and ride to power on our coattails. From a pure math standpoint, Democrats have a lot to gain by harnessing immigration as a central tenet of their campaigns.

Millennials Take Action

Millennials are leading the fight for a rational immigration system. With their new, tolerant attitude toward immigrants, they are shifting the debate away from "how tall should the wall be?" toward "how do we craft a rigorous process for illegals currently living in the United States to ensure that we're protecting their rights without opening the floodgates to new illegal immigrants?"

FWD.us, the political action group backed by Facebook CEO Mark Zuckerberg, is jumping into the fray. The group, a staunch supporter of immigrant reform, launched an app that allows users to send Congress "selfies" of themselves with messages pushing for immigration reform. The app—called #SelfiesForReform—created an engaging way for young people to speak up on an issue we're passionate about by lobbying politicians directly. Zuckerberg is just one of many technology entrepreneurs on the front lines fighting for immigration reform. Because many engineers are immigrants, it's one of the hottest topics in Silicon Valley.

For change to be possible, both parties will need to compromise. Democrats can't just pass legislation to enfranchise 11 million new voters. And Republicans can't avoid facing the political and social reality of a changing nation. Certainly, this will be one of the toughest and most important compromises of the next decade. Millennials are willing to take incremental steps towards a solution. As Brito explained, "If we can't reform immigration as a whole, we should make some small steps to improving the quality of life for at least children of immigrants."

Our generation's vision for comprehensive immigration reform is not complicated or radical. It involves detailed execution of preexisting platforms that have been largely ignored, and creative thinking in developing fathomable compromises to drive changes in public policy.

The federal government should beef up border security and make it tougher for undocumented immigrants to get into America. This does not mean that we should build a wall on the Mexican border—that's lunacy. It means increasing the number of patrol agents on the U.S. border, and purchasing drone technology, which will efficiently locate undocumented immigrants before they reach U.S. soil. It means putting up fencing near the Rio Grande, where there are currently only 15 border patrol agents. And it means increasing deportation to create a negative feedback loop for those who do make it across: in America, there is no free lunch.

"I don't think we should be condoning illegal immigration. I think we should be making it far easier than it is to become a citizen. I think we should have an easier immigration process, but we shouldn't just allow people to cross the border unsecured. I think we should make it so they don't want to because there's an easier path to citizenship," millennial leader Anna Prisco said.

Millennials are gunning for a pathway to citizenship. This path will not be easy and it will not come without challenges. Immigrants will need to pay a fine for crossing the border, must have no criminal record, and must pass the U.S. citizenship test, among other requirements. They will need to pay taxes in order to access benefits, and they will not actually become citizens for at least five years, probably longer. Undocumented immigrants will not be able to undo their decision to break U.S. law, nor will they "jump over" people waiting in line for legal immigration.

But we will not relegate them to a lower status indefinitely. Undocumented immigrants need to be accepted and integrated into society—especially those who came here by no fault of their own. We need a new system. These are some of the simplest issues in American politics—millennials would call them "no-brainers." The DREAM Act, for example, should be passed.

"A pathway to citizenship is incredibly important. I have a serious problem with people who believe that the answer is a wall or the answer is securing the border. Because the wall is an 11th century solution to a 21st century problem. You can build a wall 80 feet tall, and a man who is hungry and trying to feed his family will get over that wall," said Roberto Ruiz, a young conservative millennial whose parents emigrated from Venezuela.

At the same time, the legal immigration process needs to be streamlined. The application for immigration should be simplified and technology should be used to make the process easier. Algorithms can predict many factors—from the default risk of an applicant for a home loan to whether you are pregnant. The United States should develop a simple algorithm to predict how long it will take for potential applicants to be granted legal status—or they will never get legal status.

The United States can and should cut government jobs in the process by automating much of the immigrant review process. Of course, people will still be needed to conduct background checks. Studies show that individuals have less anxiety when they can make an intelligent decision based on known information. It is very possible that potential immigrants will wait their turn if they understand what they're in for. It is the feeling of helplessness and desperation that is one of the primary drivers of illegal immigration today.

Many young people see immigration as a key part of the American culture. "My dad was an immigrant, so I was never against the idea of immigration. I never much see an American identity. I see us as a nation of misfits. We are a nation, but ultimately, anyone from anywhere can come here. If you are from France, or Djibouti, or Morocco, it doesn't matter where you came from. You are American," Massachusetts millennial Gabriel Coll said. It is this attitude that is at the heart of why millennials are passionate and taking action to solve the crisis we face.

CONCLUSION

Immigration reform has created a wedge between the young and the old in America. The key difference between millennials and our parents and grandparents is that we've grown up with immigrant friends, classmates and role models. It's too late to stop this country's demographic transition, even if you wanted to. Today, America's schools are majority minority—and that's a good thing, because America should be a melting pot for people seeking economic opportunity and freedom.

Immigration reform taps into a distinctive view of the world that is unique to young people, one that places strong emphasis on equality and freedom for all. Millennials can and will make a substantial impact on U.S. public policy because they are tolerant of foreigners and want to create rational, fair plans to accommodate immigrants already in our country and tighten the border for the future. The question is not whether comprehensive immigration reform is passed, but rather, how fast.

Today, young people are urging politicians to join us in our battle for reform. But we're not holding our breath. We're out there making immigration reform a reality. The sooner we fix our broken immigration system, the better off we'll be. No doubt, the day will come when undocumented immigrants are able to emerge from the shadows and pledge their allegiance to the United States of America.

Less War: A Cautious Approach to Foreign Policy

PRINCETON, NEW JERSEY

ISIS is on the rise and threatens our homeland. China is flexing its muscles in the Far East. Putin is expanding his sphere of influence in Eastern Europe. The European Union is confronting numerous existential threats, the most serious since the cooperation was formed at the end of the 20th century. Today, millennials prepare to inherit a world that is reeling from instability as the U.S.'s unipolar moment comes to an end and it confronts a new geopolitical reality.

With these difficult challenges in mind, we turn our attention from entitlements to a topic with much more intrigue—but just as much nuance: foreign policy. To this end, we head over to Princeton, New Jersey, where debaters have assembled to discuss President Obama's foreign policy and its implications on geopolitics.

The tournament, taking place amidst a raging civil war in Syria and the negotiation of a complex nuclear agreement with Iran, inevitably revolves around the Middle East, terrorism and instability.

Outside of the one debate team that told us that Jews are the cause of all of the world problems—yes, apparently this debate case led to four prior victories before we defeated it—we engaged in a series of stimulating conversations with well-prepared opponents. Young people tend to support President Obama's foreign policy decisions, we learned. We were eventually eliminated by a team that presented a resounding affirmation of the Obama Doctrine—a view of the world as a fundamentally safe place, where cooperation reaps larger rewards than conflict.

In our country's history, the legacies of our leaders have often been defined by their foreign policy decisions. To millennials, the second President Bush will always be the president who waged war in Iraq and Afghanistan, which killed our friends, while FDR and Reagan are remembered for the wars over which they presided. If this trend persists, millennial leaders will either be hailed as heroes or failures, as our generation's approach to foreign policy differs greatly from those of past generations—and will no doubt shape the future of the world.

Leading from Behind: The 9/11 Generation

As New Yorkers, we frequently hear stories about 9/11—stories about people who lost their loved ones and people who miraculously did not; stories about the heroes who gave their lives on that day to save others; and stories about a nightmare that we still have not woken from. September 11, 2001, was the most important day in the life of the millennial Americans, polls show. But while our grandparents lived to see the Japanese defeated after Pearl Harbor, our generation has watched America fail to beat back terrorist threats. We send brave men and women abroad to fight for a freer world, and too many came home injured, depressed, or not at all.

"This new reality is something that our generation is going to have to deal with. ... There is never going to be a complete defeat of the people who want to harm us," said Harleen Gambir, a millennial counterterrorism analyst. 85 percent of millennials agree with Gambir, saying they cannot envision a point in their lives when terrorism will no longer be a danger.

Our generation is a patriotic one, committed to American safety. The death of Osama Bin Laden was a moment of joy for young

Americans. But we have a strong sense of "Iraq Aversion"—we are weary of foreign conflict, fearing failure and the loss of American lives. The Cato Institute called the Iraq and Afghanistan wars a "dominant historical analogy [millennials] will use for assessing future conflicts," as compared with Vietnam for boomers and World War II for the Silent Generation.[1] In place of traditional warfare, young people prefer asymmetric tactics—using diplomacy and technology to engage the enemy, without putting boots on the ground.

"We're going in there and trying to get rid of these huge, huge groups that we don't even understand fully and we're killing off their civilians," explained Washington millennial Sara Reed. "But every time we try to cause conflict in the Middle East, it just seems to back-fire every time. We went into Iraq and Afghanistan and they formed ... ISIS, which [is] much more devastating than even Al Qaeda."

Millennials don't want the United States to be a global police force. 53 percent of millennials believe that U.S. actions helped provoke the 9/11 attacks, compared with 47 percent of GenX and 39 percent of boomers. Two-thirds of millennials surveyed by Pew said "relying on military force creates hatred that leads to more terrorism." Overall, 41 percent of young people favor reducing our military presence abroad, as compared with 27 percent of Americans over the age of 55.

In our journey to understand millennial political beliefs, we asked young people why they were so hesitant about foreign engagements. More often than not, young people say they are weary of living in an America that, throughout their childhoods, was in a constant state of war.

"We went into Afghanistan and we caused panic on their country. We killed tons of their citizens, harmless people, women and children, and then after we pulled out of Afghanistan, they became our number one receiver of foreign aid," Reed said. "I see a huge cultural difference, and actually a millennial difference, to Gen X, Gen Y, where they believe in this aspect of we can go and be the heroes—whereas Gen Y specifically is just trying to clean everything up."

Instead of sending troops abroad, millennials support U.S. investment in diplomatic efforts and asymmetric warfare—like training allied personnel in the conflict zones, using drone strikes to decapitate enemy organizations by killing their leaders, and using cyber warfare. Two-thirds of millennials surveyed told Pew that "good diplomacy" is the best way to ensure peace.[2] Like the boomers before us, young Americans today are fighting against the military-industrial complex and our country's propensity to get too involved in conflicts that either don't need to be our business or are unwinnable.

A Generational Gap

A closer look at the generational divide on foreign policy reveals that millennials see the world as less dangerous than their parents do, prefer cooperation to the use of unilateral force, and are more hesitant to use military force to solve conflict.[3] By 2012, the proportion of boomers who said they believed terrorism was a critical threat reached 75 percent, compared with 56 percent of millennials who held this view. Meanwhile, 52 percent of millennials want the United States to "stay out of world affairs," as compared with just 31-39 percent for older demographics.[4] "We know our brothers, sisters, neighbors who are serving and we see those real effects," explained Emily Tisch Sussman, a former executive director of the Young Democrats of America.[5]

When we spoke with millennial leaders Jennifer Guzman from Gila Ridge, Arizona, and Laura Bishop from Oregon, the two emphasized that young people aren't against war, but believe that in order for the United States to engage itself abroad, the circumstances must be serious. "I'm not hard core in favor of war, but if they were to attack us first and our people were already in danger and communication was not working at all, whatsoever, they weren't getting back, nothing was going on, nothing was helping, no progress, then I would say to go to war," Guzman said. But even that, she said, is "pushing it for me."

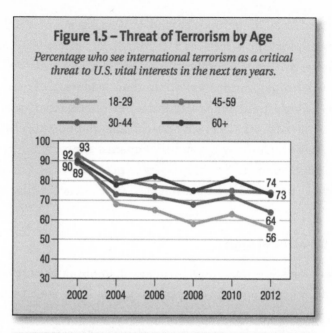

Figure 1.5 – Threat of Terrorism by Age

Percentage who see international terrorism as a critical threat to U.S. vital interests in the next ten years.

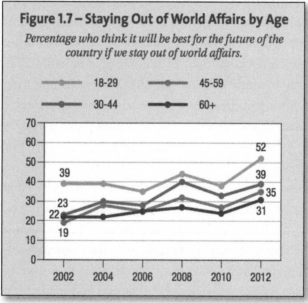

Figure 1.7 – Staying Out of World Affairs by Age

Percentage who think it will be best for the future of the country if we stay out of world affairs.

Figure: The Chicago Institute finds a growing generation gap when it comes to views on foreign policy.

Bishop, who identifies as conservative, says that despite her differences with young people on a variety of issues, she empathizes with her generation's aversion to conflict. "This generation is becoming less war-oriented and I think that's due to several reasons. I think we're becoming an increasingly global community, whereas previously, the United States was the main diplomatic superpower," she said. "But now we see that there are other nations that are developing really well, economically.... So in some of these regional conflicts, whereas previously it would have just been the United States going in, now we see that the United States can work with other nations in that area to do organized efforts which can be a lot more effective."

Is the new foreign policy of the next generation just disguised pacifism? That seemed to be the consensus when we talk to older generations about the new millennial mind-set. But Reed says our generation's new philosophy towards war is not necessarily pacifism, per se, but rather the idea that "if you are going to go into war, you'd better win."

What Does This Mean for America?

Young people tend to get more conservative over time. Compared to boomers, millennials look like a very liberal generation. Just a few decades ago, it was the boomers themselves who were radically opposed to war, spearheading the anti-Vietnam movement. Historically, foreign policy positions tend to be strongly correlated with age. Just as boomers impacted the geopolitical debate, putting pressure on the U.S. government to get out of Vietnam and de-escalate tensions in the Cold War, millennials will help carry the United States back into a multipolar world.

The rise of regional powers in the 21st century is not a millennial creation. Russia and China have long been global superpowers, and the Middle East a hotbed of conflict. While the end of America's "unipolar moment" is not a millennial creation, how our generation reacts to this new world order will shape history. In the remainder of this chapter, we'll explore how millennial views will manifest in foreign policy—from the Middle East, to Russia, China, and more. We'll also discuss how America's foreign policy toolkit has changed, and how young people will take advantage of new technologies to reshape modern warfare.

Limited Engagement in the Middle East

Millennials support limited intervention in the Middle East but are willing to put boots on the ground when homeland security is at stake.

When it comes to intervening to support democracy, the data is unequivocal. Just 12 percent of young people support intervention to spread democracy, as compared with 45 percent who oppose intervention. "I think we need to kind of go with a middle ground where we provide our input without trying to run the government," said Justin Greenman, a millennial from New Jersey. "The U.S. definitely needs to be a mediator, not like an imperialist, not invading random countries, causing coups. I think we've gotten ourselves involved in the Middle East a little bit too much. We think we're preventing terror from occurring."

On the contrary, says Abhay Ram, a millennial from Illinois, we're the ones who "lead to the rise of more terrorist organizations, because whenever you go intervene in a country, there's always going to be that group of people that disagree with that action, and you're just fostering more hate toward the U.S. We're constantly involved in the Middle East and we haven't seen much success. ... Getting involved in the Middle East is not an end to the situation, but fosters a cycle of continued violence in that area. From what we've seen in our lifetime of failures, we think it's better to leave it alone and see if it can solve itself, because historically, change doesn't come peacefully. Even dictators sometimes, oppressive dictators, have helped more than complete instability and lawlessness. If they're not posing a direct threat to us, let them go through their cycles of instability, let them get the stability out of that."

Even human rights abuse is not always a valid reason to intervene abroad, millennials say. In 2014, when President Obama was considering air strikes on the Syrians after it became clear that they were using chemical weapons on civilians, millennials opposed the move. At the time, just 28 percent of millennials supported arming Syrian rebels, as compared with 45 percent of seniors.[6] "I haven't talked to a single young person who wants to go into Syria," said Ron Meyer, a former spokesman for the Young America Foundation, in an interview with Fox News. "Picking sides in that fight doesn't make sense; wasting taxpayer dollars doesn't make sense."[7]

Rather than engage in all-out war, millennials want to see a shift in military tactics as the United States works to project power in the Middle East. President Obama has led the way in this regard, investing heavily in U.S. drone capabilities. In Yemen, for example, cooperation and intelligence sharing is widely used to target militants. "These tools were not Obama creations, but he's increased their use and he has shifted the U.S. attention full front to Afghanistan," said Thomas Sanderson, a fellow at the Center for Strategic and International Studies.[8]

When it comes to fighting ISIS, millennials believe our homeland security is at stake. Before the San Bernardino and Paris attacks, millennials were the least likely to support intervention against ISIS. Just 39 percent of millennials supported air strikes in the region, as compared with 66 percent of Americans.[9] But as the threat became more acute, support for intervention surged. Support for the use of ground troops to combat ISIS climbed from 48 percent to 60 percent among millennials, making young people the most likely demographic to support intervention.[10]

But millennials support a much more tactical, limited sort of intervention than their parents do. As college senior Hanah Oh recently wrote in her *New York Times* editorial, our generation is looking for "a clear and realistic foreign policy."[11] This involves a much more limited deployment of troops. Just 25 percent of millennials said they would send a large number of combat troops, as compared with 43 percent of Americans. Instead, millennials would support deployment solely for the purpose of advising and assisting other armies in fighting ISIS.[12]

These views are very fascinating and a great case study in the greater narrative of this book. Millennials are very thoughtful voters, offering a nuanced perspective on a very complex question, global terrorism. They are more likely to support intervention, but expect that very intervention to be limited and tactical. Rather than politicizing the question and offering ideological knee-jerk responses (i.e., carpet bombing), millennials are thinking critically about the various aspects of the conflict and drawing their own conclusions.

One could argue that millennials will allow the Middle East to collapse. Certainly, this is the rhetoric many hawks on the right would use to criticize these millennials' views. Likewise, doves will say that millennials have not truly learned the lesson of Iraq and Afghanistan and that sending American troops into Syria is signing their death warrant. But as pragmatic voters hoping to avoid the extreme options offered by either party, millennials recognize the following. First, we cannot defeat ISIS alone. So this idea that by not sending American soldiers to their deaths we're allowing ISIS to thrive is complete fiction. Second, we cannot completely abandon force. Sometimes, you need to engage tactically with the enemy, inflicting as much damage as possible while limiting your losses.

Iran and Israel: A Balanced Approach

Our generation tends to be optimistic, preferring cooperation to conflict. Predictably, millennials are strong supporters of the Iran nuclear deal and the least likely generation to believe that the program is a "critical threat" to U.S. safety. A full 65 percent of millennials support the deal, as compared with 55 percent of older Americans. And support is bipartisan.[13]

"With Iran, I have a sympathetic view. Iran is very much kind of crazy, but that craziness is largely just political rhetoric, since Iran is, in fact, a republic and does, in fact, have elections," said Gabriel Coll, a millennial from Massachusetts. "In the same sense, we have crazy politicians here who are just trying to appeal to the masses. I'm actually not that concerned about it. I kind of secretly think Iran has a lot of potential to become the next kind of model for a country in the Middle East that combines these views of Islam being part of government with the values of a republic and democracy. I very much want to see what happens with Iran."

Not all young people are as optimistic as Coll, but the demographic tends to support the Iran deal because they believe it is the only alternative to military intervention. Ending a military standoff, the Iran deal offers an opportunity to create a more peaceful region. And millennials do believe this is possible, with a majority of young people saying they believe the deal will delay or stall Iran's nuclear program. Even more important, support for this policy is bipartisan. 75 percent of millennial Democrats and 59 percent of millennial Republicans were in favor the diplomatic accords.

"These findings are the bow wave of a sea change ahead in American politics. The millennial position on Iran is not a blip but an emerging pillar of U.S. public opinion on foreign policy," said Trevor Thrall, a professor at George Mason University. Partisanship "has much less impact on their attitudes toward the Iran deal than it does on the attitudes of older Americans." Notably, younger millennials were even more supportive of the deal than the older end of the demographic. Thrall attributes the millennial viewpoint to the events of our "critical period"—adolescence—which sociologists say is important to developing our opinions and worldview.[14]

The critical approach to U.S. foreign policy taught in many schools plays a role in how millennials perceive U.S. intervention. For

Israel, this should be a deep concern. Millennials see Israel through the lens of the Six Day War and its occupation of the West Bank, not through the historical lens of the Holocaust or its dramatic war for independence. Today, more millennials blame Israel for regional violence (29 percent) than blame Hamas (21 percent). Millennials appear to be outraged by what they perceive as Israeli imperialism in its occupation of Palestinian land.[15]

Millennials have not wholly sold out Israel. Young people still say they are more sympathetic toward Israel than they are toward the Palestinians by a margin of 2:1, Pew Research found. Still, this is a sharp difference from older Americans, who are more sympathetic toward Israel by a 6:1 ratio. When Israel invaded Gaza in 2014, boomers said Israel was justified in its reaction by a margin of 55 percent to 31 percent, compared with 51 percent of millennials who disagreed, saying that Israel's action were not justified. Here, the generational difference is readily apparent.[16]

"A generation of global citizens is rising to power without the Israeli narrative embedded so firmly in its consciousness," wrote Ron Fournier in a column for the *National Journal*. "The so-called Arab Spring and the United States' diminished influence abroad has created a new set of filters through which young people will consider the Israeli-Palestinian conflict, a viewpoint that might be less inclined to favor the Jewish state."

In the next decade, Iran will legitimately pursue legal nuclear weapons. With Saudi-Iranian relations already at a standoff, nuclear proliferation is likely. Iran will remain a leading state sponsor of terrorism. Israel will remain a strong U.S. ally and will continue to receive military and economic aid, but public opinion will be increasingly divided on how to treat the "special relationship" between our nations. The entire region will be less stable and local conflict will be more likely. Rather than getting pulled into these unavoidable conflicts, millennials will choose limited intervention, with a distinct emphasis on homeland security.

Sometimes, you just can't call all the shots. You have to accept reality and do your best to cope with it. For better or for worse, that's what will happen when millennials rise to power.

China Will Gain Influence in East Asia

Young people in the United States and China have a mutual trust and respect that will allow both nations to expand their influence unencumbered. Already, China is taking advantage of this by building up its military might. By 2020, the size of China's navy is expected to exceed that of the United States'. China now owns around 190 "major combatants," which are Chinese-built vessels. This newfound naval capacity will allow China to expand its regional influence. This could lead to a global geopolitical détente between America and China.[17]

The Chinese dragon is already reemerging. According to *Foreign Affairs*, China has increased its military budget by double-digit percentages every year for the past two decades. In recent years, military spending has outpaced economic growth, with the country's defense budget reaching $145 billion in 2015. On top of that, 30-50 percent of its defense budget is off the books. Through this lens, China's budget for equipment is greater than the entire defense budgets for Japan and India. China is rapidly importing advanced fighter jets, submarines, destroyers, and transport planes. At the same, the Communist Party is investing in its local weapons manufacturing industry, presumably to increase its military capabilities.[18]

China's lack of a central command structure has long been a source of weakness for the nation. Lacking operational experience, China is increasingly investing in a Western-style command system, to better project its power. "The PLA [People's Liberation Army] is currently a territorial muddy-boots military focused on defending the rule of the Communist Party against all enemies foreign and domestic, with limited ability to fight jointly," Andrew Scobell, a senior political scientist at the RAND Corporation, told Bloomberg. "With growing attention to China's increasingly overseas interests, the U.S. model is very appealing."[19]

A recent Chinese military white paper indicates a growing focus on controlling the seas. China's growing navy will allow the country to achieve these goals, for the sake of national security and securing maritime trade. *The Economist* concluded, "China no longer accepts that America should be Asia-Pacific's dominant naval power." But for China, this is more than just a national security measure. Chinese leadership has long said that part of the "Chinese Dream" is a restoration of China's historical regional influence. This doesn't seem all too crazy, especially for a country with such a long and rich history.[20]

"Our lesson from history—those who fall behind will get bullied—this is something we will never forget," explained Fu Ying, a spokesperson for the Chinese Parliament. In China, the prevailing view is that the country's history describes belligerent Western powers using their superior military force to embarrass and weaken China. In a nod to its past—China was the first nation to travel the seas, invented block printing, and created the first compass—the Chinese hope to restore their nation's place as a first among equals in the league of great powers.[21]

Already, China is exerting its newfound might. In 2015, China dramatically increased its pace of island building. "The announcement marks a change in diplomatic tone, and indicates that China has reached its scheduled completion on several land reclamation projects and is now moving into the construction phase," said Mira Rapp-Hooper, a senior fellow in the Asia-Pacific Security Program at the Center for a New American Security. China is placing military resources on these islands to create mobile military bases.[22]

One of the key issues at stake is the freedom of navigation, especially with more than five nations claiming different territorial rights in the region. Defense Secretary Ashton B. Carter has called on China to stop its land reclamation. He said at a conference that the United States would "fly, sail, and operate" in the South China Sea to ensure freedom of navigation and flight as permitted by international law. While China has since toned down its rhetoric on the topic, it is unlikely to quit, especially as it gains military might and U.S. citizens continue to reiterate their fear of military engagement abroad. The risk of conflict in the region is now substantial, according to the Council on Foreign Relations.[23]

Beijing has strong support from citizens to expand its influence in East Asia. Australian think tank Perth USAsia Center found that a majority of Chinese citizens believes the country has legitimate claims to the Senkaku islands in the South China Sea. Seventy percent say China would win in a war against the United States, so they are not intimidated by the prospect of confrontation.[24] And young Americans are not all that worried either. American millennials said they favored a policy of building stronger trade relations with China over toughness by a margin of 69 percent to 24 percent. Boomers and the Silent Generation both disagreed.[25]

Young people on both sides of the Pacific view each other more favorably than ever. More than half of China's young people said that they held a positive view of the United States, with three-quarters saying they admired U.S. scientific advances and 59 percent respecting American ideas about democracy, an approval rate that is 15 percent higher than that of their parents, across the board. A majority of Chinese 18-29-year-olds said that it is a good thing that U.S. ideas and customs are spreading abroad.[26] Likewise, American millennials are the least likely generation to view China as a threat. Instead, young people see opportunity for cooperation.[27]

China's rise to power will lead to a new geopolitical normal, but it is unlikely to lead to outright conflict. Economic interdependence between the United States and China means that a war would be devastating for both sides. At the same time, millennials believe that China has everything to lose from an all-out war against the United States. As former Defense Secretary William Cohen explained, "A growing, stock-owning Chinese middle class, in greater commercial and intellectual contact with the world, will do more to keep Asia peaceful, stable, and eventually democratic, than any action other nations could possibly take."

Eventually, millennials envision a Cold War-like stalemate between the United States and China, but without the animosity. "China is going to have a better economy than us in the next couple of years. So with that, competition does go on," Guzman explained. "I do think we might be approaching a Cold War era, maybe not in the sense of attacking China, but in the sense that there's competition and we want to be better. And the United States is going to lose its respect, lose its dominance, lose its title as the best country in the world. And we need to make sure we're better than China, and in a sense it just becomes more of a race."

Just how much will millennials avoid conflict in Asia? A 2015 YouGov poll found that the majority of millennials believe that the United States should not have dropped a nuclear bomb on Hiroshima and Nagasaki to end World War II. From our own anecdotal experience, this is largely a function of the education system, where every single one of our professors has taught a guilt-narrative in the context of America's use of the nuclear bomb. Generally, millennials oppose military intervention, unless they believe it will serve to protect American citizens. "I think old, old school: if it doesn't affect America, there's no need to do anything. If they're just doing their own thing, then let them do their own thing," Nikko Markakos, a millennial from New Jersey, said. "But if they're doing something that threatens us, then yeah, go invade them."

Even as the countries avoid traditional war, the threat of cyber warfare will increase. In both nations, resources will be devoted to protecting infrastructure from foreign attacks and developing predatory capabilities. In 2015, the U.S. federal government sustained 61,000 cyberattacks, many of which—including a massive hack of the Office of Personnel Management—are suspected to have come from China. For the Chinese, the advantage of cyberattacks is that they are anonymous and allow for the theft of specific information, usually intellectual property. The Center for Strategic and International Studies estimates that intellectual property theft by Chinese hackers costs the United States $100 billion and 508,000 jobs annually.[28]

Even with this threat, the overall attitude among young people in both nations remains highly positive. Millennials envision building a better future for both of our countries by working together. Sixty-nine percent of millennials want to build stronger trade relations with China. Instead of being fazed by the rise of a new global super-power, millennials see this as an opportunity to build a strong new alliance that will be mutually beneficial for both nations. By cooperating on issues from the environment to nuclear proliferation and development in Africa, millennials intend to turn a new page in the Sino-American relationship.[29]

Russia Will Assert Itself in Eastern Europe

In the next two decades, Russia will regain its historical role as a force-ful global power by flexing its muscles in Eastern Europe. Though the country remains an economic backwater, with corrupt oligarchs controlling much of its economy, Russian leaders are edging for more global power. Millennials are weary of intervening to prevent a resurgence of Russian influence. Instead of engaging Russia militar-ily, millennials will restrict themselves to using economic sanctions to discourage Russian aggression. After all, most millennials aren't old enough to remember the real threat that Russia once posed. The oldest millennials were nine years old when the wall came down.

The past couple of years have seen increased aggression from Russia. First, Russia annexed Crimea, with alleged self-defense forces taking over the country and prompting a referendum to join Russia. Later, Vladimr Putin initiated a campaign to take over cities in Eastern Ukraine and wrench power from the country's Western-lean-ing leaders. Condemnation followed from the West. "America is clear-eyed when it comes to seeing the truth about Russia's destabilizing" actions in the Ukraine, explained U.S. Ambassador Samantha Power. She said that U.S. support for Ukrainians was "unwavering."

Strong language aside, millennials oppose engaging with Russia because they 1) don't perceive Russia to be threatening, and 2) tend to be hesitant about foreign engagement. When Russia invaded Crimea, for example, a minority of Americans called for military intervention, with a majority of 59 percent settling on economic sanctions as the policy tool of choice. But even in this case of blatant aggression, millennials were unwilling to intervene, even with sanctions. According to CNN, 55 percent of millennials opposed sanctions against Russia at the time.[30]

Russia's success in Crimea and the Ukraine will empower it to further exert its might in Eastern Europe. Already, Russia has announced an expansion of its naval fleet, possibly investing in new, stealthy, nuclear-capable submarines. The United States is responding by sending arms to its Eastern European allies, but the reinforcements are meager at best. "We're talking about 250 armored vehicles, tanks, Bradleys and howitzers that would not fill up the parking lot of your average high school, and they will be distributed in formations in several different countries," said one U.S. military official. "That's the scale we're talking about."[31]

Without any real threat to U.S. homeland security, millennials continue to oppose intervention. What circumstances will lead to intervention? Northwestern University undergraduate William Kirkland said they were to 1) protect human rights, 2) ensure social justice, and 3) protect our economy or global trade. Foreign aggression by Russian oligarchs didn't make the cut.

Kirkland aptly describes his perspective on foreign affairs, as influenced by the geopolitical events of the 21st century. "With all of this power comes the inevitable question of what to do with it. Since the end of the Cold War, when the United States became the world's lone superpower, four American presidents have grappled with this huge question, each choosing a slightly different foreign policy path," he said.[32]

"Both Bush presidents used American firepower to wage war against Saddam Hussein's autocratic regime, while former President Bill Clinton used it to intervene in humanitarian crises in places like the Balkans and Somalia. But in his first five years in office, President Barack Obama seems to be charting a somewhat different course." This course was a policy of nonintervention, or "leading from behind." Like it or not, this is what millennials seem to want.

"Our formative experience in American foreign policy was the swaggering neoconservatism of the Bush presidency and the quagmire in Iraq. This was soon followed, of course, by the Great Recession, an era of austerity that made expensive wars of choice seem even more nonsensical," explained Stanford undergrad Jason Willik.[33]

A New Diplomatic Toolkit

In a new geopolitical climate with a powerful Chinese dragon in the East, a new Russian sphere of influence in Eastern Europe, and regional instability in the Middle East, the U.S. diplomatic toolkit will shift. It will focus on three tactics, which we have mentioned in passing: economic sanctions, diplomatic agreements, and cyber warfare.

Economic sanctions have already begun to take their role as the central arrow in the quiver of U.S. foreign policy. The United States is and will continue to be a hub for global banking, allowing it to control the flow of financial assets throughout the world. In Eastern Europe, North Korea, and Iran, U.S. economic sanctions have proven to be a powerful diplomatic asset, likely forcing Iran to the negotiating table on its nuclear program and convincing Russia to tone down the aggression it has shown toward its neighbors. Millennials say they view sanctions as a means of exerting U.S. influence abroad without putting soldiers in harm's way. Historically, they view sanctions as having been effective in achieving U.S. goals.

Millennials will pair sanctions with global cooperation. Just as millennials seek approval in their personal lives (every photo needs a like, every tweet needs a favorite), they will seek consensus on issues of global concern (such as human rights, the environment, and in this case, peace). Global cooperation will be used to address issues ranging from nuclear proliferation, to climate change, and human rights.

As millennials avoid foreign engagement, we will increasingly rely on computer viruses and hackers to do our nation's bidding. The capabilities of cyber warfare technologies are dramatic—they could wipe out power in U.S. cities, infiltrate our nuclear facilities, shut down our Internet, and dramatically impact everyday life for our citizens. The goal of cyber warfare is not to conquer territory—that still requires boots on the ground—but it can be used to win over concessions, instill terror in a population, or in the case of a traditional war, manipulate public opinion and hasten surrender.

A recent U.S. cyberattack war game carried out by the Pentagon began with an earthquake hitting southern California, and was followed by attacks on oil and gas pipelines, Pentagon networks, U.S. banks, and commercial ports. "The question is not whether this kind of scenario will occur, but when it will occur," Coast Guard Rear Adm. Kevin E. Lunday, director of exercises and training at U.S. Cyber Command, said about the exercises. While the United States develops its cyber defense capabilities, Cyber Command is also working to develop offensive capabilities that could wreak havoc on enemy nations. Just as our parents feared a war with the Soviet Union, an all-out cyber war would be a nightmare for the American public.

Kyle Walton, a young leader in Seattle, has said that cyberattack will "absolutely" overtake conventional war as a means of conflict. "We're moving to a point where warfare is going to be almost completely destructive, and I mean everybody kind of recognizing, one country fires and then another country fires and so on and so forth," he said. "You get to a point where literally one country does something and then the rest of the world, for lack of a better word, goes to shit. So there has to be some sort of way to fight a war and go against some other country."

Instead of a conventional war, which is restricted by the idea of mutually assured destruction, nations will opt for cyber war. "Cyber terrorism can have extremely detrimental effects but it's not something that's going to destroy the environment in the kind of way that it's not going to be able to sustain human life anywhere," Walton said. Unlike conventional tactics, cyber war cannot pose an existential threat to either nation and does not require American families to send their sons and daughters off to war. This makes it much easier to justify, but also much harder to end. Though still unchartered, the potential damage of a cyber war could be very substantial.

"If Google just dropped all of its service for an entire day, could you imagine how detrimental that would be to literally everybody in the United States?" he said.

We explored this tradeoff explicitly in the final round of a regional debate tournament, around the same time as the Princeton tournament. In our closing speeches, both teams agreed that the debate effectively boiled down to a threat assessment. What is more dangerous, cyber war or nuclear proliferation? We argued for nuclear proliferation, winning the older judges on the panel. But our opponents eked out a 3-2 victory, winning over the younger judges on the panel. One of the judges, representing the majority, put it simply, "I'm more scared of Google getting shut down than Iran getting a nuclear bomb."

As we walked out of the room, we joked with our opponents—a couple of local rivals—that in a couple years, the debate would be moot. Even if nuclear war poses a greater existential threat to humanity, cyber warfare will soon command a greater share of defense spending, human capital, and political attention than conventional war.

Renewed Emphasis on Humanitarian Aid

Much of the time when millennials and boomers talk about foreign policy, they aren't even discussing the same issues. The term foreign policy for boomers tends to evoke thoughts of war and power projection. But many millennials think that humanitarian assistance should be a priority. "Coming in and searching for the American dream, I want to bring that to kids in developing nations who deserve the same things that I got—the chance that I got—but in a way that won't infringe on the individual sovereignty of their country," said Ciana Cronin, a millennial from Arizona.

This perspective seems to be a consensus among our generation. "If millennials do send their military abroad, it will often be for multilateral humanitarian intervention, perhaps overseen by the United Nations or some coalition of states. Millennials will continue to volunteer time, energy, and funds to nonprofits focused on human rights," wrote the *Diplomatic Courier* in a special report. "The gap between American ideals and actions will also increase support for candidates advocating soft power. By linking human rights violations to a loss of American influence, millennials will boost internationalist factions within the liberal camp and neoconservative candidates in conservative circles."

Divya Seth is passionate about health care, in part because she has seen her brother struggle with autism. She believes that foreign policy is a means to help other countries adopt better health systems and save lives. "The U.S. already does a pretty good job of humanitarian health care. … When we do give foreign aid, for example, sometimes the foreign aid doesn't go directly to the people," she said. "If we could instead directly provide resources like malaria nets or something … that is one of the ways that the government can solve that situation."

CONCLUSION

I hope we haven't scared you.

The rise of Russia, emergence of China, and splinting of power in the Middle East are not comforting. But it is important to acknowledge that historical trends are catching up with the United States. Millennials are increasingly weary of conflict—especially in faraway regions where our goals are uncertain or victory is unlikely. This is not a bad thing. An all-out war against Russia or China would be devastating. Conflict in the Middle East has continued for decades, and U.S. intervention has done little to solve the problem. We have spent trillions of dollars and lost too many young men and women in an effort to win unwinnable wars.

It's time for a paradigm shift. Geopolitics will be multipolar in the 21st century. The U.S. unipolar moment is over. Our generation is ready for this shift and we are not afraid. Instead, we will prioritize global cooperation, choosing war only as a last resort. This is unsettling. The world we describe in this chapter is fundamentally different from the one we've experienced over the last few decades. Rather than react in anger, declaring war and deploying troops, it is important that we internalize these changes. Older Americans need to accept their discomfort with these changes and acknowledge that they are inevitable.

Reclaiming Power: Tackling the Influence of Money in Politics

MINNEAPOLIS, MINNESOTA

"Corrupt, Fucked, and Broken." These were the words that came up most frequently in a poll of 666 millennials who were asked to describe the political system with one word.[1]

This sentiment hung over our teammates as we boarded a flight to Minneapolis, Minnesota, where we prepared to discuss the state of campaign finance in America at the annual pre-Christmas John Eddie Holiday Tournament. This tournament was always our personal favorite, not just because it was hosted in the famed "Twin Cities" but also because we always looked forward to a dinner in the Mall of America, the pleasant Christmastime cheer among opponents, and great apple cider. But when it came to the topic of the tournament—the *Citizen United* decision and the role of money in politics—something felt very different.

On flights to tournaments, we usually spend time joking about the debate topic, preparing rebuttals to our opponent's arguments, and teasing each other about our political views. Debaters are used to being ready to argue both sides of any topic. In fact, our advocacy is usually assigned based on a coin flip before each round. But we still frequently debate what the "correct opinion" is on the topic.

This image of Washington paints a damning picture of the depths to which we have sunk. Though we don't think of them that way, politicians are really no different than NASCAR drivers—they represent themselves and their sponsors.[9]

So you've figured it out: our generation is pissed as hell—and so is America. Overall, three in four Americans believe that the amount of money in elections has given rich people undue influence. Eighty percent of Americans believe that super PACs should not be able to make unlimited donations to political campaigns, with 65 percent of respondents "strongly opposed" to the *Citizens United* decision, including three-quarters of Democrats, Republicans, and Independents. No other issue claims such widespread political support.[10]

Almost half of millennials rank the role of money in politics as a decisive issue they consider when determining which candidate to support, but just 1 percent of Americans say it is the single most important issue for them.[11] This lack of political capital has slowed progress in moving the dial on reform. Meanwhile, millennials have reacted by saying they won't vote—and 26 percent of Americans overall say that the role of money in politics reduces their likelihood of voting. But of course, that's the wrong reaction. We need to fix the system and help reinvigorate our democracy.[12]

Entrenching the Elite: The Republican and Democratic Platforms

The problem with campaign finance reform is quite intuitive. We expect Congress to act on the issue—and yet, we know they won't. That's because the people in power got there because they were the ones who were best able to take advantage of loose campaign finance laws. They're good at raising money. Real campaign finance reform would make politics more competitive—a scary thought for entrenched career politicians looking to stay in power. As Sen. Lindsay Graham joked, "When I first announced for the Senate I took

Senator Thurmond's place. Anybody heard of Senator Thurmond? Yes, we change senators every 50 years."

Statistically, we know that politics today is not competitive. Incumbent politicians win their elections 90 percent of the time.[13] Lack of competitiveness in congressional elections leads to dysfunctional democracy, exacerbating corruption, entrenching politicians, favoring polarization, and preventing reform. The result is an elite bureaucracy of career politicians, largely insulated from public opinion, able to legislate against the will of their constituency. The incumbent's primary advantage is in fundraising. Incumbents usually outspend challengers by better than 3 to 1.[14] This is hugely important, according to *The Washington Post,* which found that the better-funded candidate won 91 percent of congressional races in 2012.[15]

Money also acts as a barrier to entry for new competitors. In American politics today, you must "pay to play." In the mid-2000s, it cost anywhere from $5,713 (North Dakota) to $938,522 (California) to win a state Senate campaign, according to Pew. In 2010, the average cost of a U.S. Senate seat was $9.2 million. In a crowded race, money talks. "If you've got a field with little or no name recognition," explained Neil Reiff, a Democratic election attorney, "you can drown out everyone else," he said in an interview with *Mother Jones.*[16] Because money keeps challengers from entering political races, it creates noncompetitive elections.

The result is a weakened democracy. "For the democratic framework to operate efficiently, politicians must seek reelection and must feel insecure about their prospects. When politicians perceive their seat to be 'safe,' they will often revert to legal patronage, disregarding the political will of their constituency in favor of special interests," explained Susan Rose-Ackerman, a professor at Yale Law School. With competitive elections, "Representatives have little freedom to act against their constituents' wishes," she said. On the other hand, in noncompetitive races, politicians risk becoming beholden to result of *Citizens United*, an unprecedented number of dollars have flowed from corporate coffers into the hands of politicians. Millennials believe democracy is being circumvented as corporations steal the influence that we should rightly have as citizens. "It's pretty infuriating, the idea that your opinion doesn't really matter," said Skylar Thoma, a millennial leader from Oakland, California. He described "the idea of a democracy belonging to anyone who can buy a legislator" as "a complete misinterpretation of democracy."

"The government is run by moneyed interests. Corporate lobbying groups don't care about the broad welfare of America, and prioritize policy that benefits only their bottom line," millennial journalist Tom McKay wrote for Policy Mic. "Some of the biggest corporations in America—GE, Verizon, Boeing, Honeywell and Wells Fargo—spend more on lobbying than they do on federal income taxes."

Texas millennial Cole Harper said this is the single biggest issue affecting millennials. "The way campaign finance works right now is the greatest threat to our democracy. It's something overlooked by a lot of people. Until we get it fixed, I don't think the average person on the street is going to have an equal say," he said.

Alexander Teckle, also from Texas, sees the need for reform in his hometown, El Paso. City council races there are won by margins of only a few hundred votes, he said, so large donors could have a massive impact. "There has to be a lot of campaign finance reform because city and state candidates rely on low budgets, and sometimes there might be one candidate who has a huge donor because he has a backing of a corporation," he said. In the most recent race, huge coalitions were formed around LGBT discrimination and religious exemptions for local restaurants. He said corporations spent a lot of money to prevent antidiscrimination laws from being passed—much to the chagrin of his classmates.

Shareholders aren't happy with the situation either. Shareholders' rights activists argue that political donations from general treasury funds of corporations are a misuse of funds and an improper form of political expression. But *Citizens United* ruled that companies could freely spend these shareholder dollars—without their consent—to purchase political speech. In this way, *Citizens United* opened the door to a clear abuse of managerial discretion. Following the decision, companies like Chick-fil-A and Target came under significant pressure after shareholders learned about their use of general treasury funds for political purposes.[7]

Companies aren't alone. While *Citizens United* is best known for its impact on super PACs, the decision also freed unions to campaign to the 89 percent of Americans who don't belong to them. As a result, unions have mobilized their ground troops to raise money and votes, both of which have helped them expand their influence on politics. The Sunlight Foundation, a nonprofit that tracks political spending, found that in 2013 big labor outspent big business by a margin of more than 2-to-1. "Organized labor has taken advantage of *Citizens United* to a degree that exceeds what the business community has," concluded the Accountability Project.[8]

The expanded role of unions is not a saving grace—it's part of the problem. Elections today pit big labor against big corporations, leaving broke millennials (and everyday Americans) in the dust. No wonder public employees are driving cities bankrupt, while regular Americans can barely pay their taxes and our generation can barely find jobs—let alone start a 401(k).

Mother Jones paints a surprising picture by analyzing the biggest donors to senators on both sides of the aisle. Instead of dividing the Senate along partisan lines, it divides them by their most significant contributors. Fifty-seven senators are owned (tongue-in-cheek) by the financial industry, 25 by lawyers and lobbyists, five by the health-care industry, two by labor, two by energy, and the rest are miscellaneous, with three candidates being self-funded. In the House, finance and labor are tied with 159 seats each, health care owns 26 seats, agribusiness 23 seats, lawyers and lobbyists own just 20 seats, energy owns 10 seats, defense owns seven, and the rests are miscellaneous.

Based on our research, we start to form concrete opinions. We're pretty moderate guys, but a lot of our former teammates are very liberal. So there was almost always room for conflict, which was the fun part. But here, something remarkable happened. There was a unanimous opinion on the plane, indicative of the millennial consensus.

A Broken System

Millennials have despised politics for as long as we can remember. Just look at the history. We've voted in four elections. In the first, the Supreme Court chose our president. In the second, a later discredited super PAC helped Bush win a second term. Two failed wars and a recession later, President Obama offered us hope and change— only to govern over eight of the most polarized years in American history. We're too young to remember a time when Washington actually worked—when statesmen could respectfully disagree with one another, without vilifying their opponents as being morally repugnant.

As we've grown older, the situation has not improved. Instead, it's deteriorated. In 2010, the Supreme Court's landmark *Citizens United* decision sealed the deal. In a 5-4 decision, the court ruled that campaign spending was constitutionally protected speech. Because Super PAC spending could not be construed as "quid pro quo" corruption—the direct exchange of money for favors—the court ruled that corporations, unions, and individuals could funnel unlimited donations into super PAC.

The result was devastating. The following election cycle was the "highest-spending cycle in American history, by far," according to the Brennan Center for Justice.[2] In 2012 a total of 266 super PACs pumped $546.5 million into elections, impacting the outcomes of 354 congressional and Senate races. Independent expenditures in that race rivaled those of the past decade combined.[3]

The direct impact of this money, on the local, state, and federal level, is even more corrosive. "The real danger," wrote academics at the

University of Sydney in their study on the effects of *Citizens United*, "is that unlimited corporate spending will buy hundreds or even thousands of less-publicized elections for state and local offices." Retired U.S. Supreme Court Justice Sandra Day O'Connor warned that as a result of *Citizens United* "the problem of campaign contributions in judicial elections will get considerably worse and quite soon."[4]

O'Connor was right. An Emory Law School study found a direct relationship between campaign spending on judicial elections and actual outcomes. "Every dollar of direct contributions from business groups is associated with an increase in the probability that the judges will vote for business litigants," the study found.[5] As an Ohio union official put it, "We figured out a long time ago that it's easier to elect seven judges than 132 legislators."[6]

In an essay for the *Boston Review*, Harvard Professor Lawrence Lessig argued that unlimited donations would subvert the democratic process by creating a system of dependency corruption. Money would become so fundamental to politics that even well-intentioned politicians would need to guarantee themselves strong cash flows in order to stay in office. This new form of corruption, he argued, would be just as damaging to our democracy as "quid pro quo" corruption, which is illegal.

"As with an alcoholic mother trying to care for her children, that conflicting dependency does not change the good intentions of members of Congress—they still want to serve the public interest they got themselves elected to serve," Lessig wrote. "But as with an alcoholic mother trying to care for her children, that conflicting dependency distracts members from their good intentions, directing their focus more and more toward the challenge of raising money."

Corporations and Unions: The Powerbrokers of American Democracy

With *Citizens United*, millennials are the generation that has overseen the largest expansion in legal corruption in U.S. history. As a

Senator Thurmond's place. Anybody heard of Senator Thurmond? Yes, we change senators every 50 years."

Statistically, we know that politics today is not competitive. Incumbent politicians win their elections 90 percent of the time.[13] Lack of competitiveness in congressional elections leads to dysfunctional democracy, exacerbating corruption, entrenching politicians, favoring polarization, and preventing reform. The result is an elite bureaucracy of career politicians, largely insulated from public opinion, able to legislate against the will of their constituency. The incumbent's primary advantage is in fundraising. Incumbents usually outspend challengers by better than 3 to 1.[14] This is hugely important, according to *The Washington Post*, which found that the better-funded candidate won 91 percent of congressional races in 2012.[15]

Money also acts as a barrier to entry for new competitors. In American politics today, you must "pay to play." In the mid-2000s, it cost anywhere from $5,713 (North Dakota) to $938,522 (California) to win a state Senate campaign, according to Pew. In 2010, the average cost of a U.S. Senate seat was $9.2 million. In a crowded race, money talks. "If you've got a field with little or no name recognition," explained Neil Reiff, a Democratic election attorney, "you can drown out everyone else," he said in an interview with *Mother Jones*.[16] Because money keeps challengers from entering political races, it creates noncompetitive elections.

The result is a weakened democracy. "For the democratic framework to operate efficiently, politicians must seek reelection and must feel insecure about their prospects. When politicians perceive their seat to be 'safe,' they will often revert to legal patronage, disregarding the political will of their constituency in favor of special interests," explained Susan Rose-Ackerman, a professor at Yale Law School. With competitive elections, "Representatives have little freedom to act against their constituents' wishes," she said. On the other hand, in noncompetitive races, politicians risk becoming beholden to

This image of Washington paints a damning picture of the depths to which we have sunk. Though we don't think of them that way, politicians are really no different than NASCAR drivers—they represent themselves and their sponsors.[9]

So you've figured it out: our generation is pissed as hell—and so is America. Overall, three in four Americans believe that the amount of money in elections has given rich people undue influence. Eighty percent of Americans believe that super PACs should not be able to make unlimited donations to political campaigns, with 65 percent of respondents "strongly opposed" to the *Citizens United* decision, including three-quarters of Democrats, Republicans, and Independents. No other issue claims such widespread political support.[10]

Almost half of millennials rank the role of money in politics as a decisive issue they consider when determining which candidate to support, but just 1 percent of Americans say it is the single most important issue for them.[11] This lack of political capital has slowed progress in moving the dial on reform. Meanwhile, millennials have reacted by saying they won't vote—and 26 percent of Americans overall say that the role of money in politics reduces their likelihood of voting. But of course, that's the wrong reaction. We need to fix the system and help reinvigorate our democracy.[12]

Entrenching the Elite: The Republican and Democratic Platforms

The problem with campaign finance reform is quite intuitive. We expect Congress to act on the issue—and yet, we know they won't. That's because the people in power got there because they were the ones who were best able to take advantage of loose campaign finance laws. They're good at raising money. Real campaign finance reform would make politics more competitive—a scary thought for entrenched career politicians looking to stay in power. As Sen. Lindsay Graham joked, "When I first announced for the Senate I took lobbyists, or worse, succumbing to actual quid pro quo corruption. "Opposition parties play the role of monitors, threatening to make corruption a campaign issue. Competition encourages honest policy making," Rose-Ackerman said.[17]

The conclusion is that money in politics empowers the Washington cartel. By shielding them from the influence of voters, money creates a shadow-election process where politicians become beholden to donors. No wonder American voters feel so disconnected from leaders. This problem is not minor; our leaders spend between 25-50 percent of their time fundraising, according to *The Hill*. This is corrosive to our democracy, because it literally means that our leaders are more concerned with reassuring donors of their continued support than they are with actually governing and improving America.

With all these problems, we would hope Congress would clean itself up. The last time this happened was in 2002. The McCain-Feingold Act, sponsored by maverick senators on both sides of the aisle, John McCain (R-AZ) and Russ Feingold (D-OH), banned "soft money" from political campaigns and overhauled restrictions on campaign donations. Though the bill did not go far enough, it moved the dialogue in the right direction. That was 14 years ago. Since then, the bill has been defanged by the U.S. Supreme Court, and the Washington elite have grown ever more powerful, raking in campaign donations from unions and corporations.

Today, the Washington machine is stronger than ever, churning through millions of dollars a year. American voters are angry because politics seems rigged.

But It's the Law, Right?

"Let's repeal *Citizens United*" is a common refrain we hear from millennials and boomers alike. But even though we have legitimate concerns, there's not much we can do to outside of a constitutional amendment, which is unlikely to pass.

Perhaps there is hope that the next generation of U.S. Supreme Court justices will feel differently than the current group does. But the biggest problem for millennials—a problem that we find difficult to discuss and acknowledge—is that independent campaign expenditures do appear to be constitutionally protected free speech. When you think about the decision at its core, all it says is that rich people can go on TV and try to convince voters to support the politicians they favor. As the majority in *Citizens United* noted, a ruling that limited this speech would be precedent to ban books or other materials that seemed to promote the interests of one candidate over another and were backed by moneyed interests.

From a free speech perspective, there is precedent to argue that we cannot withhold an organization's free speech rights on the basis of it being too powerful (*Buckley* and *Bellotti*). Since companies have long been considered people for the purpose of judicial case law (which makes them taxable and allows us to sue them), and indisputably have free speech rights (all of the justices agree on this), they are allowed to express their political beliefs.

Meanwhile, the concept of "political speech" is an arbitrary one, creating a subjective process in which the government must preapprove what companies say in their ads. In *Citizens United*, the court found that the complex tests applied by the Federal Election Commission (FEC) to determine which speech constituted express advocacy (and was therefore banned) were so subjective as to require speakers to ask for FEC permission before releasing information. This practice, the court ruled, is chilling to free speech.

And to make matters worse, the *Citizens United* precedent is ushering in a new set of rulings, including the 2014 *McCutcheon v. Federal Election Commission* decision. In *McCutcheon*, the court eliminated restrictions on the aggregate donations that a specific donor may make to candidates for federal office, finding that these limits did not further the interests of preventing corruption and therefore unnecessarily limited free speech. The idea behind the decision was that donating $2,000 to 10 candidates would not increase corruption more than donating $2,000 to one candidate, since none of the candidates would become beholden as a result of the donation. The impact of *McCutcheon* was to increase the total amount of money—and therefore influence—that rich Americans could donate to political campaigns.

Millennials wish that there was some way to remove the influence of corporations on politics entirely, but that seems unlikely. "If it was written in the law that the people were the sole source of funding for campaigns, then it would look like democracy," Thoma proffered.

The bottom line here is that from a purely legal perspective, millennials are stuck complaining that rich donors are stealing their influence, with few means of recourse available. The result is disheartening—voters not only say they are less likely go to the polls and vote, but it has fed an onslaught of negative campaign ads. Eighty-six percent of political campaign ads are negative, a Dartmouth University study found.[18] Professors Abbe, Iyengar, and Ansolabehere studied all of the available literature on the impact of these negative ads on voter turnout. Overall, they found that there is a 5 percent drop-off in turnout due to negative campaigning and a lower sense of political efficacy among those exposed to negative ads.[19]

Okay, so there's this massive problem that is boiling the blood of millennials across the country. How do we express our political frustration and how can we solve this issue of momentous importance? So far, millennials have expressed their anger by supporting fringe candidates and using social media to express their disappointment in establishment candidates accepting dollars from special interests. This is fascinating because it is going to be impactful in the short-term.

Already, we've seen millennials flee from mainstream candidates that they perceive to be "bought-out." This has been a major struggle for Hillary Clinton, Jeb Bush, and Mitt Romney while being a boon to the likes of President Obama and Bernie Sanders, who are seen to represent the masses. As frontrunners begin to recognize that campaign dollars from the rich come with a price, they may begin to be more careful about their sources of donations. If they do not, they will pay the price, as populist voters turn to alternatives.

Consider Bernie Sanders, a millennial favorite, who has long claimed to be an independent voice in Washington. When Sanders received a donation from recently indicted hedge fund manager Martin Shkreli, "the most hated man in America," he turned it down. In the 2016 primary race, Sanders often contrasted his donors—mostly unions—against Clinton's list of top donors, which looks more like a who's who of Wall Street. But as most candidates will still accept money and support indiscriminately—and there is a substantial risk that politicians will be beholden to their donors—campaign finance reform is necessary.

The Road Ahead: Making Elections More Competitive

Fighting corruption may be an important priority for millennial voters, but for Congress, it's taboo. That's why little to no action has been taken on the issue. Fighting corruption is a cheap talking point used on the stump and then quickly forgotten once candidates assume political office. Clearly, progress on campaign finance reform must come from the general public, and millennials are going to lead the battle. The path to restoring power over elections to the people will be a grassroots activist campaign that encourages and pressures our representatives to push forward state-level reform and eventually pass national laws regulating federal elections.

The fight to democratize politics needs to start with local government. City and statewide referendums can create publically funded elections, require full and complete transparency, and regulate lobbying. These are constitutional proposals that are popular and have proved effective. Gallop polls show that a majority of Americans support public financing of campaigns to reduce the influence of large donors.[20]

Public financing has two key benefits. First, it increases voter engagement. A study found that small donors in New York City were three times more likely to donate to citywide candidates, who benefit from public financing schemes, than to statewide candidates, who do not operate under the same system.[21] Second, public financing increases the competitiveness of races by allowing less-known candidates to throw their hats in the ring. Maine, which uses public financing for state elections, reports that 14 percent of its legislature is working class, which is five times the national average. Where it is available, public financing is often widely adopted; 80 percent of candidates in Maine used it and two-thirds of candidates in Arizona take advantage of the funding source. Public financing on a local level is so popular that some pollsters have said "it's virtually impossible to lose a ballot initiative" on the issue.[22]

But what if we literally handed people cash and told them they could use it for campaign donations? That's effectively what Yale Law School professors Bruce Ackerman and Ian Ayres are proposing. They say every American should be given $50 from government coffers to donate to political campaigns (in the form of a tax rebate). They argue that this would give voters a sense that they control their campaign dollars. This would also create a quasi-market economy for the primaries, so that political donations become an early vote on a candidacy. Too often, good candidates must drop out because they cannot afford to make it to Election Day. The total cost of this reform would be approximately $6 billion for federal elections—vs. the $4 billion currently spent by private donors.

Ackerman and Ayres go farther. They argue that limits on political donations are meaningless because candidates will always find ways to influence elections. They suggest that we raise the limits on contributions, but make them anonymous. Donations would be made to the FEC, which would use an algorithm to divide the order over a few days, so that large donations are not distinguishable. The professors say this system would be similar to the secret ballot, which was first implemented in the 19th century, to prevent widespread vote purchases by political machines. Now, of course, the secret ballot is thought to be sacrosanct.

This creates a game theory-like scenario, where candidates don't know who is supporting them. To avoid empowering super PACs, they would put in place laws that more severely separate super PACs from candidates. It is unclear what level of support such a proposal would have from the general public; there would certainly be concerns that the government was subsidizing itself. Indeed, it is highly unlikely that these proposals would even garner majority support among millennial voters. Nonetheless, as millennials continue to explore different ways to level the playing field in elections, creative solutions must be taken seriously.

Lobbying reform should come next. Proposed reforms—such as those proposed by Public Citizen, an advocacy group—include banning lobbyists from soliciting campaign contributions, banning lobbyists from sponsoring private travel for elected officials, and strengthening the ability of government watchdogs to regulate lobbying. Reformers call for a longer "cooling off" period during which former elected officials cannot join lobbying firms. Advocates say that lobbyists should have to file public disclosures online, which could be easily accessible by the general public. Such reforms are difficult to pass (largely because lobbyists already wield so much power), but they would be widely popular. Just 6 percent of Americans say lobbyists are honest, making it the least trustworthy profession in America, Politico found. Because we are the most cynical generation yet, new reforms to clean up Washington are appealing to millennial voters.[23]

To put the outsized role of lobbyists in context, just think about how desperate most congressional aides are for guidance on the issues they care about most. The average House legislative aide has worked on the Hill for just three years, has a Bachelor's degree, and is in his/her 20s. Aides are expected to cover up to a dozen legislative issues, many of which they come to with no prior experience.

In statehouses across the country, aides are even less experienced and unlikely to have the bandwidth to read and understand everything coming in front of their representatives. As a result, they turn to lobbyists for a concise view of the issues before them. Given these constraints, lobbyists will always play an important role in the political process—but it is crucial that our government maintain strong ethics by making lobbying relationships transparent and preventing conflicts of interests from emerging in the process.[24]

At the end of the day, millennials are going to push for strong campaign finance reforms in their cities and states. We'll be watching to see what is successful and will hopefully apply those lessons nationwide. For our generation, this is one of the toughest, but also the most important, issues. It must be solved.

Citizen's Equality Act

On the federal level, the Citizen's Equality Act—the legislation proposed by Harvard professor Lawrence Lessig—is a good place to begin. The legislation has three main priorities: automatic voter registration, ending partisan gerrymandering, and a new regime for public financing of federal campaigns. Millennials support all three propositions, and more. We have already discussed public financing, but the first two ideas highlight the importance of democratizing elections, beyond just a pure financial approach.

Automatic voter registration is particularly important for millennials because we directly benefit. Millennials are among the most likely to forget to vote or not put in the effort to register because we are so used to conducting our business online (and conveniently) that we do not put in the time to fill out voter registration paperwork.

"The biggest obstacle to free and fair elections is the ramshackle voter registration system," said Michael Waldman, President of the Brennan Center. Millennials are generally more disconnected from the political debate happening around them, which makes them unlikely to register to vote in advance for elections. Same-day registration, online registration, and especially automatic registration allows these young voters to cast their ballots at any point on election day, as soon as they make up their minds; no advanced planning would be necessary. We obviously support policies that would make our lives easier.

Partisan gerrymandering, which has long been a hot topic of political controversy, is the next topic for reform. Gerrymandering is the process of allocating seats in state legislatures and Congress. Usually, the party in power manipulates this process to maximize the number of "winnable" districts for their representatives. By carving out "safe" districts, the political elite create institutional sources of power. This process is widely credited with exacerbating partisanship in Congress, because it means that many representatives are catering to a very unique and nonrepresentative sample of the American public.

The solution is nonpartisan gerrymandering. By appointing independent, nonpartisan committees to carve up legislative districts, we can help eliminate congressional gridlock. A report released by former New York City Mayor Michael Bloomberg indicated that in districts that used nonpartisan gerrymandering, political races were 24 percent closer. By making races more competitive, we force politicians to be accountable to voters. Skewed districts, by contrast, encourage extreme opinions because politicians lose touch with their voters and instead become part of the Washington machine. Likewise, politicians become primarily concerned with turning away potential primary election challengers, encouraging them to adopt extreme views.[25]

CONCLUSION

Washington's inaction on campaign finance reform is to be expected. The cartel has no incentive to defund itself. America's politicians were elected on the backs of an unfair system. It takes genuine courage—and collective action—to rid Washington of corruption once and for all.

On the national political stage, the message that campaign finance reform is urgent has come from an unlikely voice. "I will tell you that our system is broken," Donald Trump said at a GOP debate. "I gave to many people. Before this, before two months ago, I was a businessman. I give to everybody. When they call, I give. And you know what? When I need something from them, two years later, three years later, I call them. They are there for me. And that's a broken system."

To cripple the Washington machine, we need to defund it. Campaign finance reform is a crucial step forward in taking back American politics for the American voter. As millennials rise to power, our generation plans to experiment with campaign finance reform, backing public financing initiatives on a local level as well as a variety of innovative proposals that some millennial leaders have already begun to propose. We can take our democracy back.

As Jack noted in his final speech during a late night debate round in Minnesota, "Unlimited campaign spending means I can keep talking. There's no debate happening—there's just me shouting over you. You talk, but I speak louder. Does that seem fair to you?"

Better Schools: Investing in Our Future

ARLINGTON, VIRGINIA

"School choice." Say these two words and many American liberals will cringe. Teachers will start to picket. Unions might even threaten to strike. The school choice movement has somehow become associated with conservative politics, what many of the Left have labeled the "corporate education agenda."

That America's education debate is so polarizing is both surprising and bewildering. The vitriol that many advocates bring to the table seems somehow inappropriate for the underlying issue—we're talking about kids going to school, after all, not nuclear war.

Because, of course, television mimics reality (kidding!), an episode of the TV series *The West Wing* best captures the difference between how boomers and millennials think about education policy. In the episode "Full Disclosure," the Democratic mayor of Washington, D.C., announces that he is in favor of issues vouchers so that low-income students can choose to attend private school.

The teacher's union is furious and this threatens to divide the Democratic Party. So President Jed Bartlett intervenes. He calls the mayor into the Oval Office and asks him to drop the issue; it's not worth the fight, he says.

The mayor turns to Charlie Young, the president's black aide. He effectively puts the decision in Charlie's hands, asking Young where he would have gone to high school, if he had the choice. Young, who went to a public school, quickly responds that he would have chosen Gonzaga, a well-respected Catholic high school.

At Gonzaga there is "never a shooting," he says. "No metal detectors. Everybody there goes to college. ..." Asked what he thinks of the proposed voucher program, Young responds, "I wish they had one when I was in school." Seeing Young's response, Bartlett concedes and Washington, D.C., moves forward with school choice.

For Young, a private school voucher offered an opportunity to rise above his humble beginnings and build a better life.

Like Young, today's millennials don't buy into the polarized education debate happening in our country. Instead, they see education as a civil rights issue and equality issue, uniting around any and all proposals that offer to fix a system that we know to be woefully flawed.

To debate this issue, we head over to Young's home city: Washington, D.C. Next door to the Capitol are dozens of failing schools and an inner city where thousands of kids are desperately fighting to break out of their cycle of poverty.

It's this backdrop that offers context to the constructive conversations we're having at a Mock Congress event in Arlington, Virginia, a metro ride away from the center of Washington, D.C.. To this conversation, we bring not just research, but personal experience.

School Sucks

In the fall of 2014, we were invited to visit a school in East Harlem and speak with members of a local student government. We talked about making the most of their role and discussed strategies they could use to better represent the student body. The students were engaged and interested, clearly intelligent people and highly relatable. We had a great time talking to them. We later found out that the school was known for low graduation rates, consistent failure on statewide exams, and even violence. These were intelligent kids, but their school was failing them and their opportunities were being stifled.

There is a deep socioeconomic divide in our schools that helps distinguish the winners from the losers before our kids even have a chance to rise from their circumstances. "My school is kind of on the border of a nicer area and a less nice area, so we have a real mix of people, and the best classes always are filled by people who live in certain areas and who fill certain socioeconomic classes. And the lower classes that the school doesn't really care about are filled by students from certain socioeconomic classes," explained Texas millennial leader Cole Harper. "It's not American. It's not fair that some people are given such ridiculous head starts in life, and that public school, something that should be the great equalizer ... is still so divided."

It should come as no surprise that America's public education system is broken. 60 percent of U.S. fourth graders are not at grade-level when it comes to reading. For low-income families, 80 percent of fourth graders are not proficient, marking a clear economic divide in educational outcomes. These numbers improve by the time we reach the eighth grade, but the outcomes are not remarkable: 22 percent of eighth graders score below grade-level. Among our OECD peers, the U.S. ranks 15th for reading and 31st for math. At the end of high school, the ACT reports that just one in four students is proficient in all four subjects it assesses: English, math, reading, and science. When it comes to education, our government is sending students a clear message: failure *is* an option.

Justin Wittekind, a millennial from California, agrees that students are getting the short end of the stick. "At the end of the day, students are some of the most disenfranchised people in America. If you live in a bad neighborhood or are from an area that is not affluent, you are already at a disadvantage. And then society says you have to go to this crappy school and you have no method of recourse. ... That makes no sense."

These disparities in K-12 educations are well documented. Only 69 percent of African American students graduate from high school in the United States, compared with 86 percent among Caucasian students (neither number is particularly encouraging). And given these dismal numbers, it's no surprise that those who do end up graduating don't make it through college; the poor foundations of their K-12 educations make it nearly impossible for many students to succeed at the college level.

Young people have no shortage of answers to America's education problems. As the generation most recently affected by our poor education system, millennials are passionate about fixing a broken system, which they believe to be a primary cause of income inequality in America. Their stories paint a vivid picture of our nation's decrepit education infrastructure.

Ohio millennial Nari Johnson, for instance, spent months volunteering in neighboring schools while in high school. In her community, she discovered hundreds of kids who lacked basic skills.

Helping Charles

"I worked at a federally mandated program called Freedom Schools, whose goal was to keep students in school and get them ready for the school year. A lot of these kids are left home all day and it's nice for them to have a place to go. I was in a pre-kindergarten classroom and there was this little boy named Charles and he was 6 years old. He didn't know how to count to 10. He didn't know his ABCs. Charles was not prepared to enter kindergarten," Nari said.

"I was working with him the entire summer and I made him my personal project. I was like okay, there's this adorable tiny child right here and I can teach his ABCs and to count to 10. And so every single day I would sit and hold his pencil with him and he would squirm around; he didn't want to be there. It was clear that no one had ever had faith in him to perform a task before; he wasn't expected to do anything. It took him a while to get past eight and we were proud. I bought him cookies, 10 cookies; he counted them as he ate them," Nari recounted.

But while Nari was proud, she had no idea of the struggles he faced at home until later in the summer, when she met Charles' family. "In the neighborhood around the school, I volunteered at a produce distribution center. And one day I saw Charles and his mom, and said, 'Hi! Did Charles show you he can count to 10? He knows his ABCs.' And his mom turned and said, 'You don't know how to count to 10?' And Charles just stared back and didn't know what to say. And his mom laughed. And she said, 'Yeah, he's always been a slow learner.' And that to me is the essence of the problem; these kids in these areas have never been encouraged by their parents. Schools need to have a stronger support system," she said.

Texas millennial Sarah Angel described the issue as a "maldistribution of resources and a fragmentation of effort along socioeconomic lines," she said. "Somebody shouldn't be bound to their economic [status]." Shruti Baxi, who hails from the Midwest, agrees. "The government should be targeting more underprivileged cities because there is a lot of potential in those areas. And that potential is really untapped because they're not getting the resources and the kinds of programs that they need. There needs to be better programs to get youth more integrated with society and teach them a lifestyle that helps them get jobs and rise up."

But how do we improve education across the board and reduce these economic and racial disparities in education?

School Choice

It's not often that three-quarters of young Americans agree on a political issue, but school choice is one of those issues, according to a recent poll by the Friedman Foundation. This is a dramatic difference from their parents, who generally support school choice only by a slim majority.[1]

Milton Friedman first articulated the idea behind school choice in 1955. In the chapter titled "The Role of Government in Education" in his classic 1962 book *Capitalism & Freedom*, the Nobel Laureate economist wrote:

"Let the subsidy be made available to parents regardless where they send their children—provided only that it be to schools that satisfy specified minimum standards—and a wide variety of schools will spring up to meet the demand. Parents could express their views about schools directly, by withdrawing their children from one school and sending them to another, to a much greater extent than is now possible. In general, they can now take this step only by simultaneously changing their place of residence."

His idea was to give parents vouchers for their children's education, which could be "spent" at a variety of institutions. This way market forces would dictate which schools succeeded. Better schools would see enrollments increase, and worse school would see parents withholding their school voucher and spending it elsewhere. As of 2014, there were more than 115,000 students participating in 23 voucher programs operating in 14 states and Washington, D.C, according to the Cato Institute, mostly limited to students with special needs.

In recent years, school choice has shifted from these voucher programs to scholarship tax credits (STCs). Under STC laws, low- and middle-income families can donate to nonprofit scholarship organizations that help enroll their children in their "schools of choice"—which are usually private schools—and receive a full or partial tax credit. As of 2014, nearly 200,000 students received tax-credit scholarships in 13 states. And these STC laws are widely heralded by millennials as a better way of educating children.

Millennial support for school choice should come as no surprise. Not only do these programs allow low-income families to escape the poor education systems of their communities, but they are also equalizing in that they allow minorities to leave what Harvard University researchers have called "apartheid schools"—schools that are virtually all nonwhite and where poverty, limited resources, social strife, and health problems abound.

This opportunity for social mobility touches the heartstrings of a generation that often has been described as America's most tolerant. 91 percent of millennials "believe in equality" and believe "everyone should be treated equally," according to MTV polls. Furthermore, 84 percent say "their families taught them to treat everyone the same no matter what race," and 89 percent believe "everyone should be treated as equals." In some senses, then, school choice is a civil rights issue.

But millennial support for school choice is about much more than equality—it's about educational outcomes. In 2013, for example, "98.6 percent of parents of scholarship recipients in Georgia reported being 'very satisfied' or 'satisfied' with their chosen school," according to the Cato Institute. Compare that number to the number of kids who fall asleep every day in New York City public schools. The contrast is staggering.

These programs even make money! Studies of the financial impact of STCs in three states found that they reduced government spending more than they decreased tax revenue. As a generation typically portrayed as liberal by the media, it may be surprising to see the millennials aligning themselves with the Cato Institute, a conservative think tank. What's going on?

Opponents to school choice argue that it "promotes the dismantling of public education at every turn."[2] They worry that if parents begin pulling their kids from poor schools, those schools will shut down, and the remaining students will be left with few options. To adults, this is scary! What happens when the education system you've lived with suddenly changes?

"One of the most problematic aspects [of it] is the idea of 'choice' itself," Karey Harwood, an ethics professor at North Carolina State University, told *Salon.* "What the [people] seem to be saying ... is that, rather than strengthen a weakened public school system because we believe in public schools as the foundation of a democratic society, the solution is to abandon public schools altogether, let them deteriorate, and replace them with alternative private schools and charter schools that can claim they cater to every possible parental preference."

Harwood's view is legitimate, but many millennials say it just represents fear of change. We have watched machines replace fast food jobs, and on-demand mobile apps render taxis obsolete. With this context in mind, the end of normal public education as we know it in favor of a more competitive system where schools have to compete for students is not all that surprising; it's just another "business" getting a 21st century wake-up call.

We're ready to let market forces dictate which schools stay open and which close. And while this inevitably means some public schools will lose traction, we are more concerned with our kids' education than with keeping an old, failing system in place. Just like cars replaced horse and carriages and televisions replaced radios, we are ready to let innovation into the education system by letting parents choose where to send their kids.

Charter Schools

By far the most successful "school choice" initiative is the charter school movement. To many millennials, these schools aren't just experiments to see if education can be done differently—they are the future.[3] Here, it's not just millennials who are ardent supporters; the general public agrees too: 85 percent of millennials and 75 percent of likely voters support growth in charter schools.[4]

Shruti Baxi went to public school in Naperville, Illinois, but found herself pleasantly surprised by the quality of education she saw being offered by teachers like her sister, who work in charter schools in inner city Chicago. Baxi says that not all charter schools are good, but the concept is effective. "I think they can do a lot of good for the community and they don't have to abide by the same rules as public schools," she said. Through helping her sister grade exams, she realizes that the students in many of these communities are facing much more substantial challenges than she does, and that charter schools can help level the playing field. "I think when you have a smaller system like that, each student gets individualized attention and you can make sure that no student falls through the cracks."

Whereas students describe charter schools in wealthier communities as being all but indistinguishable from traditional public schools, there is a visible difference in lower-income neighborhoods. Oregon millennial Laura Bishop's mom works in one such school. "Her students, for a lot of them, English is a second language, or a lot of them don't even come into school sometimes because their situation is really hard at home, or she'll have a lot of people who come in in the middle of the year. And then there's all the programs that the people are still working on. Like they have a backpack buddy system where they help provide food to take home, or sometimes she'll stay after to help the kids with subjects they're struggling on. Just providing that type of support, it really helps the students," Bishop said. "There's a lot of neglect that's going on in that system right now, which is leading to a cycle of poverty."

If charter schools can help end that cycle, then count us in. Because charter schools create opportunity for social mobility, millennials are strong supporters. In fact, many millennials are opting to teach at these schools: Teach for America, for example, which recruits its students from top universities, and sends almost one-third of its teachers to charter schools. This is primarily because millennial leaders want to be challenged and they feel stifled by the traditional public education mold.

"I feel like our generation is always moving onto the next thing," Tyler Dowdy, a 24-year-old teacher at YES Prep West, a charter school in the Houston area, told *The New York Times*, "and always moving onto something bigger and better."

"I just don't think ambitious millennials want to be in that type of system, where the amount of work they put in and results they get have no bearing on the type of career they have going forward," said Lanae Erickson Hatalsky, who analyzes public education for Third Way, a centrist think tank. "I think that especially for millennials, it's not just about money, it's about being able to challenge themselves and take on more responsibility."[5]

And they want their kids to be challenged too. That's why they're not just working at charter schools; they're sending their kids to these schools as well. For many, the draw of charter schools is academic outcomes: according to a study by Mathematica Policy Research, graduation rates at charter high schools are 7-11 percent higher than at public schools.

The impact of charter schools is especially pronounced for low-income families who have no good alternatives. "Black students in poverty who attend charter schools gain an additional 29 days of learning in reading and 36 days in math per year over their [traditional public school] counterparts," a study by the Center for Research on Education Outcomes found. "This shows the impact of charter schooling is especially beneficial for black students who [are] in poverty."[6]

Why Hipster Capitalists Love Charter Schools

The first principle of charter schools is strong, cost-effective management. Charter schools often spend a vast majority of their funding on books and teacher salaries, cutting down on red tape and auxiliary expenses. High pay for teachers is used as an incentive to lure teachers away from the stable career public schools and toward the more rigorous charter schools. Naturally, more risk-averse teachers will stay in public schools while younger, arguably more entrepreneurial teachers will make the move to charter schools, benefiting charter school students. From a business perspective, charter schools often have the chance to divide fiscal and educational responsibilities among different leaders—a rarity in public school systems. This allows business-minded (and trained) leaders to cut administrative costs and allows more focus and resources to be spent on the students. Meanwhile, the principal can focus on curriculums and standards.

Northwest of Los Angeles, at Fenton Avenue Elementary charter school, for example, former executive director Joe Lucente, now chairman of the board of directors, who has a degree in business administration and has managed a number of businesses, focused on management issues. Irene Sumida, then curriculum director and now the executive director, oversaw teachers and curriculum development. Lance Izumi and Xiaochin Claire Yan write in *Free to Learn* that "Fenton's co-leadership solves the problem that numerous charter schools have; that is, a principal who is more skilled in academic matters than management, or vice versa."

Probably the most important differentiator of charter schools is that the focus is all about achieving measurable performance. It's no wonder that schools that spend their money pushing students toward academic achievement rather than, say, renovating their facilities, will see improved performance.

At Montague Charter Academy in Pacoima, California, further northwest of Los Angeles, attention to curriculum was critical to success. Former principal Diane Pritchard sent teams of teachers to curriculum conferences before choosing the Core Knowledge curriculum, much like business sends out teams to attend trade shows in order to better understand "the lay of the land."

Charter schools often extend the school day and year, which critics call "cheating." Of course, students will perform better if given more time to study, they argue. But if that's the case, then public schools should follow suit. To date, they haven't.

The U.S. Department of Education wrote, "Because many charter schools have an extremely ambitious mission, they provide a longer school day than their local counterparts." Arts and Technology Academy charter school, for example, in Washington, D.C., adopted a 200-day school year and offered an extended seven-and-a-half-hour day, with an option to stay after school for tutoring and homework assistance.

We could go on detailing the differentiators of charter schools, but when it comes down to it, millennial support for these schools boils down to one key issue: this laissez-faire generation of what *Reason* calls "hipster capitalists" is tired of public schools with no incentive to grow and is ready to bet on a more competitive education system.

Better Teachers

Perhaps the greatest failure of the public education system—and a distinguishing factor of the charter school movement—is the lack of quality teachers in inner-city public schools. That's right: when your kids came home complaining about the teachers they hated, they weren't just "kids being kids"—sometimes, they were right! According to a report by Third Way, a majority of America's incoming teachers hail from the bottom two-thirds of their college classes. This is not to say that all teachers are bad: certainly, we appreciate the brilliant teachers we ourselves have had, some of whom we talk about later in this chapter. But unfortunately, great teachers are all too often the exception rather than the norm, especially in inner-city public schools.

Third Way asked 400 millennial college students with GPAs of 3.3 or greater about public school teachers, and only 35 percent described teachers as "smart." (Again, there are many wonderful teachers out there who defy this stereotype!) Our education systems don't have to be this way. In our high school Mandarin class, we celebrated National Teachers Day with Guan Lao Shi (*lao shi* means teacher), who taught us about the culture of teacher praise in China, based off Confucian values, that demanded students respect their teachers. Finland, which, unlike China, does not have a history of respecting teachers, overhauled its education system by fixing this very problem and is now ranked toward the top of every OECD educational ranking.

One of the biggest culprits in the American education system is the teacher certification requirement. When we were sophomores in high school, our beloved math teacher Richard Geller, who taught at Stuyvesant for 29 years and led the school's math team for nearly two decades, passed away at 65. Widely considered one of the best math teachers in New York City, if not in the country, Geller seemed irreplaceable. But lo and behold, Geller groomed one of his past students, Princeton graduate and math prodigy, John Taylor, to fill his place.

Taylor was a strong math teacher. He had a passion for proofs and had a gift for teaching. Within a few months of Geller's passing, another teacher replaced Taylor. Not because he was a bad teacher—he was one of the best. Not because he was a poor math team coach. He was excellent. But rather, he was fired because he lacked a teaching credential—instead of going to get a degree in teaching, Taylor earned degrees from Julliard and Princeton.

"Lately, I've become downright outraged as I watch bureaucracy and rules trump brains and innovation, where all too often progress is impeded by the close-mindedness of the collective," David wrote in the *Stuyvesant Spectator* at the time. "The removal of a fantastic math teacher ... mark[s] a disastrous trend in America—the decline of merit in favor of 'rules and regulations.' "[7]

Taylor would never have been removed at a comparable charter school because charter schools don't require their teachers to be licensed. In his 2001 paper "Autonomy and Innovation: How Do Massachusetts Charter School Principals Use Their Freedom," Bill

Triant reported that at some Massachusetts charter schools only 25 percent of teachers were certified.[8]

"[Certification] doesn't mean they can teach. It just means that they have taken and passed—possibly with Ds—certain courses and been through some student teaching, but I have no idea of the quality of the mentor teacher," said one principal Triant interviewed. "What I need to see is people who are highly intelligent, prestigious college background, articulate, they like kids. They are visionaries of a sort that they understand the movement and the potential that it holds and that they want to be part of creating a school. People ask and I tell them I don't care if you are certified," she said.

Even the principals Triant interviewed who prefer certified teachers saw better teacher performance. "The teachers who want to work at this school are those who want to come in at six and leave after six, who are willing to come to extra school events, who want to be on the ground floor creating processes and procedures for a school that will be around for a long time; in other words, the best of public school teachers," one teacher explained. And that makes sense. Only a risk-taker would leave a union-backed job and guaranteed pension to move to a charter school.

But even if you took the same teachers and put them in a charter school vs. a public school, they would perform better. "The problem is that those teachers in the public school system are being held under a thumb and 'no you can't do that, no, no, no, no, we can't work with that curriculum,'" another of Triant's teachers explained. "There's a lot of 'no, no, no,' because we have to do it in the same way in this building as in the other building. Does that leave the teacher with any autonomy? No."

Local governments need to unleash the potential of teachers. First and foremost, teacher certification requirements should be relaxed so that public schools can hire the best. Second, public schools should reduce bureaucratic hurdles and let teachers innovate again. Third, public schools should spend more time searching for the best curriculums.

But all these suggestions are Band-Aid solutions. And millennials don't believe in short-term fixes. We are the 10x generation, and to fix our public schools, administrators need to overhaul the very cultures of public schools. Principals should be required to innovate, like charter schools, or they should be fired. The bureaucratic school administrations of the past will not survive in the hypercompetitive, radically changing 21st century.

Teacher contracts need to be relaxed so that poor performing teachers can be removed with ease. Jack will never forget the time when he had a teacher who could not communicate effectively due to language barriers. When Jack raised his concern with a department chair, he told me that the teacher would be retiring in a year or two, so "we're just waiting him out." Bad teachers need to go.

Children spend more time with teachers than anyone else—sometimes even more time than with their parents. A prerequisite to education reform is hiring reform. Public school administrators need look no further than the charter schools down the block to realize what they're missing.

Amanda's Story

Amanda Cox, a Fresno, California, native was initially hesitant about attending a charter school. But when we caught up with her to discuss the experience, she said that she soon came to realize that the school afforded her opportunities that would not have been possible elsewhere.

"My mom first forced me to go to a charter school; obviously, I didn't go by choice. I wanted to go to public school with all my friends. I ended up going my freshman year and it was extremely weird. The people there were completely different: their mind-set was, 'I'm here to learn and I want to get things done,'" she said.

And when she began her classes, Amanda realized just how exceptional charter schools really were. "Because classes are smaller, teachers can be more one-on-one. The teachers are way better. They care more and try to personalize everything for the students."

She also noted that charter schools approach the whole academic process differently, particularly because they aren't as regulated. "I think throughout the entire year they get to enthuse students with weird things. I took two years of Latin ... and acted out things that Caesar did. ... And there are just a lot of things you can do at charter schools that you can't do at public schools because they're so regulated."

But far and away the best aspect of Cox's charter school experience was the deep concern of administrators over students' academic well-being. "I had a low C in one class. I'm not a super rigorous student, but I try hard. And it was almost a D. And they called me into the office and were like, 'Do you need me to help or meet up with me after school?' And I think the fact that you are surrounded by people who want to work, and want you to go to college, that encourages you," Cox recalled.

Technology in the Classroom

Go to any corporate office and you'll find new Mac computers and cool new tablets. Go to a public elementary or high school classroom and schools are still using projectors from half a century ago. As so-called digital natives, millennials want school districts and local governments to invest in new technologies that will help students grow.

Video games are at the forefront of education technology, as teachers use new technologies to engage their technology-obsessed students. While "gamification" is by no means expected to take over, it will be a part of the classroom of the future. In the Quest to Learn public school in New York City, for example, teachers use principles of video game design to write their curriculums.

"This curriculum—organized into missions and quests—focuses on multifaceted challenges that may have more than one correct answer, letting students explore different solutions by making choices along the way," writes *Scientific American*. Quest to Learn students even get to study video game design using Gamestar Mechanic and other computer programs.

"Games are also uniquely suited to fostering the skills necessary for navigating a complex, interconnected, rapidly changing 21st century," says Alan Gershenfeld, founder and president of E-Line Media, a publisher of computer and video games, and a Founding Industry Fellow at Arizona State University's Center for Games & Impact.

And while the vote is still out on whether this method is effective, there is a consensus among millennials that this type of experimentation in education is critical. Ask students what they want in their education, and innovation tops the list, research shows.

"We do an exit survey with our seniors, and the one comment I hear most often is the teacher is 'boring.' Why can't they make the class interesting? I understand that there are tests, etc., but one could still make the class a welcoming place instead of a dreaded one," says Barbara Jimerson, former Title VII Director of the Gowanda (N.Y.) School District. The teachers [who] are still using overhead projectors should be run out of town! Are they modeling acceptance of change? Nope, not when they're stuck in the '70s."

Take MinecraftEdu, a modification of the popular digital game Minecraft, as an example of teacher innovation. This teacher-developed program teaches students mathematical concepts and foreign languages. Likewise, SimCityEDU, a version of SimCity, a popular city-building game, has taken off as an assessment tool covering English, math, and other lessons.

This latter solution is more typical of how "gamification" is being used in the classroom in a practical way. Video games can offer useful information about student performance, providing students and their teachers will real-time scores. And best of all, they're fun. To millennials who come home from school bored, these technical innovations seem like a great way to make sure students are engaging with the material they are learning.

There are simpler ways to integrate technology in the classroom. The so-called clicker method is a perfect example. To keep students engaged in class, professors quiz students throughout their lessons. Students respond via clickers they purchase for the class. Other ways include integrating Bring Your Own Device (BYOD) policies into the classroom, in which teachers integrate the use of phones and tablets into their curriculum, having their students do research in class or work on another related project.

Technology can also be used to change the way classes operate. Flipped classrooms, for example, are the new norm on some college campuses. Instead of listening to lectures in physics, math, or even history, students tune into lectures at home and come into the classroom to solve problems collaboratively. This "Structured Active In-Class Learning" or SAIL method has been shown to improve test scores—and many students approve.

"[The effectiveness of SAIL] hit me when we were supposed to do a problem together, and after explaining a problem to someone, I understood it better," explained University of Pennsylvania student Meredith Kline.

Creativity in the Classroom

Different people learn differently. Duh! But school districts are seemingly using the same educational styles on millennials and our children as were used on our parents and grandparents. Just as millennials are looking for innovation in technology, we also are looking to see school districts and local governments adapt to changing times—and new educational methods.

"The one complaint I hear from students at South University is that they want more practical, hands-on experience and not just lectures and homework. I have worked hard to provide as much hands-on as possible," said James Anthos, the Information Technology program director at the university in Columbia, South Carolina. "In computer programming class, students start writing programs on Day 1. In systems analysis classes, students begin a term project the third week of class that culminates with a complete analysis of a hypothetical systems problem."

And millennials say this is exactly what they are looking for: 68 percent of millennials have stated that experiential learning is their most preferred method of developing new skills, according to Youth-Speak, a millennial advocacy organization. Experiential learning typically involves students working together on projects with real-world applications. For example, one public relations class put together a guide to marketing to millennials! How cool is that? Another science teacher lets her students share their work at research symposiums to show them how relevant their work is to the real world.[9]

"Letting go of the silence was the hardest thing, but I realized we have to let students work together and help each other. Now, I get uncomfortable if my class gets too quiet," Texas high school teacher Brandy Avant said.[10]

We had the chance to experience experiential, or project-based learning firsthand under the guidance of the legendary Stuyvesant High School Computer Science coordinator Mike Zamansky, who now works at Hunter College in New York City. Z, as his students call him, has made computer science so much fun that AP Computer Science classes are oversubscribed; every student takes Intro to Computer Science (it was made a requirement), and more than 100 students take post-AP college sophomore-level computer science courses.

Z's software development course is a case in point for the success of experiential learning courses. In his class, we learned to code in

Python by building our first web application within the first few months of the course. These apps were hosted online for anyone to access.

Notably, all of Z's projects are collaborative by design. Students work in teams of four, and in many ways, this is a crucial part of the class. If you ask Z, he'll tell you that coding is in its nature a group activity, because you will be working with different stakeholders who have different needs. Learning to work in teams is an integral part of project-based learning. "His students have built a movie-recommendation web site, an app that searches for language patterns in celebrity Twitter posts and Pixar-style animations," wrote *The New York Times*. "Mr. Zamansky says his best students graduate 'Google-ready.' "

In short—Z made learning fun. And any school can make this happen. In fact, Z is currently working on a nonprofit called CSTUY to make this type of opportunity available to low-income students as well. If teachers of computer science—one of the most challenging of classes—can make their curriculum so engaging that their classes are oversubscribed, so can anyone. The opportunities are limitless.

Another example of project-based learning at Stuyvesant is Kerry Trainor's "Intelligence and National Security" class, in which his students act as emissaries from foreign countries and assess threats their countries face. Each team has a planted spy to make things more interesting. Like Z does for his projects, Trainor groups students into teams to make the project collaborative and makes the projects both fun and engaging.

Josina Dunkel is a third teacher who uses this paradigm (yes, we were very lucky to have wonderful teachers in high school!). Dunkel teaches European History, which most high school students will say is dry and boring. After all, who cares about ancient Europe 500 years ago ... boring! Dunkel assigned students to be enlightenment era philosophers (David was Maximilien Robespierre, Jack was Emanuel Kant). She then asked students to write letters to each other, from the perspective of their philosopher. Suddenly, a topic that felt very much removed from our lives was personalized.[11]

There are other approaches that work well with millennials too. You've heard us called the "Me, Me, Me" generation. And when it comes to learning, that seemingly is exactly what we want—personalized attention. "In a Personalized Learning experience, curriculum stays constant. The course itself does not vary as students encounter the same flow of information in the same order as their peers," writes Helix Education. "However, a personalized guide or study plan is generated and updated as a result of pre-assessment activities to suggest which modules or topics may be skipped and where a learner should focus his or her time to develop advanced skills and knowledge."

Like experiential learning, personalized learning allows students to take ownership of what they're learning—they're not trying to please a teacher or parents, but to learn as much as possible. And as technologies advance, so is personalized learning. Now, computer systems can modularize curriculums and help students focus on the areas where they need the most work. These systems use diagnostic tests to understand prior knowledge and guide individual students toward achieving their academic goals.

For public schools to succeed, millennials will push for both government and school administrations to explore these innovative options. The price of failure would be a weakened economy, fewer jobs, and a loss in global competitiveness. We cannot afford to fail.

CONCLUSION

Millennials leaders have been hailed as disrupters in Silicon Valley, but new technologies aren't the only things that make this generation innovative. Young people are looking for leaders of our education system to think outside of the box by promoting school choice, revamping the hiring process for teachers, and introducing new educational tools such as experiential learning and personalized learning. Fixing our education system will have major ripple effects, reducing income inequality and helping to jump-start our economy.

As millennials become parents, we're seeing a major transition in the sentiment toward charter schools—and teachers unions, which may be the biggest roadblock to their acceptance. Young parents are voting with their feet, sending their children to schools to maximize their opportunities. Today, charter schools are controversial. Tomorrow, they won't be. As the data about charter school success starts to pile up, the school choice movement is becoming mainstream. Our hope—and indeed, the hope of many of our peers—is that this experimentation spreads to traditional public schools. Rather than vilifying their charter school neighbors, public schools need to start copying them.

At the end of the day, we all have the same goal in mind: to help our kids grow and succeed.

The Weed Warriors are Back: Rethinking the War on Drugs

MINEOLA, NEW YORK

I t's March and spring break beckons! Thousands of young people are flocking home from college. The lucky ones will take vacations and party with their friends. But Fort Lauderdale, Florida, the archetypal spring break destination that was immortalized in the hit films *Where The Boys Are* (1960) and *Spring Break* (1983), is no longer their destination of choice. No, today the legalization of marijuana has given Denver the momentum it needed to top the list.

"On landing in Denver—which, un-coincidentally, is now the most popular spring break destination for American students—you can call a limo from 420AirportPickup which will drive you to a dispensary and then let you smoke in the back while you cruise on to a cannabis-friendly hotel (some style themselves "bud 'n' breakfast")," reported *The Economist*, a longtime proponent of marijuana legalization, in 2016. "You can take a marijuana cookery course, or sign up for joint-rolling lessons. Dispensaries offer coupons, loyalty points, happy hours and all the other tricks in the marketing book."

To explore the nuances of the drug legalization and its military counterpart, the War on Drugs, we head upstate to Mineola, New York, for the New York State Debate Championship. Of course, the appropriate setting for this debate is a Catholic high school, chock-full of posters about abstinence and abortion.

The irony of our venue aside, the debate follows a predictable structure: everyone agrees that weed should be legal, which as we'll see is the strong millennial consensus on the issue, and the debate quickly progresses to a discussion about the War on Drugs in Latin America, and how the U.S. can mitigate the damage it's already done there.

Sex, Drugs & Rock 'n' Roll

Drugs have been a secret indulgence of young people for centuries. Boomers smoked weed at Woodstock. Their parents drank in speakeasies during Prohibition. Even Stone Age humans are said to have cultivated drugs to achieve a high. Today's young people are no different. The majority of our classmates in America are said to have used illicit drugs, with daily marijuana use at a 35-year high and cocaine and ecstasy use on the rise.[1] Meanwhile, the trend in public opinion is toward leniency in drug laws. Support for legalization of weed is at an all-time high of 58 percent. Today, four states—Colorado, Washington, Oregon and Alaska—and the District of Columbia have already legalized marijuana. An additional 14 states have decriminalized possession.[2]

The real champions of marijuana legalization are young people—including 63 percent of young conservatives and 77 percent of young liberals. The consensus is pretty astounding. Jack once spoke at a political conference in a short debate on the topic of weed legalization. At the end of the debate, the audience voted on a winner. Jack advocated for prohibition at the time and was trounced 62-2 (included his own vote). It's easy to pass off young people's support for legal weed as "kids being kids," but young people seem to have well thought-out reasons for legalization and the movement is now mainstream.

How Bad Is Weed for You, Anyway?

When pushed to explain their support for legal weed, young people say that the question of marijuana legalization comes down to a value judgment: is weed so bad for you that the government ought to ban it? As a country, we do believe that the government should, to an extent, protect individuals from themselves. That's why the drinking age is 21, prostitution is illegal, and physician-assisted suicide is banned. At the same time, the government allows adults to make bad choices: McDonald's is not illegal despite the fact that consumption of it products increases the likelihood of obesity, and alcohol prohibition was abolished decades ago. Where on this spectrum does drug use fall?

Certainly cocaine, heroin and other hard drugs seem harmful enough to be deemed illegal: these substances are widely known to cause serious health effects and in some cases, create violent tendencies in their users. Crack cocaine is widely blamed for the violence epidemic of the 1980s. Weed, by contrast, doesn't seem so bad. While studies have shown that marijuana decreases focus, can cause automotive accidents, and may have long-term effects on the brains of heavy smokers, recreational use has not been linked to violence or lethal diseases. Its short-run impacts rival those of alcohol. Drunk driving, for example, kills one person an hour—leading to more than 10,000 casualties annually.

Stephanie Brito, a millennial leader from Miami, believes that weed is no worse than alcohol. "When you compare the effects of marijuana to the effects of alcohol ... alcohol causes a lot more deaths," she said. 70 percent of Americans agree with Brito, reporting that they view alcohol as more harmful than marijuana.

Brito and her fellow legal weed proponents recognize that marijuana is a "gateway drug," encouraging users to progress to more dangerous drugs, like cocaine, heroin, and prescription drugs. Scientific studies in peer reviewed academic journals have shown that cannabinoids decrease the reactivity of dopamine reward centers later in life in mice. Rats previously administered cannabinoids were likely to react more strongly to other drugs, like morphine. But in this sense, there's no convincing evidence that marijuana is any worse than alcohol or nicotine, which have similar "gateway" effects.

Looking past health effects to social effects, alcohol could be even worse than marijuana. "When we look at social issues with marijuana and alcohol, the social issues with marijuana come from the fact that it's illegal, but the social issues with alcohol come from the fact that, for example, a family can be torn apart from someone who's alcoholic," said Brito.

Denny Baek, a California millennial leader, contrasts the effects of marijuana with cigarettes, and says that certainly from a standpoint of saving lives, he thinks cigarettes are far worse. "There's no reason that marijuana should be criminalized while tobacco is something that you can smoke before you can even drink alcohol. It destroys your body," he explained. "And yes it's a personal choice, but there's secondhand smoke; it hurts other people. ... It's an addictive substance. ... My father has tried to quit for 20-something years now and has been unsuccessful."

The New York Times endorsed this viewpoint, advocating for an end to weed prohibition in July 2014. It wrote: "It took 13 years for the United States to come to its senses and end Prohibition, 13 years in which people kept drinking, otherwise law-abiding citizens became criminals, and crime syndicates arose and flourished. It has been more than 40 years since Congress passed the current ban on marijuana, inflicting great harm on society just to prohibit a substance far less dangerous than alcohol."

But while the millennial argument that weed is "just as bad" as alcohol and cigarettes has some merit, it is not the silver bullet argument that proponents allege it to be. Just because one harmful substance is legal doesn't mean another should be too. A study of college students found that those who smoked weed had worse critical skills related to attention; memory and learning were seriously diminished. A study of postal workers found that employees who tested positive for marijuana had 55 percent more accidents, 85 percent more injuries, and a 75 percent increase in being absent from work.

Marijuana has been shown to increase the likelihood of motor vehicle accidents as well. This is itself a major concern for some millennials, who already struggle with the impacts of DUI-related accidents. "I have a lot of friends who smoke weed. ... I am personally undecided. I am leaning toward legalization and taxing and, you know, introducing it to stores, but the downside that I would see, even if it were regulated, I'm worried about things like DUIs. ... That teenagers, with whom it's so popular with, will go out and smoke and then drive," said Samantha Paul, a millennial leader from California.

And the downsides of marijuana legalization can be serious. While marijuana is technically not addicting, some of those who start using it recreationally cannot stop. Baek said he's seen this in some of his classmates. His friend is an insomniac who began smoking pot to help him relax. But after a while, he wasn't able to sleep without it. "While it used to be a struggle to fall asleep, once he had the use of this aid, it became impossible," Baek said. "After a while, marijuana wasn't working for him ... so he started to move on to harder things."

A Gateway to Jail

If millennials seem torn over the health effects, there is a consensus among young people that sending thousands of young Americans to jail for marijuana possession is disastrous for our economy and the stability of the criminal justice system and destroys families, creating a cycle of poverty and violence. Rohan Marwaha, a millennial leader from Massachusetts, said it's surprising to him that the United States is spending billions of dollars sending people to jail for minor offenses, instead of taxing marijuana. "You step back and you ask, is it really worth it considering how it affects people?" he said.

Nationwide, the police made 8.2 million marijuana arrests between 2001 and 2010, 88 percent for possession. In 2011, there were more arrests for marijuana possession than for all violent crimes put together. These arrests cost taxpayers more than $3.6 billion a year in direct costs and even more after accounting for the indirect costs of spending welfare dollars to feed the families of incarcerated bread-winners, who could otherwise contribute to the economy.[3] Meanwhile, the reallocation of limited police resources to fight drug crimes can lead to serious crimes going unpunished: half of violent crimes and 80 percent of property crimes unsolved, according to the FBI.[4] Are we making the right tradeoffs?

The biggest concern among young people regarding the prohibition of weed, however, is its implications with respect to equality and justice. Blacks in America are 3.7 times more likely to be arrested for marijuana possession, despite using the drug at approximately the same rate as whites. In Washington, D.C., blacks were eight times more likely to be arrested, before marijuana was decriminalized.[5] Likewise, blacks are 10 times as likely as whites to go to jail for drug offenses, according to the ACLU. These African Americans, particularly young black men, pay the price for years to come—with arrest records harming their job prospects and ability to support their family. Depriving boys of their fathers and preventing young black men from finding employment helps perpetuate a cycle of crime and poverty.

In her controversial book, *The New Jim Crow*, Michelle Alexander points out the "cruel paradox" of drug legalization. She said in an interview that "40 years of impoverished black kids getting prison time for selling weed, and their families and futures destroyed," and "now, white men are planning to get rich doing precisely the same thing?"

Alexander begins her book with a story about Jarvious Cotton—whose great-great-grandfather had been denied the vote as a slave, whose great-grandfather was killed by the Ku Klux Klan for attempting to vote, whose grandfather was prevented from voting by Klan intimidation, and whose father was prevented from voting through poll taxes and literacy tests. Cotton cannot vote because he is a convicted felon due to laws that prohibit marijuana possession. In South Carolina, she recounts a raid on a school in which SWAT team members handcuffed students as young as 14 and sent drug-sniffing dogs to search their book bags for marijuana. No drugs or weapons were found and the majority of those searched were students of color.

Though Alexander's comparison is provocative, it is shockingly accurate: since marijuana laws do not decrease consumption, their main effect has been to target and arrest African American men. "A classic civil rights issue is equal treatment under the law," attorney Harry Levine told *VICE News*. "If you have enforcement against some people but not other people, then you have a civil rights question," Levine said. For many cities and for young Americans, this is the primary reason to support marijuana decriminalization. [6]

"I think the idea, the excuse that authorities would use towards arresting someone who's African American and smoking is, 'Oh this is their neighborhood, this is where they come from, so we have to be harsher on them,'" Paul said. "I think it's unfair." Paul suggested that police resources would be better used elsewhere to combat rape and white-collar crime, which have low conviction rates despite causing a much greater amount of damage to their communities.

Brito sees racial discrimination in drug enforcement in her community. "When you see somebody who's a minority doing drugs, it's a stereotype; you're like, oh, this person is just smoking marijuana because they're not doing good in school, they don't care about anything, they're just on the streets causing violence, whereas you see one white suburban kid on the street smoking marijuana and you're like, oh, he's just chilling listening to Pink Floyd," she said. "I've seen it myself. There's this area in my town called Main Street and people smoke there and if you're black, you'll get arrested, whereas all of my white friends who have smoked there, they say, 'Yeah I ran into a cop and he gave me a warning.' So it's something you can see your-self when you see which people you know who are arrested for these things."

For juveniles, being arrested for drug possession can initiate or intensify a long life of crime. Researchers at Oxford University and the University of Essex have published a number of papers discussing "labeling theory," which argues that labeling young people as criminals early in their lives makes them substantially more likely to commit more violent offenses in the future, because juvenile offenders internalize societal labels and begin to conform to them. Locking up thousands of youths for minor drug offenses may also propel them toward committing more crime for practical reasons. Many former felons struggle to find work once they are freed from prison. Likewise, in jail they may learn to become better criminals and develop a criminal network.[7]

For these reasons and more, a majority of millennials believes that non-violent drug offenders should be able to have their criminal records sealed, so that they are only accessible by court order. Just 35 percent of seniors support this position.[8]

Mandatory Minimums Create Injustice

For marijuana offenders and peddlers of more dangerous drugs, the punishments can be draconian. Many states have "three-strikes" provisions in their laws that require courts to heavily penalize drug offenders after repeated bouts with the law—even if they are only arrested for minor possession. Mandatory minimums restrict judges' ability to offer what they perceive to be fair sentences, instead requiring judges to pass down "one-size-fit-all" sentences. Originally crafted by the Nixon Administration as an effort to crack down on crime, the laws are still on the books, because neither political party has the courage to abolish them. In the 30 years since the war on drugs was initiated, thousands of Americans have seen their lives destroyed by unnecessarily harsh penalties that don't fit the circumstances of their crimes. This is a miscarriage of justice.

Brenda Valencia, for example, was handed a 10-year sentence with no chance for parole after unknowingly driving her aunt to a drug deal. "This case is the perfect example of why the minimum mandatory sentences and the sentencing guidelines are not only absurd, but an insult to justice," the judge admitted afterwards. "This young lady does not need to be sentenced to 151 months without parole; however, the law is the law, and we're all bound to obey it. But it's absolutely ridiculous to impose this sentence in this case, considering the degree of participation that this defendant had in the crime."[9]

Strict enforcement of drug laws and disproportionate punishments distort justice and fail to serve the interests of the American public. No wonder that pollsters find that between 63 percent and 77 percent of Americans support eliminating mandatory minimums.[10]

The Military Front and the War on Drugs

In America, the War on Drugs is seen through the domestic lens: we view it as a war being fought in the inner cities to reduce access to drugs and lock up dealers. In fact, American demand for illicit drugs fuels violence south of the border, where cartels wreak havoc in Mexico and Central America.

Meanwhile, U.S. initiatives in the region only exacerbate the problem—pushing drugs further south and encouraging cartels to adopt more dangerous methods of pedaling drugs north. A meta-analysis of 306 studies by the Urban Health Research Initiative found that analogous to the case of alcohol prohibition in the United States, strict enforcement of drug policies in Latin America has only increased violence and organized crime in a few key ways.

Strengthening Powerful Cartels. With massive incentives to traffic drugs, U.S. enforcement only leads to a survival of the fittest scenario in which the most ruthless and violent cartels survive. As

University of New South Wales professors Lisa Maher and David Dixon explain in "The Cost of Crackdowns," "Intensive policing encourages the development of more organized, professional, and enduring forms of criminality [by] increasing the complexity and sophistication of the market, [which] encourage[es] functional specialization and hierarchical differentiation."[11]

Territorial Disputes. By disrupting existing drug markets, strict enforcement of drug laws leads to turf wars as dealers compete for market share. Researchers Bruce Benson and Paul Goldstein found that during the U.S. Merida Initiative, drugs moved south into Central America and existing trafficking networks were disrupted, expanding the "radius of violence."

In *The Economic Anatomy of a Drug War*, David W. Rasmussen found that increased drug enforcement forces cartels to spread out and develop new trafficking routes, which increases the number of cities where they wreak havoc. While drug lords cannot be allowed to run rampant, fighting their supply without reducing demand creates perverse incentives toward violence.

Relocation of Police Resources. Academicians believe that criminal networks are sophisticated. Because of the threat of jail time, criminals become aware of trends in policing and react accordingly. Researchers write that as police reallocate their resources to deal with drug crimes, criminals commit more violent and property crimes because they believe that the police are focusing on other criminals. Studies of drug enforcement in Florida in the 1980s found that increased enforcement of drug laws led to an increase in property theft and other crimes.[12]

U.S. demand for illicit drugs is destroying thousands of lives every year—leading to the death of civilians, breaking up families, and destroying communities. Kevin Casas-Zamora of the Brookings Institution writes that "35,000 people, overwhelmingly young men, at the peak of their productive and reproductive lives, may be dying in

LAC [Latin America and the Caribbean] yearly as a result of the black market in drugs that the current policies render into existence."[13]

Meanwhile, since the U.S. Merida Initiative—a security initiative among the United States, Mexico and Central America intended to combat drug trafficking—was initiated in 2007, Mexican violence increased eight-fold in the ensuing years: in 2007, there were 2,680 drug-related homicides in Mexico. This jumped to 6,837 in 2008, 9,614 in 2009, and 15,413 in 2010, according to data released by the Mexican government. Drug-related homicides increased 60 percent in 2010, and 11 percent in 2011.[14]

On the whole, prohibition-related violence has led to the death of more than 60,000 people since 2006, according to the Drug Policy Alliance, and has spread from roughly 46 municipalities in 2007 to 225 today.[15] Meanwhile, human rights allegations against the military in this region increased by 900 percent.[16] It's not a pretty picture.

U.S. drug strategy in Latin America has revolved largely around decapitation of cartel leaders. Unfortunately, cartels have reacted to the loss of their leaders by fragmenting, rather than disappearing. In 2006, there were just six major cartels operating in Mexico; by 2010, that number had doubled, according to *Nexos*, a Mexican magazine. Local trafficking organizations exploded during the same time frame, from 11 to 114.[17]

And these cartels are coming to a city near you. According to the U.S. Justice Department, Mexican cartels now operate in more than 1,000 U.S. cities.[18] Sylvia Longmire wrote for CNN that the tens of thousands of cartel members in America are a bigger national security threat than even terrorism. These cartels are silent killers, spurring violence that may be less publicized than terrorist attacks, but just as devastating in inner cities.[19]

Even nonviolent campaigns involving crop destruction seem to be ineffective. The United States' supply-side approach to eradicating drug production involves fumigating drug crops. Unfortunately, history shows that this approach fails because the potential for profit in selling illegal drugs in the United States is so high that illegal drug cultivation will simply move elsewhere. "Undiminished demand for drugs, combined with the ... inexhaustible supply of cultivatable land and extremely high levels of poverty found through Latin America, assure that new producers will arise to fill the void" when we reduce drug production in a given location, researchers at The Drug Policy Alliance explained.[20]

The prevalence of organized violence in Latin America—fueled by U.S. demand for illicit drugs—destabilizes the democratic regimes of those countries. In Mexico, the rise of cartels has contributed to corruption of public servants, a breakdown in the judicial system, and bribes to police forces that render them useless. As cartels infiltrate these democratic institutions, they weaken rule of law and public infrastructure.

"When I cross the border from the U.S. to Mexico, nothing is the same. The roads aren't built the same, the way people talk and deal with their issues, nothing is the same. It's a completely different world, and a lot of people don't see that. I go to Mexico every week, my family lives there, and we support them. It's a completely different world," explained Jennifer Guzman, a millennial leader from Arizona whose parents are Mexican immigrants.

"In Mexico, there are mixed feelings. Most people are going to tell you [cartels] are very bad, yes, very bad. I agree it's terrible, but at the same time, they are doing more for their people than the Mexican government is. They are giving back to the communities. Believe it or not, this is what they do: they do give money, they do help people out, they do a lot. The Mexican government isn't doing anything. So that's why a lot of people who are from the poorer areas of Mexico, it's really difficult to set apart," Guzman explained.

She believes that poverty helps to fuel support for the cartels, and that violence doesn't address this root cause. "We saw a lot of violence going on in Mexico, drug cartels, something that America doesn't necessarily need to get involved in," she said. "It's not uncommon in Mexico to be getting food and then two blocks down to hear gunshots."

With this grave state of affairs, it is no wonder that 82 percent of Americans believe the War on Drugs failed.[21] Instead of focusing on destroying supply, millennial leaders like Guzman believe that the United States should begin by decriminalizing marijuana and destroying demand for illicit drugs at home. Drug violence in South and Central America will not end with decreased U.S. demand alone, but the most important step the United States can take in reducing such violence is to allow for legal cultivation and purchase of marijuana.

"The U.S. should be focusing on securing [our borders]," Guzman said. "I don't think they should be going too deep into Mexico because that's not doing anything and it's not going to do anything, and it's going to stir the pot. ... And that's what they've been doing the past couple of years. ... It's not going to happen in the next couple of decades, that's just what the culture is right now; it's centered around [drugs]. Music itself, *corrido*, the most popular type of music in Mexico, it's about drug cartels."

And the violence isn't just in Mexico. As a result of the War on Drugs, violence has spread across South America. Sarah Angel, a millennial from Texas, told us about her family's story in Colombia. "Both of my parents are from Medellin, Colombia, and they grew up in the Pablo Escobar era. Especially when they were in college and med school, that was when the bombings were happening; that was when if you honked a horn, and the guy in front of you was a [drug lord], he would shoot you," Angel recalls. "And that not only affected my family, but the whole society in Latin America, and the United States."

Millennials believe that U.S. drug policy has failed both at home and abroad—that's why nearly three-quarters of our generation supports legalization. Mass incarceration is costing billions of dollars and robbing families of their breadwinners, while intervention in Latin America has done little to curb the spread of violence south of our border and failed to prevent trafficking of drugs in our cities. Nonetheless, neither Democrats nor Republicans are proposing fresh ideas to reduce cartel violence and address America's deeply flawed approach to domestic drug violations.

The Political Machine and Prison-Industrial Complex

Democrats and Republicans largely ignore marijuana legalization and the War on Drugs as important political issues. Neither party has a stated platform on the issue—in fact, most candidates share widely different views on legalization, no matter their political leaning. For most American politicians the topic of drugs is a sensitive one. The truth is that laws aside, one in two Americans has smoked weed. Current and past presidential contenders acknowledge having smoked marijuana in college, including Presidents Barack Obama, George W. Bush and Bill Clinton, and contenders Jeb Bush, John Kerry, and Al Gore.

The coalition of supporters for marijuana legalization includes progressives and libertarians, uniting across the political spectrum. But this lobby is weak and lacks funding, especially as compared with a mammoth prison-industrial complex lobbying against cannabis legalization. It's not even subtle. Police unions, private prisons, and prison guard unions have lobbied heavily against legalization measures, outspending their opponents in local legislative battles. In California, for example, the California Correctional Peace Officers Association spent $1 million fighting against a measure that would have "reduced sentences and parole times for nonviolent drug offenders while emphasizing drug treatment over prison." Joining them are the pharmaceutical lobby and alcohol companies, which generally oppose anti-vice laws.[22]

If only it were morally opposed conservatives driving the marijuana prohibition movement. At least then we could have a rational, open, respectful debate. But no—marijuana prohibition is largely driven by greed. Marijuana legalization would eliminate Byrne grants, which generated $2.4 billion for police in 2014 and property forfeitures, which sum to approximately $1 billion between 2002 and 2012, according to *The Nation*. Ironically, these police unions aren't even representing the views of their members—they are representing the economic interest of the prison-industrial complex. *Law Officer* magazine reports that 66 percent of cops support marijuana reform, while 37 percent said they favored legalization.[23]

For-profit prisons, by contrast, literally see their profit margins threatened by reducing the size of the prison population. The industry spends approximately $1 million a year on lobbying and is considered having been instrumental in "pioneer[ing] some of the toughest sentencing laws on the books today, like mandatory minimums for nonviolent drug offenders, 'three strikes' laws, and 'truth in sentencing' laws," according to *The Nation*. Likewise, prison guard unions are fundamentally opposed to prison closures, which threaten their jobs. American Federation of State, County, and Municipal Employees (AFSCME), which represents many guards in public prisons, has fought tooth and nail against prison closures in the past.[24]

Big Pharma outspends police unions and private prisons by a long shot, though their lobbying efforts are much more widespread. Drug companies are said to oppose marijuana legalization because it would threaten to cannibalize their business of selling marijuana-alternatives like Sativex, Marinol and Cesamet. Joining Big Pharma is the tobacco and alcohol lobby, which fears that if marijuana is legal, it will erode their profits.[25]

"The only difference now compared to the times of alcohol prohibition is that, in the times of alcohol prohibition, law enforcement—the police and judges—got their money in brown paper bags," said Stephen Downing, a retired LAPD deputy chief. "Today, they get their money through legitimate, systematic programs run by the federal government. That's why they're using their lobbying organizations to fight every reform." Downing said that just as with

Prohibition, the War on Drugs enriches law enforcement tasked with preventing abuse of the law.

The fact that Democrats and Republicans alike refuse to take a stance on the War on Drugs is political gamesmanship at its worst. If Republicans stand for the rule of law, then a law that is universally violated should be taken off the books. If Democrats stand for civil rights, then one of the biggest civil rights issues of the 21st century needs to be actively addressed.

Neither party sees substantial votes to be gained by taking a strong stance on the issue. So they cower and avoid discussing it. The will of corporate lobbyists is more powerful than the will of the American people. Anyway, when politicians do drugs, they get to be rehabilitated, and often get reelected. When a young African American male gets stopped for possession, his consequences are nowhere near as lenient. This hypocrisy upsets millennial leaders.

President Obama recently said that legalizing drugs would not reduce trafficking of illegal narcotics in the Americas. Instead, he called for "strong economics, rules of law, and a law enforcement infrastructure." Hillary Clinton, the presumptive Democratic nominee, is stately ambivalent on the issue, saying that she wants to "wait and see" until more research is available on the topic. It is unclear exactly what she is waiting for.

When it comes to the War on Drugs, President Obama's most notable achievement is Operation Fast and Furious—in which the Bureau of Alcohol, Tobacco, Firearms, and Explosives inadvertently helped cartels smuggle semiautomatic weapons, which are illegal in Mexico, south of the U.S. border. During the operation, the federal government intended to trace the weapons it sold to cartels to track their sources. In a cruel trick of fate, the guns were traced—only after they were used to kill a U.S. drug enforcement officer.[26]

In his 2015 budget, President Obama requested $25.4 billion to spend on the War on Drugs—to spend disrupting producers and through educational programs and drug treatment to reduce demand.

Treating drug abuse as a health issue, rather than a criminal issue or an educational issue, would be a better approach, and would cost much less than those billions.

Republicans have likewise been slow to call for marijuana legalization. Jeb Bush opposed a constitutional amendment that would have legalized marijuana in Florida, despite having himself smoked weed in college. Sen. Rand Paul—a well-known libertarian who supports marijuana legalization—bashed Bush for what he called hypocrisy.

"When Jeb was a very wealthy kid at a very elite school, he used marijuana but didn't get caught, didn't have to go to prison," Paul told *The Kelly File*. "I think it shows some hypocrisy that's going to be very difficult for young people to understand, why we'd put a 65-year-old guy in jail for medical marijuana."

Republicans have a disappointing legacy when it comes to the War on Drugs, having initiated much of its worst policies, including mandatory minimums, strict enforcement of drug laws, and support for mass incarceration, not to mention the initiation of a violent displacement strategy in Mexico that only fragmented violence and sloshed drugs around instead of meaningfully moving the dial on their eradication. In an effort to be "tough on crime," the party has initiated devastating policies that have clearly failed.

Millennials believe that we can do better. Because we acknowledge reality, young people oppose both Democrats and Republicans. Instead, young Americans support common-sense reform.

Solution: Legalize Pot

Marijuana is arguably less dangerous than alcohol and cigarettes. Instead of regulating and taxing it for profit, the U.S. government has engaged in the destructive practice of prohibiting it. As a result, prohibition has spawned a black market that fuels violence in South America and in inner cities. Nearly three-quarters of millennials believe that marijuana should be legal, in part because it is currently leading to the mass incarceration of a generation of black youth and has wreaked havoc on an entire continent. As *The New York Times* noted—the United States should have learned its lesson from alcohol prohibition a century ago. The rise of bootleggers caused far more harm than the substance being banned. The same is true today about marijuana.

But millennial support for marijuana legalization isn't only theoretical—it has practical implications. "If we have some sort of state-managed regulation of marijuana and were able to control what's going into marijuana and that it is not being sold from the street, we could use it to better our country. ... We could reduce a lot of this petty crime that's happening," Marwaha said.

Legalizing weed would have an additional benefit—it would help generate desperately needed tax revenue for U.S. states. In 2012, 300 economists, including three Nobel Laureates, signed a petition arguing that legalizing marijuana would save the United States $13.7 billion dollars—$6 billion in taxes and $7.7 billion in enforcement costs. The economists called for an "open and honest" debate on the topic. So far, that hasn't happened because politicians on both sides of the aisle are afraid to take a stance on the issue.[27]

On both sides of the political spectrum—but especially for Republicans, who struggle to find support among minorities and millennials—turning marijuana legalization into a central platform would yield strong political returns. The issue uniquely appeals to three crucial demographics: blacks, who are victims of mass incarceration; Hispanics, whose home countries bear the brunt of cartel violence; and millennials, who support marijuana legalization by the widest margins. At the same time, decriminalization is consistent with the idea of small government. It's a win-win.

Voters who oppose marijuana legalization don't tend to view it as a crucial issue. We no longer live in a time where the term "soft on crime" can end political careers. But legalizing marijuana has major upsides for both political parties. The politicians who are smart enough to recognize the political opportunity here will reap the benefits.

"Most millennials, even those who aren't involved in politics, would support legalization because of what they see online," explained Chicago millennial Eileen Brady. "I can't go on Facebook without seeing a comparison chart between the harmful effects of marijuana and the harmful effects of alcohol."

Solution: End Mandatory Minimums

Mandatory minimums have robbed too many young Americans of potentially meaningful future lives. Young people make mistakes and it is absurd that drug runners face harsher sentences than rapists and that murderers get out of jail before getaway drivers in cocaine transactions.

Young people believe in our judicial system. We are realists who recognize that a level of subjectivity is necessary for the punishment to fit that crime, and that judges are more than capable of meting out jail sentences than legislators. No judge should be forced to issue a judgment that she believes is immoral. *Rolling Stone* has called mandatory minimums "The Nation's Shame." Millennials agree.

With such strong bipartisan support for ending mandatory minimums, criminal justice reform should be a top priority for Congress. John Bennett, a blogger for *CQ Roll Call*, suggests that President Obama and Republicans in Congress could take on this issue before the end of the president's term, capitalizing on their common ground. "As Obama pushes for Congress to do even more on the issue during his final months, he just might find a willing ally in the newly installed House speaker," he wrote of Paul Ryan.

Solution: Invest in Strong Institutions

The War on Drugs in Mexico and Latin America has eased in recent years, with a welcome decrease in violence across the border. Millennials believe the United States should avoid military involvement in Mexico and instead invest in supporting strong democratic institutions south of its border. Investing in police force training and helping its neighbors build strong judiciaries will do much to help create stability. As a consequence, Mexico, Colombia, Guatemala, and other Latin American countries will be better prepared to fight their own cartels.

When it comes to supply-side enforcement, the U.S. government and its peers in Mexico and Central America should prioritize violence reduction over drug eradication. The latter policy, including crackdowns on cartels, leads to short-term escalations of violence: what has been described as a "Whack-A-Mole" game, in which drug production is not eliminated, but instead spreads.

These millennial beliefs are in line with those of South American leaders. "Enforcement resources should be directed towards the most disruptive, problematic, and violent elements of the trade—alongside international cooperation on the crackdown on corruption and money laundering," said former Brazilian president Fernando Henrique Cardoso.[28]

From a foreign policy perspective, Americans should financially support the Mexican government in its efforts to fight drug cartels—since it is American drug demand that spawned them in the first place. It should continue successful intelligence sharing with Mexican authorities and work in tandem with the police forces to arrest and eliminate drug kingpins. But restraint will be key to prevent violence escalation.

Solution: Toward a Public Health Approach

Broadly, the United States needs to begin treating drug abuse as a public health issue, as opposed to a crime issue. This paradigm shift will involve investment in needle exchange programs, rehabilitation, and education. Already, this is happening with heroin addiction in the United States, which has been called "the Ebola of northern New England."

Prevention, treatment, and recovery centers are sprouting across the country to help combat the heroin/prescription drug crisis in the United States. Today, 67 percent of Americans prefer treatment to prosecution for drug abusers, according to Pew. In Massachusetts, more than 3,000 people complete acute detox every month.[29]

Not only will a public health approach toward all drugs—not just heroin—save lives, but it will also save the state money that would otherwise be spent on incarceration. It costs $53,000 to incarcerate a prisoner for a year, as compared with $2,500 for outpatient substance abuse treatment, *The Boston Globe* reported. The National Institute on Drug Abuse reports that "every dollar invested in addiction treatment programs yields a return of between $4 and $7 in reduced drug-related crime, criminal justice costs, and theft." When savings related to health care are included, total savings can exceed costs by a ratio of 12 to 1. Talk about clear-cut.[30]

"We need to be pro-life for the 16-year-old drug addict on the floor of the county lockup," New Jersey Governor Chris Christie said. "If we're really going to be the pro-life party, we should be pro-life for the whole life, and that means giving people a chance to reclaim their lives."

In the last decade, heroin-related overdose deaths increased 286 percent. "This is the biggest public health issue of our generation," said Dean LeMire, a Delaware resident who began shooting up heroin at age 25.[31] "I did everything I could to get whatever drugs I needed just to not be sick," LeMire told *The Guardian*. "It was a horrible existence; it was incredibly lonely. I was no longer partying with or near friends. I was all alone."

Taking the Issue into Our Own Hands

As our leaders refuse to take on drug reform, millennials have decided to spearhead the fight. "The weed warriors are back," declared the *Los Angeles Times*. Young people across the country are mobilizing around pot legalization, tired of waiting for our politicians to take the lead. "We have a culture that endorses binge drinking but condemns the use of marijuana," charged Nick Watkins, a leader with Students for Sensible Drug Policy in his testimony before the D.C. City Council, when the body debated marijuana legalization. Devon Tackels, an organizer with the not-for-profit group, said that youth interest is "surging."[32]

Not everyone is happy about the end of marijuana prohibition. President Obama actually went out of his way to tell young people to stop worrying about weed. "It shouldn't be young people's biggest priority," Obama said. Of course it isn't our top priority—jobs are—but that doesn't mean young people are going to forget that the prohibition on weed has real and important damaging effects on our society. With even Democrats ambivalent about comprehensive drug policy reform, national change doesn't seem to be coming soon.[33]

But millennials aren't waiting for politicians to take the lead. We are fighting for criminal justice reform in our states. Recognizing that the vast majority of Americans, and especially young people, support drug policy reform, we are lobbying our legislators to take action on the issue immediately—and we're winning. Already, more than a dozen states have decriminalized marijuana and four have legalized it. Twenty-three states have legalized medical marijuana. Pew Research reports that as politicians fight over the "coveted millennial vote," our generation is forcing leaders to recognize marijuana as a central political issue, often for the first time.[34]

Young people are aggressively campaigning for marijuana legalization because it's such a straightforward issue—pragmatists across the board can agree that pot legalization is common sense. Already, this movement is making an impact. In December 2015, Deborah Bonello reported that loosening marijuana laws in the United States has already helped drive down the price of marijuana, cutting into cartel profits. "Small-scale growers here in the [Mexican] state of Sinaloa, one of the country's biggest production areas, said that over the last four years the amount they receive per kilogram has fallen from $100 to $30," she wrote for the *Los Angeles Times*.

Market economics are playing a key role here. As the United States eliminates the sale of illegal drugs by legalizing marijuana, we also are able to reduce violence south of the border. "Changes on the other side of the border are making marijuana less profitable for organizations like the Cartel de Sinaloa," said Antonio Mazzitelli, the representative in Mexico for the United Nations Office on Drugs and Crime. As a result, many farmers, Bonello reports, are switching over to produce more profitable crops. "The price decline appears to have led to reduced marijuana production in Mexico and a drop in trafficking to the U.S," she reported.[35]

Between 2013 and 2014, the marijuana industry grew from $1.5 billion in sales to $2.7 billion. If millennials continue pushing for reform, they can win the battle for prohibition, and likely save many lives from the threat of cartel violence. Let's hope so.

CONCLUSION

Young people are issue-based pragmatic voters, driven by values and evidence to unite around common-sense solutions. Drug legalization is a perfect case study, demonstrating how a generation of "radical realists" is uniting across the political spectrum to support an end of the decades-long marijuana ban. By placing political pressure on American leaders and taking action in their states, young people have already had a dramatic impact, changing the pace of the dialogue and moving U.S. public policy toward reform.

On the home front, this means that states are decriminalizing and regulating weed, and the federal government is moving closer to widespread criminal justice reform. On the military front, the United States is scaling back its operations in Mexico and Latin America, as a demand-based approach takes advantage of market economics to reduce drug production in Mexico. As a result, thousands of young people today will be able to avoid lives marred by criminal records they don't deserve, and fewer young Mexicans will die in the War on Drugs.

Young people need to keep fighting for change. It's working.

Equality For All: Freedom is Nonnegotiable

I f millennials had their way, we would just delete this chapter. The topics we highlight here are all of the issues that millennials believe go without saying—that women and African Americans should be treated equally, that homosexuality is not a crime against God but a personal choice, and that police violence against blacks needs to stop.

For young people, equality is reason to celebrate. For older generations, it is source of misgiving. On June 26—12 years to the day after the Supreme Court reversed a Texas ban on same-sex sodomy in *Lawrence v. Texas*—the Supreme Court legalized gay marriage.

While conservatives mourned the decision—and Kim Davis gained national notoriety for refusing to grant gay marriage licenses in Kentucky—young people started to party. In excitement that followed, millennials changed their Facebook profile pictures to show their solidarity with the marriage equality movement and hung up rainbow flags, a symbol of the movement, in the windows of their homes.

In this chapter, the final issue-based chapter in this book, we'll explore the "nonnegotiables"—social issues that unite millennials across the political spectrum. To this end, we make the last stop of our journey in Philadelphia, Pennsylvania. We're here for a debate tournament whose topic is the Voting Rights Act and civil rights in the 21 century. The city is an appropriate place to end our journey for two others reasons as well: first, it will host the Democratic National Convention in the summer of 2016 and second, it's the city where we now live and go to school.

Socialized in a Culture of Tolerance

Justin Greenman, a millennial leader from New Jersey, knows no world other than one of tolerance. He's unquestionably comfortable as we sit and talk about marriage equality, which he attributes to his age. "My dad, he grew up in the '70s. My grandfather, he grew up in the 1930s. … When my grandfather grew up he could be arrested for being a homosexual," but today homosexuality is almost universally supported by our generation. And with these changing times, our leaders need to be able to adapt to fundamentally different social norms, he said.

Just down the hall, Kyle Walton, who hails from Spokane Valley, Washington, explains just how far we've come. "I think that this is one of the first generations that's really able to unify and kind of create a movement toward equality for just about everybody," he said. "You see the rise of popularity of feminism, and the rise of respect for people with disabilities, and the rise of respect for people that suffer from depression; literally just about anything, people are a lot more accepted, and really, our generation preaches that."

Walton recognizes that change is slow, but he says there is "overwhelming" support among millennials for the idea that equality wins out. "I don't think the generation before us would have ever been talking about taking gender labels off of toys, but that's something we're talking about right now," he said. While millennials have nuanced and balanced political views regarding many of the issues that will shape America's future, Kyle says, this issue is certainly not one. Millennials will fight for social change with vigor and resilience, so much so that social change has become the new third rail of American politics.

Women's Rights

The fight for gender equality started decades before millennials were even born, but it has become a rallying cry for young men and women alike. While millennials may sometimes be overzealous in enforcing political correctness, politicians need to understand the underlying point—that millennials take equality for granted and will not vote for politicians who are overtly bigoted. Oddly enough, many politicians don't seem to have learned this lesson.

When asked how education in America became so mediocre, Mississippi Governor Phil Bryant, a Republican, responded: "I think both parents started working. And the mom is in the workplace." Former Rep. Todd Akin (R-MO) notoriously said, "If it's a legitimate rape, the female body has ways to try to shut that whole thing down." These comments help solidify the impression that the Republican Party is behind the times. Republicans are losing votes from winnable demographics by nature of their offensive comments. It's just not a rational strategy.

Even Senate Minority Leader Harry Reid, a Democrat, has made sexist remarks, calling Sen. Kirsten Gillibrand (D-NY) the Senate's "hottest member" in a speech. The late Sen. Arlen Spectator (D-PA) made waves when he told Michelle Bachman (R-MN) in 2010, "I'm going to treat you like a lady ... now act like one." None of these comments are acceptable. Not only are millennials more tolerant than past generations—having grown up with diversity—but also we recognize more sharply than ever the perils of being labeled a bigot. Republicans call this political correctness. We call it common sense.

Millennials know that there is still a lot of work to be done to create a level playing field for men and women and we want our politicians to take the lead in eliminating structural inequality. Millennials would start with equal pay. Today, women earn 80 cents on the dollar compared to men of similar backgrounds. While the wage gap is not entirely due to overt discrimination, studies have found that 19 percent of the wage gap cannot be explained by women's choice of careers or decisions about how many hours to work. In other words, there is a glass ceiling.[1]

As a society, we need to simplify the "labyrinth" that is a woman's career with good public policy. Christy Uffelman, a partner at consulting firm Align Leadership, explains that "women have specific obstacles and barriers that they have to overcome, and women of color have different obstacles than white women. It deepens and widens the further you go," she said.

Jillian Ivey understands this struggle. The 31-year-old communications strategist in Philadelphia told *The Citizens Voice* that she wants to have children, but is afraid that being pregnant and raising a child would stand in the way of a successful career. "I've seen clients walk away from my friends, saying things like, 'No hard feelings, but we need someone who's not about to pop a kid out,' " Ivey said. "Clients are contractors and vendors, not employers."[2]

Without paid sick leave or maternity leave, women are put in unfair situations. Jesske Eiklenborg, 27, a single mother from Minnesota, was fired from her job at an Italian restaurant when she became ill and called in sick. Until then, her mother had been helping with child care and she had just finished six months of unpaid maternity leave. "I've been looking for a job all month, but January is slow," she said. Relatives are helping pay her bills for now. "I'm applying for unemployment. And cash assistance."

Like Ivey and Eiklenborg, 70 percent of Americans say that workforce laws are "out of sync with the changing realities of modern families, and with the changing roles of men and women at work and at home," according to *The Washington Post*.[3] For millennials—who say their children and their spouses are their top priorities—this is a troubling.[4]

Eliminating the "motherhood penalty" that currently exists for women who give birth during their careers is a great issue for politicians because it is an achievable goal through public policy and because it has widespread, bipartisan support. First, the government should reform paid sick leave, and maternity and paternity leave. These policies will guarantee that men and women are given time to take care of their families and that low-income workers cannot be fired for being ill. Universal child care is the next battle ahead because 75 percent of women give birth while they are still working. Without access to high quality child care, many women are forced to leave the workforce to care for their children.[5]

There are a number of ways to make child care more affordable. The federal government, for instance, could use tax breaks, government-operated child-care facilities or subsidies to help mothers pay for private sector child care facilities.

President Obama has described the issue as "a national economic priority for all of us," and Americans agree. A poll conducted by Lake Research Partners found that 81 percent of Americans, including 65 percent of Republicans, support equal pay, paid family leave, and affordable and accessible child care. Paternity leave had bipartisan approval, with 62 percent of Republicans and 92 percent of Democrats supporting the idea. Widespread support for such policies indicates that Congress has a strong mandate to implement these social reforms.[6]

Americans support policies that will help working women balance family responsibilities with their careers. "We're at a tipping point, where it's increasingly difficult, if not impossible, for a family to manage the challenges of work, putting food on the table, and being there for the family," said Vivien Labaton, co-founder and co-executive director of the Make It Work campaign. "So there's very strong support for these issues. And it's worth noting that they're not partisan issues. There are significant majorities supporting these issues across party lines." Millennial women hope to reap the benefits of these policies, balancing child care with their spouses and taking advantage of universal child care to get back into the workforce after their maternity leave expires.

As women increasingly earn a majority of college degrees in the United States, they will economically reclaim an equal role in our society. Millennials—male and female—will lead the way. Early indications show that millennial families will involve a more equal distribution of child-care responsibilities. After watching their mothers struggle to balance raising children with career progression, millennials are ready to take the next step and "Lean In" on behalf of themselves, their wives, their sisters, and their coworkers.

Abortion

If gender equality is a clear-cut issue for millennial leaders, abortion is not. Ask the GOP and they'll tell you millennials are the most pro-life generation ever. Ask Democrats, and they'll say we're pro-choice. What's going on?

Abortion is deeply related with women's rights, and millennials are conflicted on this issue. Polls show that 75 percent of millennials identify as being pro-choice and 65 percent identify as pro-life. The overlap demonstrates that millennials do not believe abortion is a black-and-white issue.[7] Instead, millennials believe the government must set reasonable limits around what circumstances justify an abortion, and which do not.

Put simply, millennials believe in the availability, but not the morality, of abortion. They have effectively separated their personal views from their political views on the issue. The Public Religion Research Institute found that millennials are 1.5 times more likely to say that at least some health-care providers should provide legal abortions in their community but also 1.3 times more likely to be opposed to abortion in most or all cases. This nuance in millennial views indicates that millennials believe women have the right to choose their own destiny. In a sense, this is a vote for not forcing one's own view on others, which squares well with the idea that millennials are tolerant of diverse opinions.[8]

Generally, millennials believe that a woman should have the right to choose what she wants to do in the case of a pregnancy. Pew Research indicates that 56 percent of millennials believe that abortion should be legal in most circumstances.[9] 68 percent believe abortion should be available in their community.[10] Just 27 percent of millennials would overturn *Roe vs. Wade*.[11] Millennials are the least likely generation to identify as pro-life, and the most likely to identify as pro-choice.

In their personal lives, however, millennials disapprove of abortion. A 2010 poll commissioned by the Knights of Columbus, a pro-life organization, and conducted by the Marist Institute for Public Opinion, found that 58 percent of millennials felt abortion was morally wrong, compared with 51 percent of boomers and 62 percent of seniors.[12]

No matter their views, we know that fewer and fewer women are choosing to get abortions. In 2015, the Associated Press reported that abortions were declining in almost every state, with the rate declining by more than a fifth in some states as of 2010. "Abortions have declined in states where new laws make it harder to have them," the AP's David Crary wrote, "but they've also waned in states where abortion rights are protected." Declining abortion rates seem to be caused by cultural factors, not just legal roadblocks. Historically, we know that one-third of women will abort a pregnancy in their lifetime.[13]

Pro-life advocates take credit for this change. "There's an increased awareness of the humanity of the baby before it is born," United for Life President and CEO Charmaine Yoest said. "There's an entire generation of women who saw a sonogram as their first baby picture," she said. But Planned Parenthood and other pro-choice groups say that abortion is declining for a different reason: millennials are taking advantage of widely available birth control and sex education, reducing the need for abortions. "When birth control is affordable, women are more likely to choose the most effective method," said Judy Tabar, president and CEO of Planned Parenthood of Southern New England.[14]

For all the discussion of abortion, its salience appears to be exaggerated by Democrats and Republicans. Just 29 percent of voters say it is one of the most important issues facing our country.[15]

The debate to defund Planned Parenthood—which has recently resurfaced—is a less divisive one. Planned Parenthood is not an abortion organization; it is a women's health organization. That's why, despite uproar about Planned Parenthood transporting fetal organs across state lines, just 63 percent of Americans oppose defunding the organization. Nonetheless, Republicans in Congress threatened to shut down the government over this issue, much to the chagrin of Democratic leadership.

"It's going to be just like the shutdown over ACA. It's clear that Republicans are saying 'shut down the government unless I get my way' on an extraneous issue. And the American people are wise to that," Sen. Chuck Schumer (D-NY) told *Politico*. "It's all on their shoulders."[16]

The abortion debate won't end with millennials. Our generation is just as split as our parents were. But how we engage with the issue has changed. Millennials may choose either political camp but will still support the ability of women to use their own judgment. The religious right will always describe abortion as murder, and the Left will always disagree. The culture wars are not over. Still, if millennials shift the dialogue then at least they will have changed the conversation and brought our country forward.

#BlackLivesMatter and Police Violence

If June 26, 2015, was a monumental day for marriage equality, Nov. 25, 2014, was equally important for advocates of racial equality. As Jack walked toward the bus station in Philadelphia on his way to New York, he watched young Philadelphia residents of all colors gather in shock and anger when a grand jury in Ferguson, Missouri, chose not to indict police officer Darren Wilson in the shooting of Michael Brown. As he arrived into New York, Jack watched similar protests take place in New York. Friends in both cities slowly joined in, expressing their anger over what they felt was an injustice rooted in discrimination toward African Americans. Following the Michael Brown shooting, Americans across the country rallied and protested—mostly nonviolently, but occasionally with violence. At protests, young people were on the front lines pushing for change.

On our college campus, the reaction to the Michael Brown shooting was visceral. Students staged die-ins and even "took over" our university president's party, causing controversy. On Facebook, while millennials disputed the circumstances of the Ferguson case, they united in opposition to the racism that minorities of our generation are still experiencing. Later in the year, our friends marched through campus with a red hand around their neck and the caption "I Can't Breathe." Our West Philadelphia-based community was not alone. In St. Louis, the LOST VOICES! movement sprouted up in opposition to police brutality against black Americans and the Millennial Activists United (MAU) marched through St. Louis and made meals for protesters.

To say race is a hot topic in American politics today, especially for young people, would be an understatement. Racial tensions have come to the forefront of the national political debate, and millennials of all political leanings expect politicians to forcefully combat racial discrimination. For millennials, "equality for all" means that we do not judge others based on the color of their skin. We may be the closest generation to achieving true color blindness.

But there is still a long way to go. When we caught up with Jenna Wong, a millennial leader from Somerville, Massachusetts, she told us that despite popular notions, even her neighborhood is not that accepting. "Well, being from the Northeast, I think there is this big misconception that the Northeast is so accepting and that there is less racial tension than the South. But in reality, the Northeast is so divided by race," she told us.

"I come from a town that is really predominantly white, and all the African American kids come from the suburbs of Boston. And there is a huge cultural divide and a lack of understanding between African Americans, and whites and Asians."

Wong says that it is this misconception that is at the root of our country's racial tensions. "I think that is a huge problem that is obviously dividing the country right now with incidents of murder and police brutality. The problem is that everyone is convinced that we live in a post-racial society and that race is not something we need to be debating anymore. The burden needs to be placed more on white people to step up and say this isn't right. And as fellow members of this nation, we have an interest in advocating for equality and stopping this from happening in the future," she said.

"There needs to be more cultural mixing so that people understand the perspectives of groups other than their own and understand the experiences of these marginalized groups, who for hundreds of years faced discrimination—and there's no one really advocating for them. And it's kind of absurd that we're in the 21st century and these vestiges of the 19th century are still sticking around," Wong concluded.

Recent polls indicate that millennials distrust the criminal justice system and oppose racism at unprecedented levels. Forty-nine percent of millennials say they have little to no confidence that the judicial system can fairly judge people without bias for race and ethnicity, and a full 80 percent believe that requiring police officers to wear body cameras can be effective in curbing racial inequalities in the criminal justice system. As race tensions escalate, those who fail to acknowledge and root out deep-seated racism in the criminal justice system will find themselves on the wrong side of history. Judicial reform has been identified as the next civil rights challenge of our generation.[17]

"I think body cameras are important. People say okay, it's an invasion of privacy. But when your job involves carrying a gun around and enforcing rules, that's how we can keep you accountable," said Abhay Ram, a millennial leader from Illinois. "Because you're all over the place. You're not sitting in a desk office, you're out on the streets, and you're dealing with citizens. And with such an important job, with such honor, you should have no problem being watched. Body cameras have been key in solving cases because you can record everything that's going on. It provides accountability and will greatly reduce the number of bad cops."

Ram says that the hesitancy with which police departments are acting on the claims put forth by the #BlackLivesMatter movement will leave scars that may take years to heal. By not recognizing a need for reform and joining the movement, police departments and their officers are creating an "us vs. them" mentality that divides communities.

But millennials also think that police brutality is the symptom, not cause, of racial problems. "There is this total lack of understanding of African Americans and stereotyping because there is so much segregation ... especially in public education. We need a school system where people of all races learn together so that from an early age kids understand individual members of each race and understand there are no differences there. It's kind of cynical but I think it's too late to change the perspectives of people who are 20 or 30," Wong said.

Enfranchising African American Voters

With the resurgence of racial tensions and the 50th anniversary of the Voting Rights Act (VRA) in 2015, ensuring equality of the vote for

African Americans has gained significance as a civil rights issue for millennial voters. In 2014, the U.S. Supreme Court ruled that Section 4 of the Voting Rights Act was unconstitutional. Now, millennials believe that states are targeting African American voters to reduce turnout by implementing voter identification laws, eliminating same-day registration, and implementing laws to prevent voter fraud. New roadblocks, millennials argue, are just discreet attempts to disenfranchise black voters.

The VRA, when it was law, required that all new voting laws in southern states be precleared by the Justice Department, which allowed the federal government to prevent such abuse. But this clear breach of states' rights, the Court argued, was only justified based on "current needs." In 1965, "flagrant," "rampant," and "pervasive" discrimination was uniquely concentrated in southern states, where 44 percent of African Americans voted, compared with 72 percent in the West, Midwest, and Northeast. In 2013, however, African American voter turnout in covered jurisdictions in the south exceeded turnout in the rest of the country, as did the number of African American representatives as a proportion of the population.

U.S. Solicitor General Donald Verrilli agreed that racism was no longer more prevalent in the South than in the North. Absent uniquely "local evils," Congress could not impose stricter burdens on covered states solely on the basis of historical discrimination.[18] Hence, Section 4 of the VRA was repealed.

As the Philadelphia tournament neared its end—and teams made constitutional arguments about the old VRA and whether it should have been overturned—everyone seemed to agree on the next step. Now that the VRA has been overturned, millennials want it to be replaced. Chief Justice John Roberts wrote for the majority in the court's *Shelby v. Holder* decision that "the Fifteenth Amendment is not designed to punish for the past; its purpose is to ensure a better future." The new act will need to modify the formula to more precisely determine where abuse is most flagrant and where preclearance is necessary. As opposed to basing preclearance requirements on the facts on the ground from 1965, policies will be based on abuse in 2016. And hopefully the new law will help increase voter turnout among African Americans.

This happened in 2014. The Voting Rights Amendment Act of 2014 would have updated the formula and identified new jurisdictions for VRA coverage. Local jurisdictions that had committed five violations in the last 15 years or one egregious violation that created "persistent and extremely low minority voter turnout" would have been covered by the act—and would have been required to preclear voting regulations.

Such a new bill seemed like a logical next step given that just one-third of Americans actually agreed with the Court's initial decision to overturn the act. Not only would reinstating the VRA placate the majority of Americans, but it would also galvanize African American and millennial voters.[19] Much to the chagrin of young people, however, Republicans in Congress voted against the bill. The Grand Old Party didn't do itself any favors by opposing a bill with strong support among must-win demographics.

Voter ID Laws

One of the foremost reasons these young people so strongly support a new Voting Rights Act is to stem the tide of voter ID laws, which many young people believe are anathema to justice. Since 2010, more than 15 states have passed such laws, whose stated purpose is to prevent fraud. Ironically, voter ID laws don't address the most common source of fraud—mail-in absentee ballots. Even so, voter fraud is uncommon. In fact, according to Arizona State University, there have been just 28 cases of voter fraud convictions since 2000— hardly an epidemic. Of those, half were for absentee ballots. So the laws would prevent only a handful of fraudulent votes every year, which doesn't seem worth all the effort. That's why many millennials believe that the laws are just not-so-subtle attempts to reduce voter turnout among minorities and young people.[20]

Voter ID laws sound trivial—they simply require that citizens have valid government ID to vote. But the Brennan Center found that more than 10 percent of voters don't have the necessary ID, including one in four African Americans. Student identification is also invalid, so millennials are the next most likely group to be excluded from voting as a result of the new laws. In Texas, an African American grandmother—who could not afford to spend $25 on buying a birth certificate—was denied voter registration. Every day, African American voters were turned away because none of their IDs met the specifications of the new law.[21]

Judge Richard Posner, of the 7th U.S. Circuit Court of Appeals, has said that the laws "appear to be aimed at limiting voting by minorities, particularly blacks." The conservative judge described claims that the bill would combat voter fraud as "a mere fig leaf." "There is only one motivation for imposing burdens on voting that are ostensibly designed to discourage voter-impersonation fraud and that is to discourage voting by persons likely to vote against the party responsible for imposing the burdens," Posner said. Not everyone agrees. In a study, Nielson found that "there is little evidence that racial minorities are less likely than whites to vote when states institute voter identification requirements."[22]

Voter ID laws target young people too. In a recent article, *Washington Post* columnist Catherine Rampell, who is a millennial, wrote about the discrimination. "First they came for blacks, and we said nothing. Then they came for Latinos, poor people, and married women, and we again ignored the warning signs," she wrote. "Now, after our years of apathy, they're coming for us: the nation's millennials."

In Ohio, Republicans proposed a bill that would have prevented state colleges from distributing voter registration paperwork to

out-of-state students. In North Carolina, the state stopped allowing 16- and 17-year-olds to fill out early voter registration forms to
be automatically registered at 18. Meanwhile, out-of-state drivers'
licenses will no longer be valid voter identification.[23]

The result? North Carolina is now facing an age-discrimination
lawsuit. Texas, Pennsylvania, and other states have seen their laws
challenged under the 14th Amendment. Of course, there's nothing
foul at play, counter Republicans. "While some will try to make this
seem to be controversial, the simple reality is that requiring voters to
provide a photo ID when they vote is a common-sense idea," Governor Pat McCrory (R-NC) said after signing the law.

Apparently, most Americans ostensibly buy into this rhetoric. A
Washington Post poll found 74 percent of Americans say proof of citizenship should be required to vote. But this is limited to actual proof
of citizenship, not restrictive voter ID laws that exclude common
forms of identification like drivers' licenses. Indeed, millennials are
twice as concerned about eligible voters being denied the right to
vote as they are about voter fraud. (For Americans overall, these are
equal concerns.)[24]

Probably the worst part about restrictive new laws is the lack of
transparency. So while millennials might oppose the imposition of
new restrictions on youth and minority turnout, few of us even understand the extent to which these laws affect our states.

LGBT Equality: Our Movement

While race and gender are hot-button issues, they are movements
launched by our parents' and grandparents' generations that we have
championed as our own. Marriage equality, by contrast, is an issue
that in many ways has been fought primarily by millennial advocates.
For young people, homophobia is a dirty word, and as more and more
Americans come out as openly gay, support for the movement has
snowballed. Today, more than three-quarters of millennials support

gay marriage, which was recently legalized by the U.S. Supreme Court, and an even higher number believe that people who identify as LGBT should be accepted by society.

Older generations tend not to understand why the issue is so important. In 2010, for example, when we marched in the Gay Pride Parade for the first time, our mom asked why nice Jewish boys would be marching in the parade. She didn't oppose gay marriage—she just didn't understand why it's so important to our generation. The answer is that for us, marriage is an issue of tolerance, diversity, and acceptance. Everyone has a right to love and marriage.[25]

Our discussions with millennials, conservative and liberal, homosexual and heterosexual, highlighted two important sources of the dramatic support for LGBT rights among millennials. The first is that we are young and therefore less likely to be biased by preconceived notions. Just as our parents were the first generation to accept blacks as equal members of our society (formally, at least), millennials are open to respecting the rights of homosexuals. We are also the most likely people to have gay friends. It's hard not to be sympathetic to the cause when your friends and peers say this is their way of finding love. That's why millennials cheered on the U.S. Supreme Court decision to legalize gay marriage, sharing the hashtag LoveHasWon.

For Allie Shears, a millennial from Michigan, her perspective and that of her mom on LGBT issues are different because of their different experiences. Her mom, she said, worries that two women would not be able to raise their child in the same way that a heterosexual couple would, because children need parents of both genders. "I disagree," she said. "I don't think it's better to have both sexes. It's okay to not have both," she said. "You are growing up in a world full of people, you can meet everyone, you don't need to have that upbringing necessarily."

Many millennials, like Shears, say they can't even imagine where the notion that homosexual parents would be ineffective comes from. "There's this stigma that we shouldn't be allowing homosexual couples to have kids because 'it's unfair that the children don't get to choose.' But do you ever get to choose your parents? Do you choose if you have a mother and a father who are alcoholics, who take meth? That's not your choice either," Katherine Hu, a millennial from Plano, Texas, said.

The rapid pace of change in public opinion on gay marriage has been dramatic. Just a few decades ago in the *Lawrence v. Texas* decision, the U.S. Supreme Court ruled that it was illegal to ban same-sex sodomy. Today, states are adopting laws to prevent workplace discrimination against gays. There's no way a police officer could walk in on two gay men having sex and arrest them, as was the case for Lawrence. Our generation played no small part in this change. With the advent of social media and open communication, millennials have been at the forefront of calling for liberalization of policies that relate with the LGBT community. We also created a cultural taboo against homophobic expression. Most importantly, gay Americans have had the courage to come out and risk discrimination for the sake of their cause.

There is still much left to be done. Millennials say that the next step in the movement for LGBT equality is to pass antidiscrimination laws that prevent businesses from denying service or firing a person because of his/her sexual orientation. Today, just 22 states have passed laws that protect people from discrimination on the basis of either their sexual orientation or gender identity. Unfortunately, this didn't stop Indiana and Arkansas from passing laws to "protect religious freedom" in their states, and by extension, legitimize discrimination against members of the LGBT community. The backlash against these laws, however, has created a momentum for other states to pass antidiscrimination laws.

"I think right now gay marriage was legalized but there are a lot more things we can do to eliminate inequality. For example, a lot of states have discrimination laws in which employers can just fire employees for being gay. I think the next big fight is going to be for antidiscrimination laws," Ajay Singh explained. To combat perceived employer discrimination, many firms have launched diversity programs to target and hire employees who identify as homosexual.

There is widespread support for new laws to protect LGBT rights. Reuters found that 54 percent of Americans and 56 percent of millennials believe that businesses should not be able to refuse services to a member of the LGBT community on the basis of religious beliefs.[26] A similar ABC/*Washington Post* poll estimated that 65 percent of Americans support antidiscrimination laws that conflict with owners' religious beliefs, compared with 70 percent of millennials.[27]

Millennials are also the most likely generation to support comprehensive, federal reform on the issue, with 65 percent of millennials saying they support or strongly support such reform, and 15 percent saying that they are neutral on the issue, according to Generation Progress.[28] Among all political issues in the poll, comprehensive LGBT antidiscrimination reform ranked the highest in terms of the number of young people who said they "strongly support" the issue.

CONCLUSION

Social issues are paramount to elections because they are easily accessible to all voters and merely constitute value judgments. They govern how we live and regulate our basic freedoms. They do not require a college degree or advanced economic training to understand; they are basic ways to approach the world. For millennials, it is crucial that all people, regardless of gender, race, or sexual orientation, should be treated equally. Our generation will not stop until we achieve a fairer society that is more tolerant of divergent lifestyles and open to diversity. There is no balance to be achieved here, or compromise to be made; there is just a fight to be won.

Millennials leaders all across the country agree that our generation's support for equality is a defining characteristic. Still, young people hope that someday our views won't be so surprising. The dream is that someday, issues of equality will be less politically important—not because we forget about them, but rather because we've solved them. When millennials rule, equality issues will transcend political lines. They will be a universal truth accepted across the political spectrum.

Radical Realism: A Philosophy for the Next Generation

At each step of our journey through millennial America we peeled back a layer of the millennial platform. We started in New Haven, where we learned that millennials want reasonable restrictions placed on gun ownership, stopped in Lexington, where we discovered that millennials are free-market environmentalists and ended in Philadelphia, where we found that young people are champions of equal rights. Throughout this journey, we discovered a unique political philosophy that governs the millennial worldview: radical realism.

Radicalism is the belief that the future holds promise and—as its guarantors—young people must take action. By taking to the streets, voting, running for office, and volunteering in our communities, we can make a difference in the world. Realism, by contrast, is the understanding that policy making is difficult, and we must therefore accept pragmatic compromises to succeed.

Taken together, radical realism is a worldview, not an ideology. Over the next two decades, it will infuse into the platforms, stump speeches, and agendas of successful Democratic and Republican candidates. To understand what the future entails, we need to take a deeper dive into this philosophy and flesh out its implications.

The Rise of Radicalism: A Generation of Do-Gooders

Radicalism begins with the belief that young people are responsible for our communities. Our generation grew up with an unprecedented level of autonomy—our laptops and iPhones gave us levers with which to move the earth—and we remain convinced that our individual contributions to the causes we are passionate about will make a difference. That's why our friends fight for climate justice, join the NRA and know their rights under the second Amendment, march for equal rights, serve their country in U.S. armed forces, and run in marathons to support wounded veterans.

On our college campus, activism is even more aggressive. Every Friday of the 2015 academic year, students of all colors and backgrounds lined up on Locust Walk, the main road on our campus, for Ferguson Friday protests of racial and economic inequality. One Friday, students walked through campus with a red hand painted around their necks and the caption "I Can't Breathe." On another, a mock slave auction was hosted in front of a fraternity accused of racism. Ask students what they do when they are not in classes, and they're likely volunteering to support others in their communities. Teach for America has become a popular post-college choice for many liberal arts graduates—it's one of the top five employers on our campus alone.

Jack witnessed one particularly poignant example of this radicalism and sense of activism while in high school. He sat for 60 minutes waiting to give blood despite the fact that more than 100 volunteers were walking around to make sure the blood drive was running smoothly. But the wait wasn't due to inefficiency—there were simply more donors than anyone had expected. He wasn't in a hospital or a community center—he was sitting on the steps on the first floor of a public high school in New York City. The volunteers were students, the donors were students, and the idea to run a blood drive had come from student leaders in our community.

The millennials have often been called the civic generation because we take change into our own hands. "They are not into chasing their own ideologies as much as rolling up their sleeves and improving things," *USA Today* wrote.

Marissa, a millennial from Boston, told us about an organization she started called Art of Heal. She and her friends go to nursing homes to paint with the elderly. Stories like Marissa's are just the tip of the iceberg. For many young people, volunteerism began when Mom or Dad drove them to participate in a community service.

Civic engagement is a cornerstone of the millennial worldview. On an annual basis, three in four millennials volunteer for not-for-profit organizations. Millennials "lead the way in volunteering," according to the National Conference on Citizenship, with a 43 percent service rate, compared with 35 percent for baby boomers. Where boomers were known for their anti-Vietnam protests, millennials today are getting their hands dirty volunteering in their communities.[1]

Millennials became activists because of our unique socialization process. As digital natives, we grew up with unheard of powers. Young children can chat with their friends 24/7 and are exposed to a global community of peers far earlier than was ever possible. Millennials think that their personal intervention can make a difference—like it did when our generation came together to support the victims of Hurricane Katrina in New Orleans or to spearhead the gay marriage movement.

But millennials disavow politics as a means of change. In 2014, 62 percent of millennials said that politicians run for office for selfish reasons, 29 percent said political involvement rarely has tangible results, and 58 percent said that elected officials don't share their priorities. Young people think they will have more of an impact as issue advocates and activists than by engaging in politics through traditional means. That's why today, young people have abandoned Democrats and Republicans and have instead unified around their own platforms to take back America's future.[2]

The Rise of Realism: A Need for Compromise

Millennial optimism and radicalism is contrasted with a sobering reality. College students are burdened with an average of more than $20,000 in student loans and half will accept a job for which they are overqualified. Likewise, manufacturing jobs have not returned to the U.S. since the Great Recession, and millennials are entering a brutal job market, with the majority living paycheck to paycheck.

Meanwhile, we will inherit trillions of dollars of debt obligations and an increasingly hostile geopolitical environment, with a destabilized Syria in shambles, ISIS on the rise, and an expansionist regime in Russia flexing its muscles. These harsh realities—and the failure of our leaders to mitigate them—force millennials to take a more pragmatic, realistic approach to political change.

Realism manifests in a tendency to compromise. "The only way to solve these challenges is for popular support of reason and compromise —a bipartisan goal we can accomplish," wrote Nick Weinmeister, a student at Pitzer College. "Liberal, conservative, or any political preference could lead to legislation that puts us on track. A balanced budget, or simply a passed budget, is achievable. But until compromise is reintroduced, nothing will happen."[3]

As with our activism, millennial realism is driven by environmental influences. Millennials came of age during one of the most politically polarized times in American history. Today, gerrymandering has made districts "ideologically pure" and crazies are in power on both sides of the aisle. Party politics has torn Washington apart. Instead of fighting ideological wars, millennials want to unify around common-sense ideas: we need better jobs, safer streets, and stronger schools.

Millennials see both Democratic and Republican ideologies as flawed. Many millennials see Republicans as being behind the times on social issues and Democrats too naïve—the party's bailouts have not helped us find jobs. We'd like to find a rational middle ground. "Living in an á la carte world with unlimited options, millennials don't feel they have to choose between two limited choices," explained Michelle Diggles, a senior political analyst at Third Way, a think tank.[4]

As a result, millennials eschew political parties but crave progress. "These party lines that have been set actually limit our progress," Ciana Cronin, a millennial from Tucson, Arizona, said. "What if something that's good for the country is on the other side of the aisle? Are we really progressing, or are we just creating more conflict?" Cronin said her generation is the least likely to see a stark difference between Democrats and Republicans. "How do you determine if you're a conservative, how do you determine if you're a liberal, because you are never really one holistically. I think it's always a little bit of both," she said.

Like Cronin, two-thirds of millennials don't see a major difference between the parties and a full 50 percent identify as politically independent. Alsan Diouf, a New Jersey Democrat, explained that he didn't understand the need for voters to "pick a morality to believe in."[5]

Fighting Against Corruption in Washington

When Rob Fournier, senior political columnist and editorial director of the *National Journal*, went to Langley High School, an elite public school in Northern Virginia which caters to children of Washington politicians, he expected to find a group of engaged young people ready to get involved with politics like their parents. But when he asked a government class how many of the students planned to run for office someday, not one student raised a hand. Shayan Ghahramani, a student, bluntly said that millennials will "destroy" government and politics.[6]

Ghahramani is not alone in his disdain for politics. Vox reported that the participation of young people in politics has steadily decreased since 1964. Only 23 percent of Americans under the age of

30 told Harvard they were planning to vote in the midterm elections in 2014. When asked why they don't vote, millennials say they don't trust politicians. Sixty-six percent of millennials think that government is inefficient and wasteful and 58 percent of millennials believe that government agencies abuse their power, compared with the 2 5percent who say that they do the right thing. Only 22 percent of high school seniors think Congress is doing a good job.[7]

Even as public sector employment grows, fewer and fewer college graduates say they want a government job. In 2013, only 5.4 percent of college graduates said they would take a government job, down from 10.2 percent in 2009. According to *BusinessWeek*, seven in 10 millennials believe that government cannot solve global problems without outside support, with an even greater percentage saying business is the answer. Most telling of all, only one-third of young people think it is honorable to run for office.[8] This is because we realize that in Washington, lies, rather than honesty, have become the political norm. A recent study found that 85 percent of super PACs ad spending goes to ads that have at least one false fact.[9] Worst of all, these lies become a sort of perceptual reality, because corrections rarely succeed at changing public opinion.[10]

But millennials don't just think politicians are sellouts. We think that they are actual crooks—and for good reason.

One hot summer in high school, we agreed to volunteer for Jonathan Bing, our local state representative. Bing was a nice guy and good politician, if those even exist in Albany, but the most memorable day on the job wasn't one where we researched legislation or put together press packets—it was the day we asked our supervisor about Bing's reelection prospects. First, he just laughed, but then he let us in on Albany's dirty little secret—that incumbents in our state legislature are more likely to die or go to jail than lose their reelection campaigns.

This isn't just true of rank and file members. In 2015, New York State Assembly Speaker Sheldon Silver resigned in disgrace after being convicted on federal corruption charges. Around the same time, Dean Skelos, Silver's Republican counterpart in the state Senate, was indicted on charges of receiving kickbacks.[11]

Overall, between 2010 and 2014, 72 state-level politicians were convicted of crimes, and not just for tax evasion, although that was certainly a common culprit. State leaders were arrested for crimes ranging from child seduction to child pornography, corruption, and money laundering. Nine federal politicians have been convicted since 2009, by contrast.[12] Of course, most politicians live within the law, but you can understand why young people have such terrible impressions of politicians, especially in an age when 24/7 media coverage allows us to hear about events such as former Rep. Michael Grimm (R-NY) threatening to throw an NY1 reporter off a balcony.

Corruption has always existed in politics, but the unprecedented exposure and publicity surrounding these leaders has turned many millennials away from traditional political ideologies. Northern California millennial Arsh Sharma, for example, told us he doesn't like either party. Neither the elephant nor donkey are very good mascots to support, he joked.

Ciana Cronin said that even the good politicians, who start out well-intentioned, eventually burn out. "You start fresh and you start vibrant and you have this vitality and this stamina. You are ready to go but the longer you stay in term, I feel like you almost deplete and you realize that the action that you've taken won't be in effect in 10, 15, 20 years," she said.

Similarly, Erin Nwachukwu from Chicago's South Side said she doubts the sincerity of her city leaders, and feels mistrustful of authority figures. She's watched the government close schools, "even as they pour millions of dollars into flashy downtown parks. They don't seem like they have our best interest at heart," she said. "It seems like it's about the money."[13]

Jack Abramoff, a former lobbyist convicted of corruption, wrote in his memoir about the profound level of corruption in Congress.

"I would say a few magic words: 'When you are done working for the congressman, you should come work for me at my firm,' " he wrote. "With that, assuming the staffer had any interest in leaving Capitol Hill for K Street—and almost 90 percent of them do—I would own him and, consequently, that entire office. No rules had been broken, at least not yet. No one even knew what was happening, but suddenly, every move that staffer made, he made with his future at my firm in mind. His paycheck may have been signed by the Congress, but he was already working for me, influencing his office for my clients' best interests. It was a perfect—and perfectly corrupt—arrangement."

Combining their radical realist agenda with a disdain for the established political systems in place today, millennials are going to tear apart political norms, reconstructing the political environment as they destroy the old system.

"Millennials will produce radical reconstruction of civil institutions and government," Diggles explained. "This tension -- two parties thinking they are in the trenches dueling it out, and a burgeoning generation who reject trench warfare altogether—is, for me, the key. Washington doesn't get that change isn't just a slogan. It's about to become a reality."

Radical Realism: A New Approach to Change

The implication of radical realism is that young people see themselves as personal change agents and use their votes to support the issue-driven agenda that they believe is crucial to building a better future for their families, choosing policies from both sides of the aisle. They are realists in their willingness to compromise to achieve their goals and bypass party lines, and they are radical in their willingness to use activism and nontraditional tactics to fight for their beliefs.

Throughout our book, this theme has been present. Yong people support universal background checks, but they oppose gun control. They support the Keystone Pipeline, but oppose hydraulic fracking.

They believe in privatization of Social Security, but not in raising the Social Security age. Millennials oppose Obamacare, but don't believe in repealing it. Where Democrats and Republicans bring vitriol, infighting, and polarization, young people bring nuance. Frankly, it's a breath of fresh air.

This has important implications for our country's future. Millennials will adopt a pragmatic and centrist policy agenda with the goal of achieving tangible results. Using their newfound political might, millennials are going to translate this agenda into actual public policy. Already, this is happening, as we've noted: millennials are the driving force behind the legal weed movement and have fueled dozens of political campaigns, giving our leaders their margins of victory.

As they implement their political agenda, millennials are going to reshape the political institutions that they come to hate. "Millennials are pragmatic—they want to know what works and are willing to take ideas from each side," Diggles told *The Atlantic*. "They eschew ideological purity tests of the past. In short, they are winnable by both parties, if only policy makers understood and reflected their values."[14]

Value-Based Political Decisions: Millennials Form a Consensus

If millennials are truly moderates who crisscross the political spectrum, why do 63 percent of young conservatives and 77 percent of young liberals agree that marijuana should be legalized? Why was there such a resounding unity among millennials when the Supreme Court ruled in favor of marriage equality?

The answer to both these questions is the same: when our core values are in question—in this case, tolerance of diversity—young people unite. When a Pew survey asked millennials what distinguishes them from older generations, tolerance came in third after technology use and music/pop culture.[15]

Even these other values—like the millennial obsession with technology—affect our generation's public policy preferences. I am writing these words on my laptop as I ride on a train that I picked up five minutes ago with a ticket I bought on my phone after I boarded. I can get everything from dinner, to a movie, to a doctor on-demand.

Given this technological transformation, it should come as no surprise that millennials support experiential learning and are pushing school districts to adopt new learning platforms. Similarly, it's not surprising that gamification of curriculums—often online—is the newest trend among millennials educators.

Our technology obsession is helping millennials retool the economy and build better public policy. Roughly 85 percent of millennials describe themselves as adapting quickly to change and 60 percent of millennials say that they are entrepreneurs. Millennials have initiated the start-up revolution. "Owner" is now the fifth most popular job title on Facebook, and millennials launch 160,000 start-ups every month.[16]

When asked to describe what it means to be millennials, young people most often describe themselves as being creative. From a public policy lens, the millennial generation's affinity toward entrepreneurship and innovation encourages us to support economic initiatives that make it easier to start businesses.

But millennials aren't all work and no play. Boomers tend to view millennials as morally inept young adults who pursue their self-interest at the expense of things like happiness and religion. But underneath their selfies, millennials are value-driven people who care deeply about family, happiness, and relationships.

Millennials say being a good parent is their number one priority, followed by having a successful marriage. Surveys show that millennials consistently identify family as their most important driver of happiness. In fact, 28 percent of young people say they would most like to be remembered as a person who was loved by many people. Once again, these values affect public policy as young people rally behind universal child care and advocate for extended paid leave for new mothers and fathers.[17]

This makes sense. Millennials are the children of record-high divorce rates. We watched our parents work too hard and lose their jobs in 2008. As opposed to seeing the home as a gendered institution, millennials demand a work-life balance and expect both spouses to play an equal role. Rather than riding the corporate ladder and playing by the rules in the workplace, millennials expect companies to bend at their fingertips.

And this is exactly what's happening, with top executives at Fortune 500 companies now spending millions of dollars and thousands of hours to create a work environment that caters to millennials.

With their strong focus on values, millennials have led the rise in social entrepreneurship, creating a culture in which leaders like 23-year old Karim Abouelnaga become icons. The Cornell graduate, who we met at a recent conference for young entrepreneurs, started a nonprofit called Practice Makes Perfect that is helping close the achievement gap in inner-city schools. He has recruited hundreds of volunteers to do the teaching. Abouelnaga's initiative has been met with widespread support; he was featured by the Clinton Global Initiative and acknowledged as one of *Forbes'* "30 under 30." Like many millennials, Abouelnaga believes he can make a difference in the world.

This tendency toward social impact helps explain why young people say they support welfare and entitlement reform as a way to help people in need. For 60 percent of our generation, "a sense of purpose" defines our work life and our personal life. And 84 percent of us believe that our generation has the potential to change the world.

As millennials get older, this optimism doesn't seem to be fading. As a result, a third of millennials say that they are willing to pay more for a product or service if it supports a worthwhile cause and 90 percent say that they buy products associated with causes. After children and marriage, millennials say their third priority is helping others in need.[18]

Our desire to help others is due in part to our systematic exposure to the suffering of people at home and abroad, onset by globalization and instant communication. Long gone are the days when you could just sit holed up in your own community and ignore the plight of others. Today, our Facebook newsfeeds are inundated with stories of poverty, sickness, and inequality. At the same time, technological changes have given us the power to make a difference.

Today, the world is smaller. We can reach halfway across the world and have a concrete impact in a matter of minutes. From his home in California, Fish Stark launched the Teaching Peace Initiative, where he mobilized thousands of students across the country to help teach conflict resolution in underprivileged elementary schools.

Stark and his team fought bullies and helped students understand the importance of working together to find a middle ground. By working toward nonviolence and tolerance, these young people were able to make a difference in their communities.

CONCLUSION

As millennials look toward the future, we recognize that we will face a unique set of challenges. But instead of being guided by purist ideologies that mandate extreme views, our generation has created its own guiding worldview, one founded on the basis of activism and compromise. It's an approach that young Democrats, Republicans, and Independents can all rally around. Crisscrossing the political spectrum, millennials are uniting to take back America's future.

PART 2

Court Us If You Can

Millennials are single and ready to mingle. Fifty percent of us are political independents and the rest of us are in open relationships with Democrats and Republicans. But it's coming time for us to settle down, and choosing the party of our dreams is tougher than ever: Democrats and Republicans are so busy bickering that they both seem like jerks. That's too bad for Washington, because we're the prettiest girl on the block: in 2016 we'll represent one-third of eligible voters. "Court Us If You Can" is a how-to guide for everyday Americans who want to learn about who millennials really are and how to win our love—and votes.

Be a Champion

nside campaign headquarters, everyone is asking the same question: how do we clinch the youth vote?

There is good reason to believe that this obsession is justified; as the largest voting demographic, millennials will be kingmakers in upcoming elections—on the local, state and federal level. In this book, we've been heavily focused on issues—our goal, after all, was to reveal the millennial platform. But it's readily apparent that millennials are more than just issue advocates; we vote for candidates who share our values. If our leaders want to win millennial votes, they need to tailor their campaigns to our values.

Despite Congress' bad reputation, millennials adore certain politicians. Ron Paul, Joni Ernst, Bill de Blasio, and the 2008 version of President Obama are just a few examples of "millennial champions." Champions stand out from the crowd and have wild support among millennials, regardless of how we view the rest of Washington. In fact, the worse everyone else seems, the more we cling to our champions as the only politicians who really understand us.

Core Value: Authenticity

Millennials value authenticity and honesty above all else. Authenticity is about standing for something and meaning it. It's campaigning on one central platform and following through. It means being true to one's personality, spirit, and character. Consumer research finds that a "strong majority" of U.S. consumers believe that "being genuine and authentic is extremely important for me and for the things and people in my life."[1]

Millennials are especially keen on these values, rating authenticity and trustworthiness as two of their top five most important values, according to an Initiative survey. "Being manipulators of identity themselves, they are keenly aware that corporations, nonprofits, celebrities, politicians, and global leaders contrive 'authentic' images for themselves and prefer transparency to claims of genuineness," explained Onesixtyfourth, a consultancy.[2]

Yconic CEO Rob Henderson said that while all generations expect transparency, honesty, and integrity, "It is table stakes for millennials." We couldn't agree more. This is especially true because our generation is predisposed to assuming that politicians are corrupt. Jeff Fromm, president of FutureCast, a marketing firm, noted that young people "want to know you stand for something. ... They can spot a phony a mile away."[3]

Part of being true to yourself is being able to admit your flaws. Not all candidates are perfect in every way, shape, or form. As the 2012 FLAWSOME report noted, "Human nature dictates that people have a hard time genuinely connecting with, being close to, or really trusting other humans who (pretend to) have no weaknesses, flaws, or mistakes." If politicians are real people with real beliefs and real vulnerabilities, millennials can relate.[4]

While there are a number of authentic politicians in Washington, three stand out as best representing the millennial values of authenticity: Sen. Joni Ernst (R-IA), former Sen. Russ Feingold (D-WI), and former House Speaker John Boehner (R-OH). Their consistency, bold stances, and clear messages are strong examples of how to resonate with millennial voters.

Joni Ernst, who told voters she would make Congress "squeal" when she ran for office in 2014, gave voters one central message: she is a "mother, solider, [and] conservative." Ernst won her tight 2014 Senate race because she embodied conservative values and demonstrated that her passion came from the heart. Ernst branded herself a hawk, capitalizing on instability in Iraq and the rise of ISIS. Voters knew she was genuine—as a combat veteran and commander of the 185th Combat Sustainment Support Battalion, Ernst showed that her support for the military was nothing new. By choosing pork spending as her second key campaign issue, Ernst demonstrated that her "inexperience" was an asset. Ernst created the impression that she was a real tough woman running to do tough work; it was this authentic brand that David Polyansky, a senior advisor to her campaign, said helped her win her election.

"Joni just has the magic. There's a quality in her that even the best campaign can't teach, buy, or fake with great advertising," said David Kochel, one of Ernst's strategists. "Joni is the real deal. She's a natural leader, and people will always like her and respond to her. That's what will make her a great U.S. senator."[5]

Even David Axelrod, former advisor to President Obama, admitted that Ernst "seemed like Iowa." Axelrod hit it on the nose. Transport Ernst to any other state, and she might have lost. And that's awesome! Because an authentic candidate who fits her constituents is exactly what young people want.

Instead of parading around talking about Obamacare or balancing the budget, Ernst ran a campaign about who she was as a person and why she was the type of Midwestern conservative that voters would want to see in Washington. And that's why she won. Her campaign ads attacking corruption in Washington resonated with millennials who share her distrust of politicians.

On the other side of the aisle, Sen. Russ Feingold built a reputation as a maverick and progressive leader, whose authenticity defined his brand. Feingold was the only senator in Washington to have voted against the Patriot Act, which proponents say bolstered national security and opponents say trampled individual rights. He pushed through game-changing campaign finance reform legislation, sponsoring the McCain-Feingold Act and spending seven years to ensure its passage. And Feingold was the first senator to call for a timetable for bringing U.S. troops home from Iraq. Feingold is a man who does what he believes, not what is politically convenient. As a result, he's able to attract disenchanted young voters.

In his biography of Feingold, Sanford Horwitt writes that Feingold "represents the progressive side of the Democratic divide more clearly and authentically than any successful politician on the national stage." Horwitt says that Feingold's time in the Senate was strongly influenced by Robert M. La Follette, the legendary Wisconsin governor and U.S. Senator, known to history as "Fighting Bob."

Feingold grew up in a small Wisconsin town, where his parents led a modest life and he learned about personal integrity. This personal integrity became his defining character trait, as he defied Senate majorities and refused to succumb to special interests. Feingold was the only Democrat to vote to extend Bill Clinton's Senate trial. To quote former Wisconsin Attorney General Peg Lautenschlager, Feingold is the type of guy about whom you say, "I don't agree with him on the issues, but he's his own man" or "I'm not a Democrat, but I'm proud of him." This is an old-school type of politician—the type of politician millennials will swoon over.

Feingold is not necessarily popular among fellow Democrats, many of whom see him as arrogant and preachy. They resent his commitment to donate all funding past his $174,000 salary toward deficit reduction and his yearly efforts to prevent cost of living increases in Senate salaries. But it's this very "loner" status in the Senate that makes Feingold such a hero to millennials. Being authentic does not necessarily mean being a raging progressive, but it does mean voting your conscience. And voters, especially millennials, can tell the difference between career politician types and those who stay true to their values.

You don't have to be starkly independent and antiestablishment to be authentic, however. In fact, former Speaker John Boehner, who was the face of the political establishment during his time in the House, may be the most authentic politician of all. Boehner worked the night shift as a janitor to pay his way through college, and started mopping his dad's bar when he was 10. Later, he made millions in a small plastics business he bought early in his career, and cried when he told Americans that his whole life he had been "chasing the American dream."

Boehner's long political career may not be known for being particularly radical or different, but his genuine passion is something that really resonates with the American people. Throughout his long career in Washington, Boehner never forgot his humble roots. He frequently teared up while talking about children, saying that while he doesn't take himself very seriously, he has always taken his job very seriously. He knows that it was his responsibility to help make sure that our children have a better future. Boehner is an authentic person who had a real mission in Washington.[6]

By no means a popular political figure on either side of the aisle, Boehner left office in 2015 with a great amount of respect from his colleagues. Boehner was known as a deeply religious man committed to the core to Christian values. But maybe what left millennials with the best impression of Boehner was that 52 percent of Republican voters said he "compromised too much with Democrats." If only every politician had that problem![7]

Core Values: Optimism

Optimism is a second value that millennials look for in our leaders. The optimism that defines the millennial generation may be hard to understand realizing that we grew up through 9/11 and the 2008 recession. Still, today, young people are more secure in the future than older folks, which has not always been the case. In the 1970s, Gallop found that only half of adults under the age of 30 felt secure in America's future, compared with 70 percent of adults 30 or older. Today, half of millennials think that the country's best days are ahead of it compared with 42 percent of GenX, 44 percent of baby boomers, and 39 percent of the Silent Generation[8]

Young people are also optimistic about our financial situation, despite our difficultly finding jobs. Even while two-thirds of millennials say they aren't earning enough money to live a good life, 88 percent say they expect to earn enough in the future. This is significantly higher than the 76 percent of GenXers and 46 percent of baby boomers who share this outlook.[9] Meanwhile, 80 percent of millennials think they will be as well or better off than their parents, despite the fact that the majority of them live paycheck to paycheck and one-third of millennials are currently receiving help from their families.[10]

Millennial voters want to vote for politicians who share our optimism and offer real solutions to building a better future. The good news for politicians is that optimism is not just a way to win over millennial voters—it's a way to win elections, period. Martin Seligman, a researcher and leader of the "positive psychology" movement, has shown that optimistic politicians are statistically more likely to win elections.[11] In fact, politicians who have campaigned with optimistic messages have been particularly successful with millennials in recent years.

Elise Stefanik, for example, is optimistic to the core. The northern New York native who became the youngest woman (at 30) ever elected to Congress in 2014, counts this as strength. "I think that's where being young is a strength, because I bring, I hope, a sunny side of optimism to Congress, and a willingness to work with people. I hope I'm not frustrated after the next two years," the Republican said in an interview with CBS.

Stefanik campaigned on tolerance and compromise, saying that while she is pro-life, she respects the views of others. The Harvard graduate and domestic policy staffer for George W. Bush in the White House has worked with fellow members of Congress to get the ball rolling on key policy issues. She serves on the House Armed Services Committee.[12]

Cory Gardner, a Senate freshman from Colorado and a Republican, said his optimism is what allowed him to beat incumbent Democrat Sen. Mark Udall in 2014. He said the GOP nominee for president in 2016 will need to display optimism about the country to win. "More than anything, in this Rocky Mountain state, people want to be able to lift their eyes up to the great Rocky Mountain horizon and recognize the fact that we have an ever-hopeful state. And that's the kind of message that we had to capture to make sure that people were proud again and to make sure that we can build toward a government that we can be proud of," Gardner told ABC News.[13]

About Gardner, *The Denver Post* wrote, "Not since Mona Lisa has a smile been discussed this much." *The Atlantic* took the same tone: "A little fireplug of a man, moonfaced and brush-haired, the 40-year-old Gardner is so relentlessly upbeat it can be exhausting to spend time with him." This may all sound superficial and useless, but a Republican Congressman unseating a longtime political incumbent in a blue state is impressive—and Gardner's new message of upbeat optimism is likely what did the trick.

In a swing state on the other coast, Florida, first-term congresswoman Gwen Graham is likewise driving people crazy by being too nice. The *Tallahassee Democrat* called Graham "a serial hugger and an eternal optimist who has maintained her energy through a long, hard campaign."

Graham, a Democrat, may not have used her campaign ads to call her opponent "a nice guy," as Gardner did, but she maintained a positive outlook throughout, admitting that Obamacare was flawed, for example, but saying she would work to fix it. "I'm optimistic that by building strong bipartisan relationships with other members and strengthening relationships with the agencies that serve our constituents, we can end the gridlock and dysfunction in Congress," she told voters. Her strategy worked.

Rep. Kathleen Rice (D-NY) is an optimist and a pragmatist, the killer combination for millennial voters. "My mother, God rest her soul, was an only child and she went on to have 10 kids. She was an eternal optimist and we inherited that from her. I try to look at the way things can be and not be sidetracked," Rice told *The New York Times*.

Rice has *chutzpah*, and she pairs her optimism with toughness. In Nassau County, which elected her to Congress for the first time in 2014, Rice is known for her days as a prosecutor, where voters say she was tough on drunk drivers, creative in her drug busts, and even broke up a controversial high school cheating ring. Rice is the ideal optimist—an aggressive and ambitious congresswoman who sees a bright future and is willing to work hard to achieve it.[14]

Core Values: Tolerance

The third core value of the millennial generation is tolerance. We are the most accepting of single women having children, of gay couples raising children, of interracial marriage, of working mothers, and of non-married couples living together, for example. When it comes to being racially tolerant, Pew Research finds that young Americans are viewed as being twice as tolerant as the older generation.

Meanwhile, 70 percent of millennials support marriage equality,[15] and 85 percent of millennials believe that the government should ensure that women receive equal treatment in the workplace.[16] Millennials believe in individual choice and respect the decisions of others, believing that freedom should be prioritized above historical practices. Millennials are also tolerant of immigrants. 58 percent said that immigrants strengthen the country, compared to 34 percent of adults older than 30.[17]

Millennials are proud of being tolerant. Millennials see history through the lens of inequality, with many young people believing that it is the role of their government to correct racial, gender, and sexual inequality. And they are unlikely to vote for intolerant politicians, who they view as backward, racist, and unfit for leadership. Young people are so passionate about tolerance that the racist or sexist comments of even one politician can reflect poorly on his entire political party.

On the flipside, millennials are inspired by the politicians who are on the front lines fighting for equality in the United States. Some of America's standout tolerant politicians are Sen. Rob Portman (R-OH), Rep. John Lewis (D-GA), and Sen. Tammy Baldwin (D-WI).

Even though he was one of the initial sponsors of the Defense Against Marriage Act in 1996, Rob Portman is a man who knows how to adapt to changing times. When his son came out of the closet in 2011, Portman grappled with the tough question of gay marriage. After "family soul-searching," Portman became the first Republican senator to openly support gay marriage in 2013.

"I feel very comfortable in taking a position of respecting people for who they are," Portman told the Associated Press, "which is what I think ultimately same-sex marriage is about." Portman cast a crucial vote with Democrats to support the Employment Non-Discrimination Act (ENDA), a bill that bans discrimination against homosexuals in the workplace.[18]

Since his change of heart, Portman has been a lightning rod for anti-gay hatred, and his political ambitions have been jeopardized. Many pundits believe that Portman, an Ohio native, would have been Mitt Romney's first choice for vice president in the 2012 elections, but was not selected because of his views on gay marriage.

Portman's future presidential plans, and even his reelection for senator, are likewise thought to be in great jeopardy because of his position on gay marriage. Just 47 percent of Republicans told CBS that they would consider voting for a candidate who doesn't share their views on gay marriage. The National Organization for Marriage has already pledged to defeat Portman in 2016. He may yet lose, but not without a fight and not without a huge outpouring of support from millennial voters who agree with his position and respect his courage.[19]

John Lewis, for his part, is a civil rights hero. The rest of Congress should follow his lead. He is the only living "Big Six" leader of the civil rights movement. In the 1960s, Lewis led what is now known as Bloody Sunday, a peaceful protest in Selma, Alabama, in which the police used tear gas and clubs to attack protestors. Lewis, who suffered a skull fracture that day in 1965, is now a 13th-term Democratic congressman from Atlanta. As a young man, he led the voting rights act movement. Now he's fighting the *Shelby County v. Holder* Supreme Court decision, which overturned the Voting Rights Act.

In his amicus brief to the Supreme Court, he noted "the high price many paid for the enactment of the Voting Rights Act and the still higher cost we might yet bear if we prematurely discard one of the most vital tools of our democracy." In July 2011, Lewis began fighting voter ID laws, which he compared to poll taxes. (In 2012, U.S. Attorney General Eric Holder would make the same comparison.) Since he got to Congress, Lewis has been a civil rights champion. The fight for civil rights is not yet over, as Lewis himself knows very well. Millennials are looking for politicians who will appreciate the importance of equality and will fight to protect the rights of minorities.

Finally, Tammy Baldwin, a Democrat, is fighting for the rights of gay Americans. As the first gay or lesbian elected to the Senate, Baldwin not only embodies the fight for gay rights, but she also is fighting on the floor of the Senate for her gay peers. She was the first senator to speak in support of the ENDA.

"The citizens of Wisconsin made history, electing our state's first woman to the United States Senate, and electing the first out gay or lesbian person to the United States Senate in the history of our great nation," Baldwin told her fellow senators. "But I didn't run to make history, I ran to make a difference—a difference that would give everyone a fair shot at achieving their dreams." Giving everyone a chance at the American dream is what millennials are all about.

Conclusion: How to Be a Champion

Authenticity, optimism, and tolerance are keys to winning the trust and support of young Americans. We firmly believe that winning millennial votes is as much about values as it is about issues. As a mentor of ours once explained, "Politicians can change their mind on issues, but they'll never change who they are."

"Millennials will align with somebody regardless of political labels based on values," Rob Shepardson, founding partner of the advertising agency SS+K, told *Adweek*. We hope the examples above help highlight some of the most important values for millennials.[20]

Politicians may never be as tolerant as Tammy Baldwin, as authentic as John Boehner, or as optimistic as Cory Gardner. But by combining the values of tolerance, optimism, and authenticity, they can become a champion—a hero for millennials, a mentor, and a role model.

Leaders can become millennial sweethearts by demonstrating that they share the same values as millennials and taking pragmatic approaches to policy. Three politicians have done this extraordinarily well: Ron Paul, John Kasich, and Narendra Modi.

Ron Paul: Fighting for Individual Rights Since '35

How does the oldest candidate in a presidential race win the plurality of young voters? How does an isolationist politician who believes in returning to the gold standard and thinks Social Security is unconstitutional stand a chance?

You'll just have to ask Ron Paul, the 80-year-old physician who won 47 percent of millennial voters in the 2012 New Hampshire Republican primary and 48 percent in the Iowa Caucus.

The man is genuine to the core: a consistent libertarian who has the courage of his convictions and bases his policy choices on his steadfast belief in individual rights. Think he's crazy? Maybe he is, but young people certainly don't think so. He's a man worth watching, if only to understand how he has managed to build the sort of cult of personality that draws huge crowds every time Paul shows up at a college campus.

"When Ron Paul came to Tampa, he brought with him the youngest delegation in the history of the Republican Party," explained *Mic* reporter Hamdan Azhar. "They weren't lawyers or political hacks or millionaires—they were college students, actors, teachers, techies, and hipsters." [21] They were ordinary kids who had a dream that they could make a difference. Adam Sullivan, former editor-in-chief of *The Daily Iowan*, the student newspaper at the University of Iowa, which endorsed Paul, said that young people were so passionate about Paul's vision that those who lived out of state would come back to Iowa just to vote for Paul in the caucus. [22]

Paul's core belief system is rooted in an appreciation for individual freedom and responsibility, and it is consistent. Forty years ago, Paul believed in the same laissez faire economics he campaigned on in 2012. Unlike mainstream Republicans, Paul does not preach small government and states' rights, and then argue for federal regulation of abortion, marijuana use, and marriage. His views are consistent across the board: no government in bedrooms, no government in boardrooms, and no government in war rooms.

"Ron Paul's ideological consistency is remarkable, almost unheard of in modern politics," James Picht wrote for *The Washington Times*. "It isn't the hobgoblin consistency of small minds, but the intellectual consistency of an honest mind."

To add to this allure, Paul is strong on the issues young voters care about: Paul is pro-gay marriage, wants to save us from the national debt, wants to bring troops home, and wants to dramatically reform the tax code. Not only does Paul focus on issues important to young people, but he also makes the effort to reach out to millennials. Paul, reported *Forbes*, has repeatedly made statements along the lines of "Republicans are going to be neglectful if they say: 'Oh, you don't need Independents, you don't need the young people.' That's where the excitement is, and that's where the changes are coming about."[23]

Explaining millennial support for Paul, 26-year-old Kenneth Christiansen told NPR, "I think it's just the concept of freedom, being able to choose what you want with your life."[24] Millennial Ron Gray agreed, saying that Paul gives him hope "that not everyone is a sell-out; not everyone is controlled by special interests. There are people who still stick to their principles."

Paul is an optimist. He inspired an entire generation of Americans to believe that the future was bright, and that if we restored our basic freedoms, the economy would start working again. His vision and his principles were a refreshing change for millennial voters.

The lesson to take away from Paul is not to be a semi-racist, isolationist politician who advocates for legalizing heroin and abolishing the Federal Reserve. But if a conspiracy theorist who blames 9/11 on U.S. foreign policy can inspire a generation of voters, anyone can do it.

Paul shows just how desperate millennial voters are for a breath of fresh air, for a politician who isn't a crony, who isn't owned by special interests, who is real, genuine, and authentic. He illustrates the power of consistency and direction. Paul is a millennial champion because he is someone we can look up to and respect.

John Kasich: The Pragmatic Governor

Paul's foil is Gov. John Kasich (R-OH), a 2016 Republican presidential candidate who won the millennial vote by a margin of 15 points in his successful reelection bid in 2014. He shows that a pragmatic candidate can use optimism, authenticity, and tolerance to generate historic electoral returns. Kasich is even more interesting because he lost millennials in 2010 by 10 points.

The mandate with which he won reelection shows how candidates can change and adapt to develop a public image that is amenable to millennial support. Kasich's win is fascinating for a different reason too: Ohio is a swing state that President Obama won in 2008 and 2012, so winning millennials by such a huge margin is a real coup.

In his first term as governor, Kasich accomplished significant achievements: he balanced the budget, cut taxes, and reduced regulation. Though a conservative, Kasich counts himself a realist, focusing on prosperity for the people of Ohio above all else. Like Paul, Kasich espouses a core mission.

He told *The Economist* that he believes "conservatism must have a moral purpose."[25] This purpose, he says, is to celebrate success and help others achieve it. Kasich believes job training and school reform are two important answers to this question. (As we note in our chapter on the economy, these are the types of solutions millennials are seeking.)

Kasich makes a genuine effort at tolerance, even if this is not central to his image. He says that Ohio is trying to help grant state contracts to minorities, and says that the job of government is to help the people who "live in the shadows"—including drug addicts, the homeless, and ex-cons.

The governor's can-do attitude exudes optimism. Kasich was the only Republican gubernatorial contender to focus entirely on what he could do for Ohio, without much effort spent attacking President Obama. An economic conservative, he appeals to the aspects of the Republican Party that young people love—the party of economic opportunity, of wealth, of balanced budgets, and of low taxes. When criticized for accepting Medicaid funding, he retorted that his critics were unchristian for proposing that he reject money that could help the poor. This sort of realistic approach to policy-making is very much a staple of what makes a good millennial candidate. It embodies our own philosophy of radical realism.

On the campaign trail, Kasich stays real—which is what helped him court so many Democratic voters. When *The Economist* asked him what he thought about winning 25 percent of the African Amer-ican vote in 2014, he responded, "I'm flabbergasted by it." Later he joked, "When I said [during the campaign] that we need to respect the president of the United States, the reporter [for the Associated Press] nearly passed out." Kasich says he understands blue-collar voters. When he goes into their communities, he can say, "I get your values. I grew up next door to you."

Kasich talks explicitly about wanting to help the next generation. He told voters, "There's a certain magic that comes from teamwork. There's a magic that comes from pulling together. We have managed our budget, we've managed the size of the state government, we've reduced taxes, we're up now almost a quarter of a million jobs, that's our moral purpose. I think that Ohio's greatest legacy is that the next generation is better off than the generation we're in; that's what I want for my children. We're doing better and better and better and as result of that, it's lifting everybody."

And his moral purpose, jobs, is exactly what millennial voters want their politicians to be talking about and focusing on. This realistic appraisal of priorities is dynamite. No wonder he won the millennial vote by such a wide margin.

Narendra Modi: The Middle-Class Dreamer

Though not a U.S. politician, India's Prime Minister Narendra Modi is a champion of young voters and a social media guru.

The 65-year-old embodies our core values of authenticity and opti-mism, and his vision of hope and prosperity allowed him to achieve a landslide 2014 electoral victory, despite his intolerance. Modi took the world by surprise when his BJP party took an outright majority in the Lok Sabha, India's lower house of parliament. Modi's grassroots support is credited with helping achieve this dramatic victory—and young Indians were essential. American politicians have much to learn from Modi about running a successful political campaign.

Young Indians supported Modi by the largest margin of any age demographic.[26] These young Indians grew up in the modern India. Young people across the board are better educated, more ambitious, and more empowered than previous generations. Like America's millennials, India's youth are frustrated with their country's slowing economic growth. Modi's aggressive campaign for change resonated with these youths.

"For the first time, I thought, this was an able leader for the youth, who can take us out of our doldrums," Sanjay Yadav, a 24-year-old journalism graduate student in Mumbai, told the *Los Angeles Times*.[27] As young Indians look to remake their country, Modi is their "swaggering hero," so much so that pundits have dubbed India youth the "Modi generation," *The Guardian* reports.[28]

Modi appeals to this generation because he speaks to their struggles—high unemployment, desperation, a longing to join the middle class, and anger at an entrenched political system with no vision of the future. In the age of the Internet and connectivity, all young voters are results-oriented.

"The young voter is a no-nonsense, delivery-focused voter," pollster Yashwant Deshmukh of CVoter told *The Times of India*. "For them, governance is a product, and proven governance is a proven product. Modi's answers would always begin with what he had done in Gujarat, India's western-most state. That image of the doer seems to have clicked big time with the youth."[29] Modi told voters that economic growth was possible—that he would help them find work.

Modi's masterful use of social media should serve as an example for politicians everywhere. After the election, *The Telegraph* wrote, "The BJP and Modi ran a breathless and tech-savvy campaign that dazzled and engaged voters directly through social media."

Modi took selfies with voters, appeared as a holograph at campaign rallies, and is a longtime Twitter user. His opponent, Rahul Gandhi, never took to Twitter, and the Indian National Congress party only started tweeting in 2014.[30]

Modi's campaign team launched "Mission 272," a social media campaign and an app that energized his base and made it clear that Modi would not stop until his BJP party controlled the majority of the parliament.[31] On India272.com, Modi's web platform, he organized bloggers, lawyers, artists, and supporters to pitch the mission as a "historic opportunity to transform our nation." The vision was multi-platform: Mission 272 included viral videos, volunteer opportunities, Facebook and Twitter campaigns, and news updates.

Modi's consistent message and record of results were essential to his campaign. Throughout the entire campaign, Modi hearkened back to the same core value proposition: he cleaned up Gujarat and he would fix India's economy by reforming. His record as a clean and competent administrator defined him as a candidate. And his modest upbringing demonstrated that he understood the struggles of regular voters. As a child, Modi sold tea at a train station for his impoverished family, before rising through the ranks of the BJP to eventually become Gujarat's Chief Minister. "It is easy to pick up a broom and start cleaning but it takes a real leader like Modi to infuse enthusiasm in people," a student told *The Times of India*.[32]

At the end of the day, however, it was Modi's optimism and hope for India's future that made him such a hit with India's youth. Modi told crowds, "I welcome all of you and there are several opportunities waiting for you in India. Times have changed very quickly. [The] world is seeing India with immense hope and optimism."

Modi's talk of industrialization and jobs, creating new economic opportunity, and controlling inflation, raised expectations. Modi did not talk about corruption and the structural problems facing India in its race to create jobs for a bulging population, instead focusing on a vision for a strong, more confident India.

"I will make such a wonderful India that all Americans will stand in line to get a visa for India," Modi told voters. His ability to inspire passion in voters through a specific, tangible vision of his country's future and a clean record of good administration made Modi the youth champion.

American politicians have many important lessons to learn from Modi. Modi's focus might be the most important one. Modi did not run on social issues. He did not talk about gay rights at campaign events, even though they are important. He didn't focus on the environment. Modi did not tackle every issue possible. He focused on one central issue: cleaning up corruption to reform the economy.

This is the type of narrow, focused message young people are seeking. It is difficult to be authentic and optimistic when you are addressing every issue under the sun. Politicians need to focus on the issues that matter most to their constituents, and for millennials, that issue will be creating jobs.

CONCLUSION

The millennial generation is sick and tired of politics. Voters are cynical and hardened by gridlock and incompetence in Washington. In a telling headline, *Bloomberg BusinessWeek* wrote, "Politicians: Millennials Won't Vote Because They Hate You." To appeal to voters, politicians need to break through this cynicism and establish a relationship based on trust with voters. To do so, politicians need to resonate with millennial values by being authentic and relating with their struggles, being optimistic about building a better future, and being tolerant of those who share different views.

The best politicians will be champions. These leaders will combine millennial values with pragmatism to build rock-solid campaigns. By combining optimism, authenticity and tolerance, America's next generation of leaders can earn millennial support. Once our leaders adopt millennial values, they need to learn how to communicate with millennials on our platforms about our issues—which we'll talk about in the next chapter.

Mobilize Millennials
on Social Media

Millennials were born to be marketers. Getting a date on Tinder is literally a lesson in Marketing 101. You have four pictures. Most people will decide whether to swipe right or left entirely based on their first look at your profile picture. If they're on the fence, they'll click to see the other pictures and a one-sentence description of who you are and who your mutual friends are. The goal is to maximize your real estate and drive sales from that first impression.

If politicians realized that crafting a great Tinder profile is a prerequisite to winning political office, they would be much better off. Winning millennial support starts with getting noticed. Politicians need to get out in front of voters with a positive brand that resonates with millennials to get a "right swipe," and even have the chance to talk to us. For millennials, social media is often the first line of defense. Effective politicians use social media to sell their brands long before they get out on the campaign trail.

"That's Ashley Swearengin, state controller, more jobs! And that would be freakin' awesome!" announced a deep-voiced man on Pandora, an Internet radio service. Swearengin, a two-term mayor of Fresno, California, and 2014 state controller candidate, gets an A+ for creativity. Pandora users are captive listeners and any political advertisements are memorable because the medium is unique.[1] But using terms like "freakin' awesome" isn't enough to win over millennial voters. We care about content—how are you going to get us jobs? Do you have experience or are you just full of hot air?

In this chapter, we'll address how social media can turn young people into voters and advocates for political campaigns. We'll touch on tactics and content, highlighting how candidates can galvanize their base, win over independent millennials, and accomplish goal #1: build loyalty among millennial voters.

Social Media: Do or Die

Social media is no longer peripheral: it is the modern day town square, where 18-34-year-olds spend approximately 3.8 hours every single day. "It's become part of my wake-up routine. Shut off the alarm, roll over, and check the weather. Scroll through Facebook, make sure I didn't miss any texts from last night, and then finally—the part that makes the impending 10 a.m. lecture bearable—check Yik Yak," wrote college sophomore Dani Blum in an editorial.[2]

Because social media is the lens through which millennials digest the world around them, it is also a powerful tool for political engagement. Overall, 66 percent of social media users have engaged in civic or political activities online, 38 percent use it to promote political content, and 35 percent use the web to encourage people to vote.[3] Facebook newsfeed are hotbeds for political controversies and great ways to measure political sentiment. Bernie Sanders, for example, found his core supporters by chatting with them on Reddit.

But the most important reason that social media can generate exponential political returns is that it can be used to galvanize supporters. Facebook has reported that its users are 57 percent more likely to persuade a co-worker to vote, 2.5 times more likely to attend a rally, and 43 percent more likely to vote than the average American.

In 2010, when Facebook introduced an "I Voted" box that individuals could check off for their friends to see, it said that it sent an additional 300,000+ people to the polls. In 2012, 45 percent of eligible voters were encouraged to vote through social media, and 22 percent let their friends know on social media that they voted.[4]

Social networks are ripe for exploitation by effective organizers. But most politicians get an "F" for social media engagement. Check out the average senator's Twitter page, and you'll find nothing more interesting than photos of him/her shaking hands with various leaders, unions, and local political groups.

On social media, different people play different roles. We all have our friends, who we connect with via organically overlapping networks on social media. On Facebook, I have my high school friends, college friends, childhood friends, summer friends, colleagues, and then friends of friends who I consider a part of my network. On Twitter, I follow my friends, celebrities, newspapers, and political candidates. Twitter is less personal than Facebook and is therefore a more difficult place to catch my attention. It serves a different role.

The first step to engaging millennials online is recognizing the purpose and boundaries of each social media site. Facebook is "a place where young people are having a dialogue mostly amongst themselves,"[5] Rep. Joaquin Castro (D-TX) aptly said. Twitter, by contrast, is a noisy mess of self-promoters, vying for our attention. (Read: it is much harder to engage millennials on Twitter than on Facebook, but politicians spend more time on the former and less on the latter.) Instagram is used to keep track of friends and live vicariously through their experiences—traveling around the world, going to concerts, or eating delicious food.

No matter the platform, the core idea behind social media is about building a personal brand. For regular teens, the brand could be the girl who loves to post pictures of herself at the beach, the science fair wiz who posts pictures of all his or her awards, the varsity basketball player, the skater bro, you name it. A brief glimpse at a millennial's social media presence can tell a lot about the person. Politicians should invest time and money in building a brand that will resonate with millennial voters. This is harder than it seems: most politicians' social media profiles have no central theme and fail to attract or engage voters.

Take Sen. Kirsten Gillibrand, for example. The maverick is a self-described feminist, and her Facebook page holds no punches. Repeatedly, she condemns sexism in the military and on college campuses. She writes about her legislation intended to combat sexual assault in the military and on college campuses. When she isn't brandishing her core value proposition, she shares photos of her family. Slowly but surely, even staunchly independent millennials begin to associate her with these issues. Eventually, they begin to cite her in their own Facebook conversations and link to her page.

Many politicians think that if they dump enough money into Facebook advertising and a campaign consultant, they'll master this new "wild west" of political campaigns. They could not be more wrong. If Facebook demonstrates anything, it is that you cannot buy support. Buzz is organic, and a straightforward, resonant image will cultivate genuine supporters. If, in the course of our regular social media interactions, we come to view a politician as a friend and an ally, then we will develop an allegiance to a candidate, just as we are loyal to our friends. This type of relationship is much stronger than traditional politician-supporter bonds, and is much more resilient to the ebb and flow of every news cycle. It also creates opportunities for stronger organization in the future, with these young people organizing their peers and actively volunteering for political campaigns.

The campaign to elect Bill de Blasio as mayor of New York City in 2013 is a second example of strong social media positioning—and his unexpected victory demonstrates its power to be a game-changer. Early in the campaign to replace three-term Mayor Michael Bloomberg, de Blasio—a small-time public advocate—was polling in fourth/fifth place. The candidate rarely received media coverage, and early in the campaign cycle, most people could hardly pick him out of a lineup. But millennials knew who he was. De Blasio was the income inequality guy. My friends said they were going to volunteer for him. My debate coach—then an NYU student—said the media was crazy for missing the potential in this guy. And his social media presence was consistent—every one of his posts told a story about "a tale of two cities." Then "out of nowhere"—de Blasio swept the polls.

The media were shocked. Where did he come from? How did he lead the pack? A lot of credit was given to an ad that features his son, Dante de Blasio, who told New Yorkers that he would support de Blasio "even if he wasn't my dad." While calm and controlled Dante certainly helped create buzz around de Blasio (the clip was shared wildly on social media), it was only successful because it contributed to a sustained and consistent messaging campaign about income inequality, an issue that resonated with New Yorkers and especially with millennials.

Successful social media campaigns are mission-driven. Vote for de Blasio because early childhood education helps the poor. Vote de Blasio because affordable housing helps the poor. Vote de Blasio because fighting for African Americans helps the poor. Each issue boils down to one unifying idea. Vote Kirsten Gillibrand because she's fighting against rape in the military. Vote Kirsten Gillibrand because she's fighting against rape on college campuses. Vote Kirsten Gillibrand because she cares about families. Social media users have very limited attention spans. Most posts to social media will never garner the attention of users. But over time, the posts we do see help us build deep impressions of candidates. These impressions are very hard to change after the fact. They are invaluable.

In the 2016 presidential primaries, Sanders took the lead in capturing the millennial vote. Sanders spent months holding real-time Q&As with supporters on Reddit, a popular question-answer site. This strategy early in the election season was successful for two reasons: first, young people respected him for being a trailblazer;

he was an early adopter of a less mainstream social media site. The second reason is that young people see Sanders as an accessible candidate; while Hillary Clinton goes around raising millions from fat cat donors, Sanders spends his time on young people. (Clinton didn't change voters' impressions when she copied his strategy.)

Candidates like Sanders and Paul before him—fringe candidates with radical ideas—have galvanized young voters by engaging them in the political process. They tell young people that we are important and that we don't have to buy into the canned platforms of mainstream Democrats and Republicans. From a purely tactical standpoint, these candidates are on the front lines of social media, engaging us every day.

New Media

They say that Washington always prepares for the last war, instead of the current one. That couldn't be truer of political campaigns and the approach to social media campaigning. Everyone is so busy fighting over who can have the better Facebook or Twitter page, they are missing the larger picture: engaging millennials holistically on all platforms.

Campaigns should use Instagram, Reddit, Pandora (as Swearengin successfully did), and especially Snapchat in addition to just Facebook. Any message on a fresher platform will make the candidate and his/her campaign look more advanced.

Most campaigns today have Snapchat accounts where they post cultivated stories, and I hope this is a practice that will filter its way to all elected officials. Snapchat stories are quick and easy ways to deliver a memorable message, and if they're funny, can even become fairly popular. If these videos are candid (scarfing down a piece of pizza after a long day stumping for votes), they can attract consistent viewers. It's much easier to get to know a candidate by seeing literal snapshots of his/her day than to read cultivated PR garbage from campaign teams.

On these platforms, the spin will need to be toward authenticity and away from traditional "leadership" or "experience" messages.

Candidates often struggle to balance including their family members in the campaigning process, and this is a tough decision to make. We personally think politicians should err on the side of inclusion, and as Michelle Obama's role in her husband's campaign demonstrates, many political consultants seem to agree with us. For politicians who have young kids (which many do), including the family in the social media presence is an important humanizing tactic.

New apps like Periscope—which allows users to upload live videos to the web—can be used to capture funny moments in real time. And since everyone knows that political messages are canned anyway, politicians can plan out what their families are going to do in the videos.

Television ads have always been an integral part of political campaigns and they receive the most funding by far. Apparently, data shows that they are very successful. A 30-second TV spot, usually filled with negative information about the opponents, if we're honest with ourselves, can leave a lasting impression with voters and help change their opinions.

So there's a huge problem that needs to be addressed—I haven't turned on a television in more than 12 months. For my friends, that period may not be so long but the message is the same—millennials are increasingly choosing to watch television on Netflix and generally avoiding traditional "prime-time" shows, instead choosing political comedy like #jonvoyage, if anything.

What's the solution? The obvious answer is to reallocate budget toward "digital," which is the biggest cliché of them all. While this will naturally happen to some extent, we actually think it's the wrong approach. Anecdotally, based on our conversations, millennials say they are already so inundated by political messaging that they are unlikely to voluntarily click on an advertisement (whereas we are more likely to click on an ad for a product we think might be interesting).

Instead of diverting TV funds toward mobile and web ads, we think campaigns would be well advised to spend money on more costly YouTube advertisements. These ads would need to be more expensive because they need to be catchy enough to attract viewers, or they are useless. But if done right, they will generate repeat views without the need to shell out cash in the future—the videos live forever.

Sen. Marco Rubio (R-FL) did this right when he released a video of Rick Harrison—the TV celebrity who runs the show *Pawn Stars*—endorsing his campaign for presidency. The video could definitely have been more engaging or fun to watch (it was more than a little dry), but the idea was on the right track. *Pawn Star* fans jumped to click on the video, which generated thousands of likes and views on YouTube and generated buzz in the media and on talk shows like *Hannity*.

This success all came with what was clearly a sub-par video, Rubio sounded canned, Harrison sounded bored, and it didn't feel genuine to the show ("F-" for the media consultant who filmed it). Other campaigns need to follow suit—and hopefully they'll hire better folks to do their filming.

Content: What Should You Be Talking About

When we first shared our story about Swearengin's Pandora ad, we warned that the content of the radio advertisement was not up to par. I don't care for "that's freakin' awesome," and when I recounted the ad to potential voters, their almost universal reaction was to call the line condescending.

Millennials are a highly educated generation in American history, and politicians often have trouble squaring that with our love of hashtags, use of superficial dating apps, and jokes as if we don't know what we're talking about. That's why politicians and the media love to make fun of the millennials—"they are so stupid," people like to say. The problem for these politicians is that millennials are intelligent. Campaigns need to offer coherent arguments to win our votes.

So our recommendation for politicians when approaching content is to think about using a platform that's fun and shareable, but to use hard facts in their ads. Swearengin was ranked one of the top 10 mayors in California—why didn't she tell us that? And she was right to identify jobs as the most important message to get across, but has she actually created jobs? What are her platforms? How is she going to win?

These are all questions that need to be answered. Sharp statements are effective. Short and clear. Carly Fiorina—a political novice who ran an upstart Republican presidential primary campaign in 2016 and did better than many pundits expected—hits this on the nose. I'm Carly Fiorina, she said, and I believe in opportunity. I rose from secretary to CEO and I want to protect the American dream. Her argument is powerful and clear.

Millennials are issue-oriented voters looking for authentic candidates to deliver real results. They are radical realists—the opposite of partisan ideologues—who are interested in casting an educated ballot. As such, millennials tend to be undecided swing voters who have a disproportional impact on electoral outcomes.

The result is that traditional "Get Out the Vote" campaigns won't cut it. Having a compelling thesis and a personalized argument about why millennials should bother voting for you is more important than ever. Politicians cannot get away with throwaway talking points or aggressive attacks at the opponent.

Finally, prioritizing millennial issues is crucial. All too often politicians offer us the same message as everyone else. With targeted advertising, politicians can be much more audience-driven. They should feed into the optimism of the millennial generation and propose that they are our champions. Most of this book focused on our policy platforms, and it is a guide to how to approach these issues. If getting us jobs, protecting us from gun violence, and giving our generation a voice in the political process are themes of the campaign, then millennials will buy into the message. In millennial America, content is king.

Top 10 Social Media Tips

The key four elements of social media use that we have focused on in this chapter are branding, organizing, getting out the vote, and engaging with voters. We have developed a set of 10 actionable recommendations for using social media to appeal to voters. While many of these may be obvious, we think that the vast majority of politicians, including major 2016 presidential contenders, do not follow these rules.

1. **Be Real:** Don't try to be fancy. Be a regular person. Talk about eating pizza and getting stuck in traffic. If a Twitter page sounds like a real person, it is believable. If content sounds cultivated, people will not listen. Politicians, they're just like us.

2. **Everyone Counts:** Don't discount your Twitter followers and ignore them. They form the backbone of your campaign. You don't have to respond to everyone, but be respectful and treat everyone as important. This is New Jersey Senator Corey Booker's forte—he responds to tweets within minutes, joking with random tweeters, not only his fellow senators.

3. **Understand the Ecosystem:** Social media is an ecosystem. Understand who lives around you—bloggers, pop stars, and family members—and live like a neighbor. If you treat social media like a one-way platform for you to sound your ideas, fewer people will pay attention. If you understand the environment, you will find volunteers and supporters rising to action on your pages.

4. **Make Friends:** No one will see your posts if they are not in your network. Politicians should work diligently to encourage supporters to "friend" them or like their pages. Often, good content is the best way to drive views, but this is a place where digital media consultants really can deliver.

5. **Post Regularly:** Post at least once a day. Obviously this depends on your audience and the quality/type of each post, but generally three to five posts per day on Facebook cannot hurt. On Twitter, the sky is the limit. You need to generate buzz and to do it frequently. If you consistently appear in voters' newsfeeds and they like your posts, you will rise to the top of their feeds.

6. **Share Exclusive Information:** Generic tweets are no fun. Tell us something new that is unique to you. Whether that is your opinion, breaking news, or behind-the-scenes photos, social media users are going to be attracted to information that feels different. Remember, we are scrolling through Twitter and Facebook and stop at interesting posts. Your content has to be so different that it causes us to stop in our tracks.

7. **Images Speak Louder than Words:** There's a reason BuzzFeed became so popular so fast. It is easier to digest images and GIFs than words. Posts that include photos generate 180 percent more engagement than the average post. Especially on Facebook, a post without an image is almost guaranteed to get lost in the crowd.[6]

8. **Be Cool: Use Videos:** Nike's #MakeItCount video took NikeFuel to the next level. Instead of creating an advertisement, Casey Neistat and Max Joseph took the money Nike gave them and traveled around the world to make the money count. Their travel video went viral. Melbourne's transportation authority created a video about "Dumb Ways to Die." The video has 95 million views on YouTube. Videos are substantially more powerful than

images or words. So if you are thinking about making a video, #MakeItCount.

9. **Don't Say Stupid Things:** Given the state of national politics, this must be said. Topics not to talk about: Religion, rape, abortion, and gays. Always proofread tweets and Facebook posts and if in doubt, run a post by a staff member. Gaffes made online will never be forgotten. Imagine that every tweet you make is immediately sent to *The New York Times* and archived.

10. **Damage Control:** Use social media to undo gaffes. Post quickly and frequently to correct mistakes. One of President Obama's senior advisors accidentally tweeted a racial slur on his social media account. A few minutes later, he corrected himself: "Obviously a horrendous typo in my previous tweet. My apologies." Twitter forgave him because he acted quickly, before the situation got out of control. Notice the severity of the response—he made sure the twitter-sphere knew how seriously he treated the "horrendous" mistake.

CONCLUSION: ENTERTAIN US, PLEASE

Politicians need to entertain us. I recognize that this is far cry from the ribbon-cutting ceremonies that most politicians think are the most exciting parts of their online presence. In an age of connectivity, politicians need to realize that they are competing with celebrities for attention. It doesn't cut it to just be a boring public servant. The coolest politicians can build cult followings online—and the lame ones, well, we don't even know their names.

In this realm, young politicians have an advantage. When Rubio reached for a water bottle during his response to the State of the Union address in February 2013, the media jumped on this "amateur" move, calling it a "duck and dive" as the video went viral. Rubio turned the gaffe into a fundraiser, selling Marco Rubio water bottles for $25

Patrick Meehan ✓ 🐦 Follow
@RepMeehan

Honoring some of the winners of the #Delco Senior Games at Maris Grove in Glen Mills yesterday

11:50 AM - 22 Jul 2014

1 RETWEET 1 FAVORITE

Susan W. Brooks 🐦 Follow
@SusanWBrooks

Excited to hear Lowe's is bringing a new customer support center to Indy. Nice to see #IN05 attracting new jobs!

11:49 AM - 22 Jul 2014

4 RETWEETS 5 FAVORITES

"Most politicians have clumsily used social media as just another means of self-promotion or extended press releases. Most posts by politicians on social media take the form of a congratulatory note after a meeting..." —*Buzzfeed*

When the EPA accidentally tweeted a score from a Kardashian game, Dingell killed it with his reaction.

each, posting to his website the following message: "Send the liberal detractors a message that not only does Marco Rubio inspire you ... he hydrates you too."[7] Rubio then posted the Poland Springs bottle he was drinking from to Twitter, where the photo was re-tweeted almost 5,000 times. The media (not to mention us cynical young folk) ate it

EXCLUSIVE

I'M COMING HOME

Rep. John Dingell ✓
@john_dingell   🐦 Follow

With the House adjourned for the week, I'm taking my talents back
to Michigan to spend time with constituents. #MI12

2:45 PM - 18 Jul 2014

239 RETWEETS 211 FAVORITES   ↩ ↻ ★

After LeBron James announced he was "coming home" to Cleveland, Dingell
took to Twitter to mock the celebrity.

up.[8] Millennial voters are better able to relate with young candidates
like Rubio because they look, sound, and feel like our friends.

But age can be overcome. In fact, Buzzfeed's favorite politician
was American's oldest congressman, until he retired in 2015. Then
88-year-old John Dingell (D-MI) saw his Buzzfeed feature go viral on
Facebook soon after it was published. And for good reason: Dingell
is hilarious. "The longest serving member of Congress is better on
Twitter than all of us. Rep. John Dingell, the 88-year-old Michigan
Democrat first elected in 1955, has quickly solidified himself as the
best politician on Twitter," Buzzfeed's Andrew Kaczynski wrote.

Many politicians have their interns or staff members manage
social media profiles. That may allow for mediocre posts, even good
ones, but rarely allows for the true character of the politician to shine
through. And fake politicians always get caught. Dingell is a funny
granddad. That personality animates his Twitter profile—and his daily

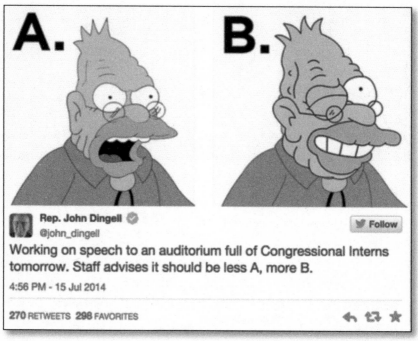

Dingell can be self-deprecating. We are all laughs.

encounters. The comments Dingell's constituents left on Buzzfeed demonstrate the genuine nature of his Twitter personality. Kendra Anspaugh, a community college teacher, posted to Facebook about Dingell, "When I was on an 8th-grade class trip to DC, he came and met our group outside the Capitol and snuck us in a side entrance to avoid the long lines to get in. Best. Congressman. Ever."

Jessica Carreras, digital media coordinator for the City of Dearborn, Michigan, posted on her wall, "Dingell is my representative—met him a handful of times, and he really is hilarious. I once took a picture of him with our city's police chief (I take photographs for our city) and he turned around and said 'OK, Chief, now I want a picture with her.' Awesome."

Dingell is not alone. Over the past couple of years a number of politicians have used social media to effectively generate engagement.

Texas state Sen. Wendy Davis, for example, became the first politician to crowd-source her filibuster, asking followers to share their stories and testimonials. Her request for submissions was re-tweeted 9,000 times. Sen. Rand Paul took to Twitter to celebrate Fesitvus (the made-up holiday from *Seinfeld*) by airing his grievances—from the lack of puppies in politics, to President Obama's failure to abide by the Fourth Amendment. His friend Corey Booker (with whom he frequently engages in Twitter banter) is famous for using Twitter to resolve the concerns of his constituents—like filling potholes.

When it comes to engaging the public online, politicians may have something to learn from the private sector about timing. Oreo stood poised to act during Super Bowl XLVII. When a 34-minute power outage angered 100 million viewers across the country, Oreo took to Twitter. It tweeted, "Power Out? No problem. You can still dunk in the dark." The post was re-tweeted 16,000 times and received 20,000 Facebook likes. Politicians are afraid of gaffes—but keeping up with the times and cracking good jokes will keep their names in front of young voters.

Build a Grassroots Army

The first day I walked into the campaign offices of Carolyn Maloney (D-NY) during her 2010 Congressional reelection bid, I was absolutely shocked. The room was packed with millennials in high school and college at the time, getting ready to canvas or make calls on Maloney's behalf. Later, I found out that when we volunteered on our first political campaign with Maloney, we joined more than 300 New York City teens—the largest campaign team in the history of New York State, according to the campaign organizers—in what was effectively an uncontested primary race. The Maloney for Congress campaign was a textbook study on how to build a grassroots movement using social media—and it wasn't even a tight race!

Anyone can build a campaign energized by millennial volunteers; it just takes effort and sweat to build support among students, who are often looking for work to do over the summer anyway. These volunteers can be incredible advocates for any political campaign. They provide a successful organizer unparalleled manpower to knock on doors and organize phone banks. The result is that these campaigns are able to reach more voters and spread their message. On the Maloney for Congress campaign we each had the opportunity to manage 30 interns, all really intelligent high school students from around the city. In a single day, our teams could call 20,000-30,000 homes across the city. If we went out canvassing, we could knock on more than a thousand doors in a day. In this chapter, we focus on how and why any campaign can mobilize millennial volunteers to build incredible, innovative, and winning campaign teams.

The power of organizing grassroots volunteers from among millennials is that these young people are enthusiastic about the change they believe in. I will never forget my first day of high school, because it coincided with the day of the primary election. I spent the day shuttling back and forth between campaign headquarters at 3 a.m., school, and back to knock on more doors along with dozens of peers. Together, a bunch of semi-random young people with no knowledge helped our congresswoman get elected. Talk about #Impact.

Millennial volunteers can later become strong community advocates, especially in smaller towns. Peers of ours say that the best leaders intentionally bring in volunteers from diverse neighborhoods to cultivate ambassadors who will spread their message beyond just a core constituency. As luck would have it, much of our initial campaign team went on to do great things; our 16-year-old office manager went on to run Christine Quinn's mayoral campaign; Jack's co-team leader was the only Intel Science Finalist in New York City; one of the most successful interns on the campaign went on to manage 300+ interns on a Missouri Senate race—all before graduating from high school. Recruiting can create talent pipelines and community goodwill in any district.

We always pay attention to which campaigns try to recruit students during every election cycle because the campaigns that have the best outreach arms tend to win. It is ironic for us to watch candidates lose tight races, knowing full well that they could have had 100 high school students knocking on doors for them full-time from June through August—and were simply not motivated enough to build this grassroots army. What a mistake!

Businesses love to talk about how millennials believe in volunteering, so much so that many companies now have volunteer days, when all employees do community service instead of their regular work. When they come to recruit on campus, many of these businesses spend half their pitch discussing all the opportunities for us to engage our communities and give back while on the job. These companies recognize that millennials are civically minded and care about making a difference in our communities. Politicians should realize that social media is a platform that makes grassroots campaigning easy. Millennials are volunteers ripe for the picking.

Get Out the Vote: Driving Voter Turnout

All of these tactics are important for politicians to develop loyal support among millennials. But come Election Day, the most important issue becomes driving voter turnout. Get out the vote strategies can often make the difference between the winners and losers in terms of tangible votes. There are two key elements for organizers to consider: registering voters, and then getting them to go the polls and cast their ballots.

Millennial voters do everything online, and converting voter registration into an easy task that can be completed in a few button clicks can dramatically improve turnout. The last time I filled out a paper application was when I applied for a visa to travel to China—in the spring of 2014. I applied to college online, apply for jobs online, applied for a credit card online, and submit my assignments online. Right now, only 21 states allow for online voter registration. National campaigns and local campaigns in these states should take advantage of online voter registration to bring millennials to the polls. The remaining 29 states should pass laws to legalize online voter registration as soon as possible.

Adults may take registering to vote for granted, but when you are 18 and just graduated from high school, there are many things on your mind—and voting is usually not on the top of that list. This makes voter registration drives crucial to actually getting young voters to the polls. Political parties should conduct voter registration drives online and partner with local Young Democrats/Young Republicans groups to drive turnout. Focus should be placed on taking advantage of the existing network of volunteers and using their existing relationships to spread the word about voting online.

When it comes to getting voters to the polls, the value of strong marketing is often overlooked. At the University of Pennsylvania, a referendum on divestment from fossil fuel garnered higher voter turnout than midterm elections. Because students could see the tangible impact of the referendum, they voted. Because the midterm candidates never reached out to us or explained why voting for them would help us, many students didn't vote. Even your authors, who are clearly politically involved, were not exposed to even one single advertisement in our local congressional race. Likewise, the competitive mayoral race in Philadelphia barely scratched the surface of engagement on campus. With more than five colleges in Philadelphia, and thousands of potential voters, candidates missed out on a key demographic. It isn't rocket science—millennials will vote when given a concrete reason to go to the polls.

Social media sites are especially effective for driving voter turnout because they take advantage of a psychological phenomenon known as "social proof." In *The Small BIG*, Steve Martin, Noah Goldstein, and Robert Cialdini explain that individuals are more likely to conform to what they perceive as positive social norms when they believe that those similar to them are abiding by the same norms. For example, when Britain changed its tax collection letters for non-submitters to tell them that the vast majority of their community members paid their taxes on time, the tax clearance rate rose from 57 percent to 86 percent. All because the government added one sentence to its tax collection letters!

Likewise, researchers tested four ways to improve energy conservation. Homeowners were asked to place one of four signs on their front doors to remind them that: a) conservation benefits the environment, b) conservation protects future generations, c) conversation helps residents save money, and d) the majority of their neighbors were conserving energy. After a month, the researchers found that reminding homeowners that their peers conserve energy was the most effective way of reducing energy use. The other methods barely worked at all.

If people are motivated by a belief that others conform to socially beneficial norms—such as paying taxes or conserving energy—it seems reasonable to believe that social media could encourage all voters—not only young people—to register to vote. Voter registration, like environmental conservation and taxes, is a civic duty that may be time-consuming and may not yield immediately foreseeable benefits. The best way to encourage people to be civically engaged is to remind them that their friends are doing it.

Because young people are most closely bound to their social networks, they are most likely to be influenced by "social proof," or peer pressure. Empirically, social media has improved turnout among young voters. In the first election after Facebook was founded, in 2006, Facebook and Rock the Vote joined forces to drive voter registration. This helped lead to a 10 percent turnout boost as compared with 2002, the last midterm election. National statistics point to an overall trend of increasing voter turnout among young people—and 2014 was no exception. Still, in 2016 it will be up to local politicians to drive turnout in their home districts.

CONCLUSION: CONVERTING THE ARMY INTO A TEAM

Once a political campaign is finished, grassroots engines turn off and volunteers return to their daily lives. Outside of the occasional newsletter, politicians forget the activists who helped them win their political office.

In millennial America, successful politicians will convert grassroots armies of young volunteers into longtime supporters and even staff. Millennials want to volunteer their time for the causes they believe in, and in a world where many of them must seek out internships to be competitive in the job market, politicians have the opportunity to engage a larger team in delivering services to their constituents. Especially in local governments, this gives politicians the ability to deliver real value for voters and expand their political footprint.

New York City Councilman Ben Kallos, a Democrat, is a good case study. When I was told by a group of New York City high school students that the councilman had more than 20 people working in his district office, I laughed. I thought they were crazy. City council offices can barely afford a couple of legislative aides, let alone more than five social workers, a dozen interns, and a sizable policy team. But soon I learned that Kallos has managed to exponentially increase the impact of his office by using strong management to convert motivated millennials into free volunteers. His practice—long used by political campaigns to lower costs—is to have interns and volunteers train each other, with more senior volunteers training newer ones. As a result, Kallos is able to address election-winning convenience issues like overfilled garbage cans. Kallos demonstrates that building ties with the millennial community will see political careers benefit greatly.

Afterword: Decision 2016 and Beyond

Our goal in this book was to take a deep dive into millennial political beliefs to better understand where this generation is leading our country. From marijuana legalization to gun control, we have explored some of the most complex issues in American public policy. But we keep getting an additional question, and we want to take the chance to answer it. That question is: Knowing what we do about millennials political beliefs, which party is going to win millennial votes?

We think we have made a persuasive case in this book that the answer is anyone. Millennials are an unclaimed generation. They are politically independent. Especially for political candidates, party affiliation may be less important than specific policy positions. In local and national elections, the door is wide-open to the candidates who are able to adopt a "radical realist" perspective. Compromise, moderation, and fierce action-oriented advocacy are the keys to winning over the hearts and minds of millennial voters.

Of course, we have not answered the question entirely. It is valid to realize that U.S. elections by nature favor a two party system, because our "first past the post" process means that congressional elections are winner takes all. Right now millennials favor Democrats.

Even with half of millennials identifying as independent, 51 percent of millennials surveyed by Pew Research said they lean Democratic, while 35 percent lean toward Republicans. Frankly, Democrats have done a better job courting millennial votes than Republicans have. This should come as no surprise—millennials helped elect President Obama in 2008 and 2012.

But millennials still say they are politically unclaimed because they don't like either party. They choose Democrats at the polling booth more out of necessity than choice; hence, the refusal to identify as Democrats. But with millennials getting older, things are changing. Economists say party affiliation is "sticky." The more often you vote for a specific party, the more likely you are to vote for the party in the future. Economists Ethan Kaplan and Sharun Mukand describe this trend as "persistence of political partisanship" in a recent academic paper, which studied the party affiliation of young voters in the years after they registered to vote.[1]

This should be a call to action for both parties. As millennials enter a new phase in our lives, we're suddenly no longer going to be known for texting or selfies. We're going to be America's parents, lawyers, construction workers, welders, and doctors. This transition is happening right now—so both parties need to be urgently courting young people. Instead, Republicans and Democrats are alienating our generation, further entrenching our cynicism. This may lead to the worst possible outcome of all—a new normal where millennials simply don't turn out to vote. Civic engagement is sticky too, so if people start deciding to consistently opt out of elections, this could continue later in life.

Instead of cultivating millennial support, both parties are pushing us away. Let's start with Democrats. It's probably no surprise that Hillary Clinton is not a "millennial champion." Clinton embodies the pessimism, phony politics, and cynicism that our generation so strongly opposes. Though millennials support her in polls, and will likely come out to deliver her a majority in November, we really don't like her. That's why millennials came out in favor of Bernie Sanders during the 2016 Democratic primary race by a predicted 16-point margin, forming the core of his base. It wasn't that Sanders' policies so starkly differed from Clinton's, but that he is a straight talker with new ideas.

Republicans, meanwhile, are fighting for the future of the GOP, which is running the risk of becoming totally irrelevant. That's ironic because when we really look through the millennial platform, a lot of it is straight out of the Republican playbook. Millennials are "hipster capitalists," as Reason noted, and radical realists. They generally favor markets over government and their top policy priority is the economy. Socially, they are family-oriented. They believe in small government. This is hardly a generation of bleeding heart liberals. It's a generation that needs hope and wants change, after growing up in the shadow of terrorism and the 2008 recession.

Big wedge issues are turning millennials away from the GOP. The party establishment likes to talk a lot about gay marriage, illegal immigration, and hawkish foreign policy views. Rather than highlighting places where millennial swing voters tend to agree with the Right, the views that get the most attention are social policies that millennials fundamentally disagree with. It then becomes easy for Democrats to turn national elections into demographic battles they know they can win. Latinos and millennials are just too important to ignore.

On the flip side, we have House Speaker Paul Ryan. Ryan's message is really simple. He believes in "opportunity for all." He's a budget hawk who cut his teeth on reducing government spending and working to create jobs in the United States. Ryan's focus on poverty plays to millennial preferences, capturing the balance between small government and the importance of equality. The Wisconsin congressman gets what it takes to be a unifying figure. After Donald Trump suggested banning Muslims from immigrating to the United States, Ryan held a news conference to remind voters that this is not the stance of the GOP.

"We are going to do all we can so working people get their strength back and people not working get their lives back. No more favors for the few. Opportunity for all—that is our motto," Ryan said when he accepted the role as House Speaker. Millennials really buy into this message. That's why early in the 2016 election cycle, millennials consistently ranked Paul Ryan as their first choice for president, until it became clear that he would not run.

We are journalists, not pollsters. We cannot predict the future. But with a comprehensive picture of how millennials think about political issues, a firm understanding of their importance in the political process, and a framework for reform, the ingredients are all here. Instead of complaining about why millennials' political views don't make any sense, it's time Washington politicians began to cater to America's most powerful generation.

Regardless of which party absorbs the millennial vote, the generation itself will cause a profound shift in this country's politics. Because social issues draw such a unified consensus among millennials, issues like marriage equality, environmental protection, and marijuana legalization will soon be met with concrete public policy. Meanwhile, income inequality will continue to gain steam as a hot-button political topic. This issue has become a rallying cry for the generation that spearheaded the Occupy Wall Street movement. Likewise, criminal justice reform, gun control, and economic reform will gain traction.

Looking outside our boarders, foreign policy issues are positioned to become some of the biggest challenges facing millennial leaders. Tensions in the Middle East between Israelis and Palestinians seem to be sparking after what seemed to be a decade of relative peace. Iran continues to raise red flags as analysts worry about a potential arms race in the region, despite the recent nuclear deal. Meanwhile, cyber-attacks from China and tension between China and U.S. allies in East Asia threaten to destabilize the region, while Russia continues to exert itself in Eastern Europe. As these tensions escalate, a nation of young people will explore a new set of diplomatic tools—from cyber warfare to economic sanctions—rather than engage militarily.

The millennial generation will have an important role to play in translating its obsession with technology into public policy, innovating within the education system, and developing methods to make college more affordable. If there is any guarantee when it comes to our enigmatic generation, it is that our leaders will disrupt Washington—not only through these technologies, but also as public servants changing the very nature of American political discourse.

Looking forward to the future, the country will rely not only on millennial voters, but also on millennial leaders. Starting with the 2020 electoral race, millennials will no longer be the youngest demographic; the centennial generation, born after 2000, will vote in their first election, likely choosing between a slate of new millennial challengers and older incumbents. Already, leaders in Congress have formed a caucus of young leaders who are at the forefront of change. These radical realists will introduce a new philosophy that will hopefully revitalize our nation.

We live in a trying time. Americans are more divided than ever. Today, the bickering of Democratic and Republicans politicians is being pushed to the wayside. In its place, a new millennial consensus will be implemented, as young people reimagine the future of their nation. Dear America, adults are fired—the kids are taking over.

Acknowledgments

This book would not have been possible without the support of our life coach, Jerry Cahn, and our debate coach, Julie Sheinman. A special thank you to both of them for supporting us throughout this whole process. Thanks to our mother Dina for her encouragement and our brother Daniel for constantly challenging our ideas and pushing us to reconsider our premises.

The Junior State was instrumental in giving us the opportunity to form our political views at their conferences and in helping us schedule interviews and meetings with student leaders from across the country while we prepared our manuscript. Thank you to Jeff Harris, Elizabeth Ventura, Kyle Simmons, Lisa Shuman, and to Junior State members and alumni everywhere.

We appreciate all the work done by our agent Jennifer Cohen, who fought tirelessly to help us translate this idea into a reality. Thank you our editor Rachel Shuster and to all of the folks at Post Hill Press for their dedication and commitment to our book, especially Anthony Ziccardi and Gavin Caruthers.

Endnotes

Introduction

1. Ingraham, Christopher. "Five Really Good Reasons to Hate Millennials." *Washington Post*. May 5, 2015.

2. Sheets, Connor Adams. "Will Millennials Determine The 2016 Presidential Election? New Poll Looks At Their Voting Plans." *International Business Times*. October 9, 2014.

3. Draplin, Derick. "Young Republican Voters Helped Midterm Election's Red Wave, Exit Polls Show." The College Fix. November 7, 2014. Tuccille, J.D. "GOP Senate Pickups: 7 and Counting. It's a Republican Day." *Reason*. November 4, 2014.

4. Rampell, Catherine. "Millennials' Mysterious Support for Permissive Gun Laws." *Washington Post*. December 7, 2015.

5. Perez, Esten. "Likely Millennial Voters Up for Grabs in Upcoming Midterm Elections, Harvard Institute of Politics Youth Poll Finds." Harvard Kennedy School. October 29, 2014.

6. "Low Midterm Turnout Likely, Conservatives More Enthusiastic, Harvard Youth Poll Finds." The Institute of Politics at Harvard University.

7. Fournier, Ron. "The Outsiders: How Can Millennials Change Washington If They Hate It?" *The Atlantic*. August 26, 2013.

Safer Streets

1. Findlehor, David, Heather Turner, Richard Ormrod, Sherry Hamby, and Kristen Kracke. "Children's Exposure to Violence: A Comprehensive National Survey." PsycEXTRA Dataset.

2. Findlehor, David, Heather Turner, Richard Ormrod, Sherry Hamby, and Kristen Kracke. "Children's Exposure to Violence: A Comprehensive National Survey." PsycEXTRA Dataset.

3. Washington Times Staff. "142 School Shootings since Sandy Hook Massacre in Newtown, Conn." *Washington Times* (Washington, DC), October 1, 2015.

4. "Changing Norms and Behavior." Cure Violence Changing Norms and Behavior Comments.

5. Parsons, Chelsea, and Anne Johnson. "Young Guns: How Gun Violence Is Devastating the Millennial Generation." Generation Progress. February 2014.

6. Parsons, Chelsea, and Anne Johnson, *op. cit.*

7. "Protect Children Not Guns 2013." Children's Defense Fund. 2013.

8. Hawkins, Awr. "Pew Study: Majority of Millennials Oppose Gun Control—Breitbart." *Breitbart News*. March 10, 2014.

9. "Poll: Majority of Young People Considering Gun Ownership." American University. January 14, 2013.

10. "The Impact Of The 1994 Federal Assault Weapon Act." Brady Center to Prevent Gun Violence. March 1, 2004.

11. Dube, Arindrajit, Oeindrila Dube, and Omar García-Ponce. "Cross-Border Spillover: U.S. Gun Laws and Violence in Mexico." *American Political Science Review*. 2013: 397–417.

12. Koper, Christopher, Daniel Woods, and Jeffrey Roth. "An Updated Assessment of the Federal Assault Weapons Ban: Impacts on Gun Markets and Gun Violence, 1994–2003." Report to the National Institute of Justice, United States Department of Justice, 2004.

13. Ekins, Emily. "Poll: Americans, Especially Young Ones, Say People "Should Be Allowed" to Own Assault Weapons." *Reason*. January 31, 2013.

14. Weinger, Mackenzie. "Mitt Romney's Stance on Gun Control." *Politico*. July 20, 2012.

15. Levy, Robert. "Gun Control Measures Don't Stop Violence." *CNN*. January 19, 2011.

16. "More Guns, Less Crime Again." NRAILA RSS. September 15, 2010.

17. "NRA-ILA: Statement on President Obama's Proposed Executive Actions on Gun Control." *NRA-ILA*. January 5, 2015.

18. "Who Put The NRA in Charge of Our National Security?" Children's Defense Fund. December 4, 2015.

19. Wintemute, Garen J. "Prior Misdemeanor Convictions as a Risk Factor for Later Violent and Firearm-Related Criminal Activity Among Authorized Purchasers of Handguns." *JAMA* 280, no. 24 (1998): 2083.

20. "Gun Safety and Public Health: Policy Recommendations for a More Secure America." The National Physicians Alliance and the Law Center to Prevent Gun Violence. September 1, 2013.

21. Ibid.

22. Ibid.

23. "Universal Background Checks & the "Private" Sale Loophole Policy Summary." Law Center to Prevent Gun Violence. September 10, 2015.

24. Ibid.

25. Wintemute, Garen J., Anthony A. Braga, and David M. Kennedy. "Private-Party Gun Sales, Regulation, and Public Safety." *New England Journal of Medicine*: 508–11. "Protect Children, Not Guns: The Truth About Guns." Children's Defense Fund. 2013.

26. "Gun Safety and Public Health: Policy Recommendations for a More Secure America," *op. cit.*

27. Ibid.

28. Webster, Daniel W., Jon S. Vernick, and Maria T. Bulzacchelli. "Effects of State-Level Firearm Seller Accountability Policies on Firearm Trafficking." *Journal of Urban Health* 86, no. 4 (2009): 525–37.

Better Jobs

1. Ark, Casey. "I Studied Business and Programming, Not English. I Still Can't Find a Job." *Washington Post*. August 27, 2014. November 29, 2015.

2. Trumbull, Mark. "Have Degree, Driving Cab: Nearly Half of College Grads Are Overqualified." *The Christian Science Monitor*. January 28, 2013. December 2, 2015.

3. Davis, Owen. "Millennials And Their Money: Portrait Of A Generation." *International Business Times*. October 01, 2015.

4. Sweeney, Brigid, and Stephen Serio. "The Millennials: Educated. Ambitious. Screwed?" *Crain's Chicago Business*. October 18, 2014.

5. Malcolm, Hadley. "Job Outlook for 2014 College Grads Puzzling." *USA Today*. May 19, 2014.

6. Sanburn, Josh. "4 Ways Millennials Have It Worse Than Their Parents Did." *Time*. December 4, 2014.

7. Malcolm, Hadley. "Job Outlook for 2014 College Grads Puzzling." *USA Today*. May 19, 2014.

8. O'Sullivan, Rory, Konrad Mugglestone, and Tom Allison. "In This Together." *Young Invincibles*. January 2014.

9. "Left Behind; The Jobless Young (Youth Unemployment in Developed Countries)." *The Economist*, September 10, 2011.

10. Steinberg, Sarah Ayres. "The High Cost of Youth Unemployment." Center for American Progress. April 5, 2013.

11. Langer, Gary. "Exit Polls: Economy, Voter Anger Drive Republican Victory." ABC News. November 02, 2010. "Young Voters: Least Convinced That the Stimulus Worked." Crossroads Generation. June 21, 2012. Halpin, John, and Ruy Teixeira. "Election Results Fueled by Jobs Crisis and Voter Apathy Among Progressives." Center for American Progress. November 4, 2010.

12. Greszler, Rachel. "Job Creation: Policies to Boost Employment and Economic Growth." The Heritage Foundation. April 18, 2014.

13. Madhani, Aamer. "Harvard Poll: 57% of Millennials Disapprove of Obamacare." *USA Today*. December 04, 2013.

14. Nolte, John. "Poll: Young, Poor and Independents 'Strongly' Agree ObamaCare's Got To Go—Breitbart." *Breitbart News*. July 02, 2012.

15. Volsky, Igor. "GOP Survey Of Young People Reveals They Support Progressive Policies." *ThinkProgress*. June 3, 2013.

16. "Democratic Gains Dissipate, Youth Vote Back to Swing Voting Bloc." The Institute of Politics at Harvard University. 2014.

17. Rai, Arti, Stuart Graham, and Mark Doms. "Patent Reform: Unleashing Innovation, Promoting Economic Growth & Producing High-Paying Jobs." U.S. Department of Commerce, 2010.

18. Simon, Ruth, and Caelainn Barr. "Endangered Species: Young U.S. Entrepreneurs." *Wall Street Journal*, January 2, 2015, Business sec.

19. Ibid.

20. Duffy, Jim. "Cisco Quietly Downsizing through Outsourcing." *Network World*. March 12, 2009.

21. Scott, Robert. "The China Toll: Growing U.S. Trade Deficit with China Cost More than 2.7 Million Jobs between 2001 and 2011, with Job Losses in Every State." Economic Policy Institute. August 23, 2012. January 6, 2015.

22. Scott, Robert. "The China Toll." Economic Policy Institute. Briefing Paper #345 (2012).

23. Barshay, Jill. "Reflections on the Underemployment of College Graduates." *Washington Monthly*, August 4, 2014.

24. Kavoussi, Bonnie. "Average Cost Of A Factory Worker In The U.S., China And Germany." *The Huffington Post*. March 8, 2012.

25. Reinecke, Gerhard. "Is Globalization Good for Workers? Definitions and Evidence from Latin America." *International Labor and Working-Class History* 70, no. 01 (2007): 11-34.

26. Bessen, James. "Workers Don't Have the Skills They Need—and They Know It." *Harvard Business Review*, 2014.

27. Jaschik, Scott. "'Academically Adrift'" *Inside Higher Ed*. January 18, 2011.

28. Dua, Andre. "Voice of the Graduate." McKinsey. 2013.

29. Brownstein, Andrew. "New Study of the Literacy of College Students Finds Some Are Graduating With Only Basic Skills." American Institutes for Research. January 19, 2006.

30. Nemko, Marty. "America's Most Overrated Product: The Bachelor's Degree." *Chronicle of Higher Education* 54, no. 34 (2008): B17.

31. Sanchez, Claudio. "Should Everyone Go To College?" NPR. July 15, 2009.

32. Nemko, Marty, *op. cit.*

33. Mutikani, Lucia. "RPT-FEATURE: So Many US Manufacturing Jobs, so Few Skilled Workers." *Reuters*. October 13, 2011.

34. Sweeney, Brigid, and Stephen Serio, *op. cit.*

35. Mutikani, Lucia. "RPT-FEATURE: So Many US Manufacturing Jobs, so Few Skilled Workers." Reuters. October 13, 2011.

36. Sweeney, Brigid, and Stephen Serio, *op. cit.*

37. Sweeney, Brigid, and Stephen Serio, *op. cit.*

38. Sweeney, Brigid, and Stephen Serio, *op. cit.*

39. Fottrell, Quentin. "40% of Unemployed Workers Are Millennials." *MarketWatch*. July 7, 2014.

40. "As Sequester Deadline Looms, Little Support for Cutting Most Programs." Pew Research Center for the People and the Press. February 22, 2013.

41. Ossola, Alexandra. "Why Millennials &%#@! Love Science." *The Atlantic*. December 29, 2014.

42. Ibid.

43. Press, William, and Hunter Rawlings. "Why Science? An Unemotional Argument for Federal Investment in Research." *Huffington Post*, June 20, 2014.

44. National Institute of Health. "Our Society." U.S National Library of Medicine. March 10, 2016.

45. Atkinson, Robert, Jacek Warda, and Luke Stewart. "We're #27: The United States Lags Far Behind in R&D Tax Incentive Generosity." The Information Technology & Innovation Foundation. July 19, 2012.

46. Tan, Avianne. "Texas Kids Told 'It's Illegal' to Sell Lemonade Without a Permit." *ABC News*. June 10, 2015.

47. Zaru, Deena. "Texas Cops Shut down Kids' 'illegal' Lemonade Stand." *CNN*. June 11, 2015.

48. "Over-regulated America." *The Economist.* February 18, 2012. Accessed January 7, 2016.

49. Sinensky, Michael. "Why Over-Regulation Of Small Businesses Actually Hurts Employees The Most." *Business Insider.* February 11, 2011.

50. "What You Need to Know About the New Crowd-Funding Bill." *Reuters.* December 11, 2011.

51. Frier, Sarah, and Zachary Mider. "Getting a Visa Took Longer Than Building Instagram, Says Immigrant Co-Founder." *Bloomberg.* April 8, 2015.

52. Katsomitros, Alex. "The Global Race for STEM Skills." The Global Race for STEM Skills.

53. Kim, Anne. "Three Ways to Bring Manufacturing Back to America: The Much-Ballyhooed "In-Sourcing" Trend Is Real Enough. but It Won't Amount to Much Unless Washington Acts." *The Washington Monthly*, March 1, 2013.

54. Mankiw, N. Gregory. "Economists Actually Agree on This: The Wisdom of Free Trade." *The New York Times.* April 25, 2015.

55. Poushter, Jacob. "Americans Favor TPP, but Less than Those in Other Countries Do." Pew Research Center. June 23, 2015.

56. Office of Public Affairs. "U.S. Exports Support a Record 11.3 Million Jobs in 2013." Department of Commerce. February 25, 2014.

57. National Economic Council. "Moving America's Small Business & Entrepreneurs Forward." WhiteHouse.Gov. May 2012.

58. Shacklett, Mary. "What's behind Enterprise Insourcing of IT?" TechRepublic. November 25, 2012.

59. Kim, Anne. "Three Ways to Bring Manufacturing Back to America: The Much-Ballyhooed "In-Sourcing" Trend Is Real Enough. but It Won't Amount to Much Unless Washington Acts." *The Washington Monthly*, March 1, 2013.

60. Rose, Joel. "Study: College Grads Unprepared For Workplace." NPR. May 28, 2010.

61. Wojciechowska, Iza. "A Major Push on Advising." A Major Push on Advising. August 6, 2010.

62. Rodkin, Jonathan. "Skipped Your College Internship? You're Far Less Likely to Get a Job in Business." *Bloomberg Business Week.* August 15, 2014.

63. "IBM P-TECH." The Aspen Institute. Accessed March 10, 2016.

64. Ayres, Sarah, and Ben Olinsky. "Training for Success: A Policy to Expand Apprenticeships in the United States." Center for American Progress. December 2, 2013.

65. Fain, Paul. "Federal Job Training Programs Encourage Collaboration with Employers." Putting Community Colleges to Work. April 17, 2014.

66. PBS Newshour. "How Oregon Is Investing in the next Generation of Blue Collar Workers." *PBS.* January 3, 2016.

Less Debt

1. Kurtzleben, Danielle. "Just How Fast Has College Tuition Grown?" *US News.* October 23, 2013.

2. Cary, Mary Kate. "Why the Government Is to Blame for High College Costs." *US News*. November 23, 2011.

3. Howard, Beth. "Schools Take On Stress." *US News*. September 22, 2014.

4. Asay, Paul. "Youth Culture Update: 'Til Debt Do Us Part." Christian Talk Radio, The Word 100.7 FM. June 4, 2013.

5. "The State of the Nations Housing 2014." Joint Center for Housing Studies of Harvard University. 2014.

6. Douglas-Gabriel, Danielle. "How Student Debt Became a Presidential Campaign Issue." *Washington Post*. May 24, 2015.

7. Cook, Nancy. "The Debt Dilemma." *The Atlantic*. June 8, 2015.

8. Ibid.

9. Belkin, Doug. "What's the Best Way to Make College More Affordable?" *Wall Street Journal*. September 15, 2015.

10. Tierney, John. "How to Win Millennials: Equality, Climate Change, and Gay Marriage." *The Atlantic*. May 17, 2014.

11. Schumpeter. "How to Make College Cheaper; Schumpeter." *The Economist (US)*, July 9, 2011.

12. Morgan, Julie Margetta. "Making College More Affordable." Center for American Progress. February 2, 2012.

13. Ursta, Karlee. "5 Things Millennials Were Thinking During #SOTU." *Millennial Action*. January 22, 2015.

14. The White House. "Free Community College." *Facebook*. January 8, 2015.

15. The White House. "Remarks by the President on America's College Promise." The White House. January 09, 2015.

16. Mason, Kyla Calvert. "Obama: Community College Should Be 'as Free and Universal in America as High School.'" *PBS*. January 20, 2015.

17. Baima, David. "America's College Promise Act of 2015." American Association of Community College. July 8, 2015.

18. Hammer, Melissa. "Strong Support for President Obama's Free Community College Plan." *Harvard Political Review*, April 29, 2015.

19. Carolyn Heinrich, and Christopher King. "How Effective Are Workforce Development Programs? Implications for US Workforce Policies."Workforce System Strategies, 2011.

20. Davis, Janel. "Millennials Value College Education More than Older Generations." AJC. July 15, 2015.

21. YouGov. "Three-fifths Want Taxes to Fund Debt-free College." YouGov: What the World Thinks. August 12, 2015.

22. Donald, Donte. "Young Adults Say College Is More Important than Ever, But Harder to Afford." *Demos*. November 9, 2011.

23. Quinlan, Casey. "Everything You Need To Know About Martin O'Malley's Debt-Free College Plan." *ThinkProgress*. July 08, 2015.

24. Frizell, Sam. "Martin O'Malley Unveils Debt-Free College Plan." *Time*. July 8, 2015.

25. KAMENETZ, ANYA. "How Going To College Could Change Under Hillary Clinton's New Plan." *NPR*. August 11, 2015.

26. Fain, Paul. "Bill Haslam's Free Community College Plan and How Tennessee Is Grabbing the Spotlight in Higher Education Policy." *Inside Higher Ed*. August 26, 2014.

27. Cota, Adam, Andre Dua, and Martha Laboissiere. *The Atlantic*. February 24, 2012.

28. Ibid.

29. Graves, William H., and Carol A. Twigg. "The Future of Course Redesign and the National Center for Academic Transformation: An Interview with Carol A. Twigg." January 27, 2006.

30. Dhoul, Tim. "Understanding and Meeting the Needs of Millennials | QS Digital Solutions." *QS Digital Solutions*. July 17, 2015.

31. Smith, Ashley A. "Nearly Half of Four-year College Graduates Attended Two-year College." *Inside Higher Ed*. March 26, 2015.

Environmental Protection

1. Ganley, Elaine. "Worldwide Climate Rallies Draw Hundreds of Thousands." *The Big Story*. November 29, 2015.

2. Tindall, D. B. "How Protesters Kept the Pressure on at the Paris Climate Talks." *IPolitics*. December 23, 2015.

3. Marlowe, Lara. "COP21: Thousands Defy Paris Ban to Join Protest." *The Irish Times*. December 14, 2015.

4. Chaisson, Clara. "The Voice of a Generation." *OnEarth*. July 26, 2015.

5. "COP21: Digital Map Launched by UNICEF Helps Young People Tell Their Climate Change Stories." UN News Center. December 03, 2015.

6. Thomas, Joelle. "Climate Change and Millennials: The Future Is in Our Hands." *Scientific American*. December 8, 2015.

7. "World Leaders Make History with Climate Deal in Paris." *Al Jazeera English*. December 2015.

8. Mooney, Chris. "Poll: Millennials Are No More Convinced about Global Warming than Their Parents." *Washington Post*. April 30, 2015.

9. Timm, Jane C. "Millennials: We Care More about the Environment." *MSNBC.com*. March 22, 2014.

10. Koch, Wendy. "Poll Finds Generation Gap on Energy Issues as Millennials Voice Climate Concerns." The Great Energy Challenge Blog. October 30, 2014.

11. The Age of Stupid. Directed by Franny Armstrong. Performed by Pete Postlethwaite, Jeh Wadia, Alvin DuVernay. New Zealand, 2009.

12. Zwingle, Erla. "Alps, Global Warming, Melting Glaciers—National Geographic." *National Geographic*.

13. "Threat of Himalayan Extinction." News24.May 19, 2006.

14. McGarrity, John. "US Military Says Climate Change Could Increase Wars, Conflict." *Climate Change News*. June 06, 2014.

15. Annan, Kofi A. "The Anatomy of A Silent Crisis." Global Humanitarian Forum. 2009.

16. Vidal, John. "Global Warming Causes 300,000 Deaths a Year, Says Kofi Annan Thinktank." *The Guardian*. May 29, 2009.

17. Cardoni, Salvatore. "WTF?!? Climate Change Denier Claims." *TakePart*. August 12, 2013.

18. Ibid.

19. "Millennials Demand Action on Climate, Will Punish "Ignorant" Politicians Who Deny Climate Change." Democracy Corps. October 31, 2014.

20. "Scientific Consensus: Earth's Climate Is Warming." *NASA*. Accessed March 11, 2016.

21. Ruelas, Gus. "Koch Industries: Secretly Funding the Climate Denial Machine." *Greenpeace*. Accessed March 11, 2016.

22. Fischer, Douglas. ""Dark Money" Funds Climate Change Denial Effort" *Scientific American*. December 23, 2013.

23. Chait, Jonathan. "Obama Might Actually Be the Environmental President." *New York Magazine*. May 5, 2013.

24. Koprowski, Gene J. „Millennial Voters Want Results, Not Regulations." *The American Spectator*. August 11, 2015.

25. Kessler, Glenn. „Will Keystone XL Pipeline Create 42,000 'new' Jobs?" *Washington Post*. January 6, 2015.

26. Snyder, Benjamin. "What You Need to Know about the Keystone Pipeline." *Fortune*. January 09, 2015.

27. Benderev, Chris. "Millennials: We Help The Earth But Don't Call Us Environmentalists." *NPR*. October 14, 2014.

28. Stepp, Matthew. "Millennials Re-envisioning Environmentalism and Climate Policy." Chelsea Krost. March 24, 2014.

29. Ekins, Emily. "61 Percent Favor Building Keystone Pipeline." *Reason*. April 18, 2014.

30. Doe, Hilary, and Zachary Kolodin. "The Blueprint for the Millennial America." Roosevelt Institute. 2015.

31. Newport, Frank. "Americans Still Favor Nuclear Power a Year After Fukushima." *Gallup*. March 26, 2012.

32. Boisvert, Will. "The Diablo We Know—The Case for Keeping California's Last Nuclear Plant." The Breakthrough Institute. August 4, 2015.

33. Lucas, Natalie, and Mia Zhou. "Why Millennials in the United States and China Are Partnering for the Paris Climate Talks." *Sierra Club*. August 26, 2015.

34. Sierra Club. "SSC Executive Committee of 2015-2016." *Sierra Club*. 2015.

35. Yardley, William. "Here's What the Paris World Climate Agreement Will Do— and What It Won't." *Los Angeles Times*. December 12, 2015.

36. Yardley, William. "Here's What the Paris World Climate Agreement Will Do and What It Won't." *ArcaMax*. December 12, 2015.

37. Corbyn, Zoë. "Stanford Students Begin 'indefinite' Sit-in over Fossil Fuel Divestment." *The Guardian*. November 16, 2015.

38. Henn, Jamie. "Growing Fossil Fuel Divestment Protests Hit Colleges Nationwide." *MSNBC*. April 18, 2015.

39. "Campuses & Organizations That Have Divested." University of Wisconsin. 2015.

Entitlement Reform

1. Ekins, Emily. "Millennials Prefer Small Government If Large Government Requires High Taxes." *Reason.com*. June 10, 2014.

2. Ekins, Emily. "What Millennials Think Government Should Do." *Reason.com*. July 10, 2014.

3. Olsen, Hanna Brooks. "But Seriously, Let's Talk About Millennial Poverty." *Medium*. January 09, 2015.

4. Ibid.

5. Associated Press. "Young Americans Committed to Volunteering, Poll Finds." *Washington Post*. December 29, 2014.

6. Ekins, Emily. "Millennials The Politically Unclaimed Generation." *Reason*. July 10 2014.

7. Holland, Joshua. "Why Americans Hate Welfare." *BillMoyers.com*. March 4, 2014.

8. Reddy, Patrick. "Smart fixes to reform welfare: U.S. can repair cracks in system and lift people out of poverty by requiring work, increasing benefits for two-parent families." *Buffalo News*. September 22, 2014.

9. "83% Favor Work Requirement for Welfare Recipients." *Rasmussen Reports*. July 18, 2012.

10. Harden, Blaine. "Two Parent Families Rise After Changes in Welfare." *New York Times*. August 12, 2001.

11. Madhani, Aamer. "Harvard poll: 57% of Millennials disapprove of Obamacare." *USA Today*. December 4, 2014.

12. Lee, Patrice. "Why is Healthcare So Expensive." *Generation Opportunity*. September 2, 2015.

13. Keckley, Paul. "What Do Millennials Want From The Healthcare System? The Three Imperatives." *The Keckley Report*. March 17, 2014.

14. Madhani, Aamer, *op. cit.*

15. Smith, Ben. "Obama Prepare to Screw His Base." *Buzzfeed*. February 10, 2014.

16. Coombs, Berta. "Want a clearer medical bill? Act like a millennial." *CNBC*. May 7, 2015.

17. "Millennials' Lukewarm Support For Health Care Bills." *Pew Research*. February 4, 2010.

18. Touryalai, Halah. "More Americans Say 80 Is The New Retirement Age." *Forbes*. October 23, 2012.

19. Taylor, Paul. "Millennials in Adulthood." Pew Research. March 7, 2014.

20. Avik, Roy. "Saving Medicare from Itself." *National Affairs*. Summer, 2014.

21. Lange, Jason. "Main fund for U.S. Medicare program to run out of money in 2030." *Reuters*. July 22, 2015.

22. Biggs, Andrew. "Disabling Entitlement Reform." *The Wall Street Journal.* September 7, 2015.

23. Palmer, Brian. "Democracy or Gerontocracy." *Slate.* January 2, 2013.

24. Ekins, Emily. "Millennials Favor Private Accounts for Social Security Even if Benefit Cuts to Current Seniors Required." *Reason.* July 17, 2014.

25. Parker, Kim. "The Big Generation Gap at the Polls Is Echoed in Attitudes on Budget Tradeoffs." Pew Research Center. December 20, 2012.

26. Foroohar, Rana. "2030: The Year Retirement Ends." Novim. July 19, 2014.

27. Oakley, Diane and Kelly Keneally. "Pensions and Retirement Security 2013." National Institute for Retirement Security. February 2013.

28. Kingkade, Tyler. "Millennials Favor Preserving Social Security Over Reducing Deficit, Despite Skepticism: Pew Poll." *Huffington Post.* December 31, 2012.

29. Murray, Sarah. "Baby Boomers and Millennials: Two generations prepare for retirement." *Retirement Town Hall.* May 28, 2015.

30. Chandrashekhar, Chetan. "Young voters crave intelligent discussion about entitlements." *The Seattle Times.* October 16, 2012.

31. Ekins, Emily. "58 Percent Oppose Minimum Wage Increase if it Costs Jobs, but 51 Percent Would Accept Higher Prices." *Reason.* April 29, 2014.

32. Butler, Stuart and Henry J. Aaron. "The Future of Medicare: 15 Proposals You Should Know About." *AARP.* May 2012.

33. Barnes, James. "61% Of Those Making Minimum Wage Are Millennials Living In Poverty: Here's The One Thing That Would Get Them Out." *Thought Catalog.* March 8, 2014.

34. Berman, Russell. "Where the Minimum-Wage Fight Is Being Won." *The Atlantic.* May 4, 2015.

35. Schmitt, John. "Why Does the Minimum Wage Have No Discernible Effect on Employment?" Center for Economic and Policy Research. February 2013.

36. Neumark, David and William Wascher "Minimum Wages And Employment: A Review of Evidence From the New Minimum Wage Research." National Bureau of Economic Research. November 2006.

37. Saltsman, Michael. "Raising minimum wage won't lower poverty." CNN. September 16, 2011. Gitis, Ben "The Steep Cost of a $10 Minimum Wage." American Action Forum. October 23, 2014. "The Effects of a Minimum-Wage Increase on Employment and Family Income." *CBO.* February 18, 2014. Morath, Eric. "Minimum-Wage Increase Could Slow Future Hiring, Employment Survey Shows." *Wall Street Journal.* March 19, 2014.

Immigrant Opportunity

1. Fry, Richard, and Jens Manuel Krogstad. "Dept. of Ed. Projects Public Schools Will Be 'majority-minority' This Fall." Pew Research Center. August 18, 2014.

2. Lerman, Judi. "Millennials' Attitudes Toward Immigrants and Immigration Policies." *Opportunity Agenda.* August 2012.

3. Ibid.

4. Passel, Jeffrey, and Jens Manuel Krogtad. "5 Facts about Illegal Immigration in the U.S." Pew Research Center. November 19, 2015.

5. Riley, Jason L. "The Mythical Connection Between Immigrants and Crime." *Wall Street Journal*, July 14, 2015. Reston, Laura. "Immigrants Don't Drain Welfare. They Fund It." *New Republic*. September 3, 2015.

6. Anchondo, Leo. "Top 10 Myths About Immigration." American Immigration Council. 2010. Accessed December 28, 2014.

7. "Reagan-Bush Debate." *WPA Film Library*. 1980. Accessed January 8, 2015. https://www.wpafilmlibrary.com/videos/121506.

8. Suls, Rob. "More Prioritize Border Security in Immigration Debate." Pew Research Center for the People and the Press. September 03, 2014.

9. Parker, Christopher. "The (Real) Reason Why the House Won't Pass Comprehensive Immigration Reform." The Brookings Institution. August 04, 2014.

10. Congressional Budget Office. "The Economic Impact of S. 744, the Border Security, Economic Opportunity, and Immigration Modernization Act." Congressional Budget Office. June 18, 2013.

11. Shierholz, Heidi. "Immigration and Wages: Methodological Advancements Confirm Modest Gains for Native Workers." Economic Policy Institute. February 4, 2010.

12. Stanek, Becca. "7 Quotes Show Why the Tea Party Just Doesn't Get Millennials." *PolicyMic*. November 03, 2014.

13. Ibid.

14. Ponnuru, Ramesh. "Immigration Polling." *National Review*. October 30, 2014.

15. Bennett, Brian. "High Deportation Figures Are Misleading." *Los Angeles Times*. April 1, 2014.

16. Lerman, Judi, *op. cit.*

17. Rodriguez, Laura. "Executive Order from President Obama Revives Dreams for Undocumented Youth." *Millennial Latina Narratives*. February 12, 2013.

18. Peri, Giovanni. "How Immigrants Affect California Employment and Wages." Public Policy Institute of California. February 2007.

19. "Common Myths Common Myths About Undocumented About Undocumented Immigrants." National Council of La Raza. 2006.

20. Gonzalez, Daniel. "Birthright Citizenship Ban Could Hamper U.S. Military Recruiting." *Arizona Central*. March 23, 2011. Marcos, Cristina. "Divided GOP Rejects Allowing Illegal Immigrants in the Military." *The Hill*. May 14, 2015.

Less War

1. Thall, Trevor and Erik Goepner. "Millennials and U.S. Foreign Policy." CATO Institute. June 16, 2015.

2. "The Generation Gap on Foreign Policy and National Security Issues." Pew Research. November 11, 2011.

3. Thall, Trevor. "Millennials and U.S. Foreign Policy: The Next Generation's Attitudes toward Foreign Policy and War (and Why They Matter)." CATO Institute. June 16, 2015.

4. Smeltz, Dina. "Foreign Policy in the New Millennium." The Chicago Council. 2012.

5. Snyder, Christopher. "Millennials from both sides of the aisle agree US intervention in Syria is not a good option." *Fox News*. August 28, 2013.

6. Ekins, Emily. "Poll: If We Arm Syrian Rebels Americans Say 78% Chance Weapons Will Be Used Against US Eventually." *Reason*. October 16, 2014.

7. Snyder, Christopher, *op. cit.*

8. Associated Press. "Obama Has Increased Drone Attacks." *CBS News*. February 12, 2010.

9. Ekins, Emily. "Poll: 66% Favor Airstrikes Against ISIS, but 52% Oppose US Sending Ground Troops." *Reason*. October 10, 2014.

10. Kaplan, Rebecca. "Poll: After Paris attacks, millennials want ground troops to fight ISIS." *CBS News*. December 10, 2015.

11. Ekins, Emily. "Poll: 66% Favor Airstrikes Against ISIS, but 52% Oppose US Sending Ground Troops," *op. cit.*

12. Ibid.

13. Thrall, Trevor, and Erik Goepner. "Millennials Support Iran Deal." Cato Institute. July 27, 2015.

14. Thrall, Trevor, and Erik Goepner. "Millennials Strongly Back Iran Deal." *Philly.com*. July 26, 2015.

15. Palumbo-Liu, David. "Millennials Are over Israel: A New Generation, Outraged over Gaza, Rejects Washington's Reflexive Support." *Salon*. August 1, 2014.

16. "More Express Sympathy for Israel than the Palestinians." Pew Research. August 28, 2014.

17. "At the double." *The Economist*. March 15, 2014.

18. Bitzinger, Richard. "China's Double-Digit Defense Growth." *Foreign Affairs*. March 19, 2015.

19. Bloomberg News. "China's President Xi Solidifies Power with Overhaul of Military." *Bloomberg*. August 31, 2015.

20. "Who rules the waves?" *The Economist*. October 17, 2015.

21. AFP. "China defence budget to grow 'about 10 percent': govt." *The Express Tribune*. March 4, 2015.

22. Wong, Edward and Jane Perlez. "As Tensions With U.S. Grow, Beijing Says It Will Stop Building Artificial Islands in South China Sea." *The New York Times*. June 16, 2015.

23. Brown, Harold. "Chinese Military Power." Council on Foreign Relations. May 2003.

24. Keck, Zachary. "Most Chinese Say Their Military Can Crush America in Battle." *The National Interest*. March 13, 2015.

25. Kohut, Andrew. "Section 8: Domestic and Foreign Policy Views." Pew Research. November 3, 2011.

26. Kohut, Andrew. "Chapter 2. Attitudes Toward American Culture and Ideas." Pew Research Center. June 13, 2012.

27. "2015 Millennials: Interactive." *Bloomberg View*. December 8, 2015.

28. Gorman, Siobhan. "Annual U.S. Cybercrime Costs Estimated at $100 Billion." *The Wall Street Journal*. July 22, 2013.

29. Winograd, Morley and Michael D. Hais. "Want To See Better US-Chinese Relations? American and Chinese Millennials Could be Key." *New Geography*. December 17, 2012.

30. "CNN Poll: 59% approve of sanctions against Russia." *CNN*. March 10, 2014.

31. Lubold, Gordon. "U.S. Sends Tanks, Military Equipment to Deter Russian Aggression." *Wall Street Journal*. June 23, 2015.

32. Kirkland, William. "Kirkland: What would millennials fight for?" *The Daily Northwestern*. May 11, 2014.

33. Willick, Jason. "The Other Generation Gap." IVN. September 4, 2013.

Reclaiming Power

1. Miles, Chris. "Corrupt, Fucked, and Broken. What Young People Really Think of the Political System." Policy Mic. July 15, 2014.

2. "Super PAC spending." *Los Angeles Times*. November 20, 2012.

3. "2012 Candidate Super PAC Spending." *Wall Street Journal*. 2012.

4. Skaggs, Adam. "Buying Justice: The Impact of Citizens United on Judicial Elections." Brennan Center for Justice. May 5, 2010.

5. Kang, Michael. "The Partisan Price of Justice: An Empirical Analysis of Campaign Contributions and Judicial Decisions." Emory University School of Law. December 8, 2012.

6. Brandenburg, Bret. "What's the Best Way To Pack a Court?" *Slate*. November 14, 2008.

7. Raskin, Jamie. "A shareholder solution to 'Citizens United." *The Washington Post*. October 3, 2014.

8. Mauer, Richard. "Alaska labor unions take advantage of Citizens United ruling." McClatchy DC. November 26, 2012.

9. Gilson, Dave. "Who Owns Congress? A Campaign Cash Seating Chart." *Mother Jones*. September/October 2010.

10. Eggen, Dan. "Poll: Large majority opposes Supreme Court's decision on campaign financing." *The Washington Post*. February 17, 2010.

11. Frumin, Aliyah. "Money has too much of an influence in politics, Americans say." *MSNBC*. June 12, 2015.

12. Moore, David. "Widespread Public Support for Campaign Finance Reform." *Gallop*. March 20, 2001.

13. Harsanyi, David. "Let's Stop Kidding Ourselves: 90 Percent of Congressional Incumbents Will Win Re-election." *Reason*. June 20, 2014.

14. Smith, Bradley. "Why Super PACs Are Good for Democracy." *US News*. February 17, 2012.

15. Lowery, Wesley. "91% of the time the better-financed candidate wins. Don't act surprised." *The Washington Post*. April 4, 2014.

16. Kroll, Andy. "The Super-PAC Steamroller: Coming to a Town Near You!" *Mother Jones*. April 25, 2012.

17. Rose-Ackerman, Susan. "Political Corruption and Democracy." Yale Law School. January 1, 1999.

18. Beckel, Michael. "Study: Super PACs aired more ads than candidates." Center for Public Integrity. May 3, 2012.

19. Lau, Richard R., Lee Sigelman, and Ivy Brown Rovner. "The Effects of Negative Political Campaigns: A Meta-Analytic Reassessment." *The Journal of Politics* 69, no. 4 (2007): 1176–209.

20. Saad, Lydia. "Half in U.S. Support Publicly Financed Federal Campaigns." *Gallup.* June 24, 2013.

21. Gripp, Andrew. "2016 Will Make the Strongest Case for Publically Funded Elections." *IVN.* June 22, 2015.

22. Silver, Josh. "All Is Not Lost: How to Win Money-in-Politics Reform." *Huffington Post.* April 4, 2014.

23. Kopan, Tal. "Poll: Lobbyists rank last on ethics." *Politico.* December 16, 2013.

24. Drutman, Lee. "How to Reform Lobbying: Transparency." *Pacific Standard.* August 1, 2011.

25. Goodman, Douglas. "Non-Partisan Redistricting Can Help Break Congressional Gridlock." *Policy Mic.* March 22, 2012.

Better Schools

1. Bedrick, Jason. "Support for School Choice Continues to Grow." CATO Institute. August 19, 2014.

2. Rawls, Kristin. "The ugly truth about 'school choice.'" *Salon.* January 24, 2012.

3. Neff, Blake. "Poll: School Choice Super Popular With Minorities And Millennials." *Daily Caller.* January 30, 2016.

4. Beck Research. "Re: School Choice Survey Research Results." American Federation for Children. January 28, 2016.

5. Klein, Rebecca. "Millennials Have Pretty Depressing Things To Say About Teachers." *Huffington Post.* April 29, 2014.

6. Ozimek, Adam. "The Unappreciated Success Of Charter Schools." *Forbes.* January 11, 2015.

7. Cahn, David. "Moratorium on Brains." *Stuyvesant Spectator.* December 12, 2011.

8. Triant, Bill. "Autonomy and Innovation: How Do Massachusetts Charter School Principals Use Their Freedom?" Thomas B. Fordham Institute. December 1, 2001.

9. Dhoul, Tim. "Understanding And Meeting The Needs Of Millennials." *QS Digital Solutions.* July 17, 2015.

10. "An Innovation Odyssey: Students at the Center." *Intel.*

11. "Making the French Revolution Meaningful." *The Teaching Channel.* 2014.

The Weed Warriors are Back

1. Diehl, Caleb. "Study: Daily Marijuana Use among College Students at Highest Rate in 35 Years." *USA Today.* September 1, 2015. Wadley, Jared. "College Students' Use of Marijuana on the Rise, Some Drugs Declining." *University of Michigan News.* September 08, 2014.

2. Gao, George. "63% of Republican Millennials Favor Marijuana Legalization." Pew Research Center. February 27, 2015.

3. "The War on Marijuana in Black and White." American Civil Liberties Union. June 2013.

4. "Marijuana Arrests by the Numbers." American Civil Liberties Union. June 2013. Harris, James W. "New FBI Report: Savage U.S. Marijuana War Continues, Despite Majority Support for Re-Legalization." The Advocates for Self-Government. November 12, 2014.

5. Cheney-Rice, Zak. "4/20 Is Over, and America's Weed Laws Are Still Racist as Hell." *Mic*. April 20, 2015.

6. Cherney, Max. "Philadelphia Is Decriminalizing Marijuana Possession | VICE News." *VICE News*. September 14, 2014.

7. Plummer, Ken. "Labeling Theory." Historical, Conceptual, and Theoretical Issues. Philadelphia: Brunner-Routlegde, 2001.

8. Ekins, Emily. "Poll: 77% of Americans Favor Eliminating Mandatory Minimum Prison Sentences For Nonviolent Offenders; 73% Favor Restoring Voting Rights." *Reason*. October 21, 2014. "America's New Drug Policy Landscape." Pew Research Center for the People and the Press. April 02, 2014.

9. Families Against Mandatory Minimums. "Mandatory Sentencing Was Once America's Law-and-order Panacea. Here's Why It's Not Working." Prison Policy.

10. Ekins, Emily, *op. cit.*

11. Maher, Lisa, and David Dixon. "The Cost of Crackdowns: Policing Cabramatta's Heroin Market." Center for Problem-Oriented Policing. July 2001.

12. Benson, Bruce L., Ian S. Leburn, and David W. Rasmussen. "The Impact of Drug Enforcement on Crime: An Investigation of The Opportunity Cost of Police Resources." *Journal of Drug Issues* 31, no. 4 (October 2001): 989–1006.

13. Casas-Zamora, Kevin. "Drugs and Democracy: Toward a Paradigm Shift." The Brookings Institution. April 22, 2009.

14. Molzahn, Cory, Viridiana Ríos, and David A. Shirk. "Drug Violence in Mexico Data and Analysis Through 2011." Trans-Border Institute. March 2012.

15. Saldaña, Jeronimo. "¡No Se Puede! California Latinos Are Done with the Failed Drug War." Drug Policy Alliance. May 22, 2014.

16. "OHCHR Submission to the 30th Session of the Human Rights Council (Resolution A/HRC/28/L.22) in Regards to the Special Session of the UN General Assembly on the World Drug Problem (UNGASS) 2016." Women and Harm Reduction International Network. May 15, 2015.

17. Hastedt, Glenn P. *Readings in American Foreign Policy: Problems and Responses*. Rowman & Littlefield Publishers, 2015.

18. Ibid.

19. Longmire, Sylvia. "Drug Cartels in U.S. as Big a Threat as Terrorism." *CNN*. December 9, 2010.

20. "The Drug War Across Borders: US Drug Policy and Latin America." Drug Policy Alliance.

21. "82% Say U.S. Not Winning War on Drugs." *Rasmussen Reports*. August 18, 2013.

22. Dilley, Sara. "The Top 5 Industries Lobbying Against Cannabis Legalization Will Infuriate You." *Leafly*. January 21, 2015.

23. McKay, Tom. "These 5 Groups Are Standing in the Way of You and Legal Marijuana." *Mic*. August 07, 2014.

24. Elk, Mike, and Bob Sloan. "The Hidden History of ALEC and Prison Labor." *The Nation*. August 01, 2011.

25. Fang, Lee. "The Real Reason Pot Is Still Illegal." *The Nation*. July 02, 2014.

26. Pavlich, Katie. Fast and Furious: Barack Obama's Bloodiest Scandal and Its Shameless Cover-up. Washington, DC: *Regnery Pub.*, 2012.

27. Berman, Jillian. "Pot Legalization Could Save U.S. $13.7 Billion Per Year, 300 Economists Say." *The Huffington Post*. August 28, 2012.

28. Cardoso, Fernando Henrique. "Five Ways to End the Drug War; Start by Decriminalizing Drug Use." *The Huffington Post*. September 10, 2014.

29. "America's New Drug Policy Landscape." Pew Research Center for the People and the Press. April 02, 2014. Siddiqui, Sabrina. "Heroin Crisis: Presidential Candidates Forced to Confront Issue on Campaign Trail." *The Guardian*. October 10, 2015.

30. Rose, Carol, and Cheryl Zoll. "State's Opioid Crisis Needs a Public Health Approach." *Boston Globe*. November 12, 2014.

31. Siddiqui, Sabrina, *op. cit.*

32. Students for Sensible Drug Policy. "Nick Watkins Testifies before DC Council on Marijuana Legalization." *YouTube*. November 3, 2014. Hill, Corey. "Marijuana Laws Are Crippling America, But Millennials Will Lead the Revolution." *Mic*. October 11, 2013. Skelton, George. "Recreational Marijuana Proponents Are Pushing a False Narrative." *Los Angeles Times*. November 12, 2014.

33. "Obama Says Pot Legalization Shouldn't Be Young People's 'Biggest Priority'" *NBC News*. March 17, 2015.

34. Gao, George. "63% of Republican Millennials Favor Marijuana Legalization." Pew Research Center. February 27, 2015.

35. Lopez, German. "Marijuana Legalization Is Already Making Mexican Drug Cartels Poorer." Vox. December 31, 2015. Bonello, Deborah. "Mexican Marijuana Farmers See Profits Tumble as U.S. Loosens Laws." *Los Angeles Times*. December 30, 2015.

Equality for All

1. "Women Deserve Equal Pay." National Organization for Women.

2. Roman, Stephanie. "Millennial Women Beginning to Close the Gender Wage Gap." *Citizens Voice*. August 16, 2015.

3. Schulte, Brigid. "Voters Want Paid Leave, Paid Sick Days, Poll Shows. Obama, Too. Will Congress Oblige?" *Washington Post*. January 21, 2015.

4. "Parenting a Priority." Pew Research Center. March 24, 2010.

5. Bakst, Dina. "Pregnant, and Pushed Out of a Job." *The New York Times*. January 30, 2012.

6. Mertens, Maggie. "Will Millennial Women Ever Get Paid Maternity Leave?" *Refinery29*. January 28, 2015. Schulte, Brigid, *op. cit.*

7. Meier, Sam. "75% Of Millennials Are Pro Choice, And 65% Are Pro-Life. Wait. What?" *Mic.* January 18, 2013.

8. Ibid.

9. "Chapter 2: Generations and Issues." Pew Research Centers Social Demographic Trends Project. March 7, 2014.

10. Murphy, Jan. "Roe v. Wade: Millennials' Support for Reproductive Rights Encouraging to Abortion Rights Advocates." *Penn Live.* January 21, 2014.

11. Dimock, Michael, Luis Lugo, Alan Cooperman, and Carroll Doherty. "Roe v. Wade at 40: Most Oppose Overturning Abortion Decision." Pew Research Center. January 16, 2013.

12. Greenberg, Jon. "Ralph Reed: Millennials More Pro-life than Boomers or Seniors." *PolitiFact.* March 11, 2014.

13. "Abortions Decline across US—in States with New Restrictions and without Them." *The Guardian.* June 07, 2015.

14. Crary, David. "AP Exclusive: Abortions Declining in Nearly All States—The Boston Globe." *Boston Globe.* June 8, 2015.

15. Jones, Robert P., Daniel Cox, and Rachel Laser. "Committed to Availability, Conflicted About Morality." Public Religion Research Institute. June 6, 2011.

16. Everett, Burgess, and Jennifer Haberkorn. "GOP Support Grows for Hardline Planned Parenthood Strategy." *Politico.* July 30, 2015.

17. Diehl, Caleb. "Harvard Poll Finds Millennials Have Little Faith in Government, Media." *USA Today College.* April 29, 2015.

18. "New Target In Voter ID Battle: 1965 Voting Rights Act." *NPR.* August 2, 2012.

19. Sink, Justin. "Poll: Only One-third Support Supreme Court's Voting Rights Ruling." *The Hill.* July 03, 2013.

20. Childress, Sarah. "Why Voter ID Laws Aren't Really about Fraud." *PBS Frontline.* October 20, 2014.

21. Iyer, Keesha Gaskins, Sundeep. "The Challenge of Obtaining Voter Identification." Brennan Center for Justice. July 18, 2012. Owen, Sue, and W. Gardner Selby. "Eric Holder Says Recent Studies Show 25 Percent of African Americans, 8 Percent of Whites Lack Government-issued Photo IDs." *PolitiFact.* July 11, 2012.

22. Childress, Sarah, *op. cit.*

23. Rampell, Catherine. "Millennials Get Cut off at the Polls." *Washington Post.* July 7, 2014. Apuzzo, Matt. "Students Joining Battle to Upend Laws on Voter ID." *The New York Times.* July 05, 2014.

24. "Fear of Voter Suppression High, Fear of Voter Fraud Higher." Washington Post. August 13, 2012. Mitchell, Quinlan. "Study Reveals Millennials See Voter Disenfranchisement As A Bigger Issue Than Voter Fraud." *Generation Progress.* November 24, 2014. Schwartz, Herman. "The Public Doesn't Support Restrictive Voter ID Laws, but Many New Ones Will be in Force in 2016." *The Great Debate.* December 08, 2015.

25. Cloutier, Catherine. "Almost 3 in 4 Millennials Support Same-sex Marriage—The Boston Globe." *Boston Globe.* June 26, 2015.

26. Holland, Steve. "Most Americans Side with Gays in Religious Freedom Disputes: Reuters/Ipsos Poll." *Reuters.* April 09, 2015.

27. Lorenz, Brandon. "New National Poll Shows Americans Still Reject LGBT Discrimination." Human Rights Campaign. April 9, 2015.

28. McBride, Sarah, and Zenen Jaimes Pérez. "Millennials Overwhelmingly Support Comprehensive LGBT Nondiscrimination Protections." Center for American Progress. April 7, 2015.

Radical Realism

1. "Executive Summary." National Conference on Citizenry. August 27, 2009.

2. Harvard Public Opinion Project. "Survey of Young Americans' Attitudes Toward Politics and Public Service: 25th Edition." Institute of Politics, Harvard University. April 29, 2014.

3. Weinmeister, Nick. "What Happened to Compromise." *Seersucker Mag.* Accessed May 7, 2016.

4. Diggles, Michelle. "Millennials: Political Explorers." *Third Way.* March 20, 2014.

5. Wofford, Carrie. "Why Millennials Will Save Politics." *US News.* April 22, 2014.

6. Fournier, Ron. "The Outsiders: How Can Millennials Change Washington If They Hate It?" *The Atlantic.* August 26, 2013.

7. Ekins, Emily. "Millennials Think Government Is Inefficient, Abuses Its Power, and Supports Cronyism." *Reason-Rupe.* July 10, 2014.

8. Kitroeff, Natalie. "Politicians: Millennials Won't Vote Because They Hate You." *Businessweek.* October 31, 2014. Accessed December 30, 2014.

9. Kiesel, Meghan. "Vast Majority of Attack Ads Include False Claims." *ABC News.* June 22, 2012.

10. Nyhan, Brendan, and Jason Reifler. "When Corrections Fail: The Persistence Of Political Misperceptions." *Political Behavior* 32, no. 2 (2010): 303–30.

11. Brown, Stephen Rex. "Sheldon Silver, Dean Skelos convictions uncovered 'deep problem of corruption in Albany,' says Preet Bharara." *New York Daily News.* December 14, 2015.

12. "List of American state and local politicians convicted of crimes." Wikipedia. Accessed January 1, 2015. "List of American federal politicians convicted of crimes." *Wikipedia.* Accessed January 1, 2015.

13. Irvine, Martha. "Millennials Are 'Alienated' And Less Trusting Than Generation X Was." *Huffington Post.* November 4, 2014.

14. Fournier, Ron, *op. cit.*

15. Ibid.

16. "The Millennial Generation Research Review." U.S. Chamber of Commerce Foundation. 2012.

17. "Parenting a Priority." Pew Research Center. March 24, 2010.

18. Ibid.

Be a Champion

1. "The Importance of Authenticity." White Hutchinson Leisure & Learning Group. July, 2012.

2. Thompson, Anne Bahr. "Rewriting Our Cultural Story for Brands—One Mash-up at a Time." *CultureQ*. 2011.

3. Gianatasio, David. "Tapping Millennial Political and Social Passions Ahead of the Midterm Elections." *AdWeek*. October 6, 2014.

4. Luna, Tania. *Surprise: Embrace the Unpredictable and Engineer the Unexpected.* New York, NY. Perigee, 2014.

5. Jacobs, Jennifer. "10 reasons Joni Ernst won Iowa's open U.S. Senate seat." *Des Moines Register*. November 6, 2014.

6. 60 Minutes. "Meet The Next House Speaker, Rep. John Boehner." *CBS News*. December 9, 2010.

7. "What John Boehner's Resignation Means For The House of Representatives." *Millennial Vote Blog*. October 12, 2015.

8. Coy, Peter. "No Faith. No Country. No Marriage. Still, Millennials Are Optimistic." *Bloomberg Businessweek*, March 7, 2014.

9. "Confident. Connected. Open to Change." *Pew Research*. 2010.

10. Shin, Laura. "4 In 5 Millennials Optimistic For Future, But Half Live Paycheck To Paycheck." *Forbes*. December 5, 2014.

11. Goleman, Daniel. "For Presidential Candidates, Optimism Appears a Winner." *New York Times*. May 8, 1988.

12. "Optimism at Forefront for Youngest Woman to Serve in Congress." *CBS News*. January 5, 2015.

13. Bell, Benjamin. "Sen-Elect Cory Gardner: After Taking Congress, GOP Must 'Govern Maturely.'" *ABC News*. November 9, 2014.

14. Berger, Joseph. "Nassau County Prosecutor's Decision to Seek House Seat Is Rooted in Family." *New York Times*. March 20, 2014.

15. Kingkade, Tyler. "Millennial Support For Gay Marriage Hits All-Time High: Pew Research Center." *The Huffington Post*. March 21, 2013.

16. Teixeira, Ruy, and David Madland. "New Progressive America: The Millennial Generation." *Center for American Progress*. 2009.

17. "Confident. Connected. Open to Change." *Pew Research*, 2010.

18. Bondioli, Sara. "Gay Marriage Now Linked With Sen. Rob Portman And His Possible 2016 Bid." *The Huffington Post*. November 17, 2014.

19. Rothman, Noah. "Poll: GOP Voters More Flexible on Abortion, Climate, Gay Marriage, and Min Wage Than Dems." *Mediaite*. February 27, 2014.

20. Gianatasio, David, *op. cit.*

21. Azhar, Hamdan. "Love and Politics: Why I'm Voting for Ron Paul." *Mic*. November 4, 2012.

22. Resmovits, Joy. "Ron Paul's Iowa Caucus Conundrum: Can He Get Out The Youth Vote?" *The Huffington Post*. December 24, 2011.

23. Richer, Stephen. "Can Ron Paul Sweep the Youth Vote in New Hampshire?" *Forbes*. January 10, 2012.

24. Smith, Robert. "Ron Paul: Why The Young Flock To An Old Idealist." *NPR*. May 16, 2011.

25. "A Big Win for John Kasich; Lexington." *The Economist*. November 8, 2014.

26. Vaishnav, Milan. "India Election: Is There a Surge of Support for Narendra Modi?" Carnegie Endowment for International Peace. February 25, 2014.

27. Bengali, Shashank. "India's Young Voters Look to Narendra Modi for Change." *Los Angeles Times*. May 26, 2014, World/Asia sec.

28. Dasgupta, Swapan. "Narendra Modi Embodies the Change Young Indians Crave in the Election." *The Guardian*, April 2, 2014, Opinion sec.

29. "Election Results 2014: Youngsters Vote for 'doer' Modi—The Times of India." *The Times of India*. May 17, 2014.

30. Associated Press. "India Election Results 2014: Five Reasons Why Narendra Modi Won." *The Telegraph*. May 16, 2014.

31. Kumar, Vinay. "BJP All Set to Launch 'Mission 272-plus.'" *The Hindu*. December 24, 2013.

32. "'Motivator Modi' Inspires Youngsters." *The Times of India*. November 8, 2014.

Mobilize Millennials on Social Media

1. Shams, Sharokina. "Campaigns Use Social Media to Engage Voters." *KCRA*. October 8, 2014.

2. Blum, Dani. "There's a Yak for That." *The Daily Pennsylvanian*. September 29, 2014.

3. Ibid.

4. "Facebook Tips, Tricks and Politics." Social Media Breakfast Madison. January 19, 2013.

5. Said, Heba. "Politicians Focus on Social Media to Engage Voters." *The Shorthorn*. July 2, 2014.

6. "5 Ways Social Media Will Change Political Campaigns in 2014." *IVN*. December 30, 2013.

7. Harris, Paul. "Marco Rubio Survives His Water Bottle Moment with Style." *The Guardian*. February 16, 2013.

8. Rubio, Marco (marcorubio). "#GOPResponse #SOTU #gop #tcot." 13 Feb 2013, 03:59 UTC. Tweet.

Afterword

1. Mukand, Sharun, and Ethan Kaplan. "The Persistence of Political Partisanship: Evidence from 9/11." January 26, 2011.

About the Authors

David Cahn and Jack Cahn are millennial journalists and activists who have been featured in *The New York Times*, *The Wall Street Journal*, *Time*, and *New York* magazine, and have appeared on CBS, Nickelodeon and Al Jazeera's "America Tonight." Experts on millennial political beliefs, the twins were nationally ranked debaters between 2010 and 2014 and have served as national leaders of the Junior State of America and as organizers for national and local campaigns. Today, they write for the *Huffington Post*, where they are accomplished journalists. Jack won Columbia's Gold Circle Award for News Reporting in 2015, and David received Scholastic's National Gold Medal for Persuasive Writing in 2014.